The Pat Conroy Cookbook

The Pat Conroy Cookbook

• Recipes of My Life •

Pat Conroy

with Suzanne Williamson Pollak

NAN A. TALESE

DOUBLEDAY

New York London Toronto Sydney Auckland

PUBLISHED BY NAN A. TALESE
AN IMPRINT OF DOUBLEDAY
a division of Random House, Inc.
1745 Broadway, New York, New York 10019

DOUBLEDAY is a registered trademark of Random House, Inc.

Essay "A Hometown in the Low Country," © Pat Conroy, first printed in *House Beautiful*.
Reprinted by permission of Pat Conroy
Essay "Honeymoon," © Pat Conroy, first printed in *Gourmet* magazine.
Reprinted by permission of Pat Conroy
Essay "Southerner in Paris," © Pat Conroy, first printed in *Southern Living* magazine.
Reprinted by permission of Pat Conroy
Essay "Oyster Roast," © Pat Conroy, first printed in *Gourmet* magazine.
Reprinted by permission of Pat Conroy
Essay "Men Grilling," © Pat Conroy, first printed in *Gourmet* magazine.
Reprinted by permission of Pat Conroy
Essay "Frank Stitt," © Pat Conroy, adapted from introduction by Pat Conroy to *Frank Stitt's
Southern Table: Recipes from Highland's Bar and Grill*, published by Artisan, a Division of
Workman Publishing, September 2004
Recipe for "Barbeque Shrimp and Rosemary Biscuits" is from *From Emeril's Kitchen* by Emeril
Lagasse, copyright © 2003 by EMERIL'S FOOD OF LOVE PRODUCTIONS, LLC, reprinted by
permission of William Morrow/HarperCollins Publishers, Inc.

Book design by Elizabeth Rendfleisch
Illustrations by John Burgoyne

Library of Congress Cataloging-in-Publication Data

Conroy, Pat.
The Pat Conroy cookbook : recipes of my life / Pat Conroy.—1st U.S. ed.
p. cm.
1. Cookery, International. 2. Conroy, Pat—Biography. I. Title.

TX725.A1C57574 2004
641.59—dc22
2004053692

ISBN 0-385-51413-1

PRINTED IN THE UNITED STATES OF AMERICA

December 2004

First Edition in the United States of America

1   3   5   7   9   10   8   6   4   2

This book is dedicated to the cooking partner of my life,
Cassandra King

I would like particularly to thank Jennifer Josephy, the superb editor of Doubleday/Broadway's excellent line of cookbooks, for her guidance through this project. Without her, my longtime editor, Nan A. Talese—who is all right with words but hardly an expert on food—would have been lost.

CONTENTS

I Encounter Escoffier

The subject of food is nearly a sacred one to me. It never surprises me when I read stories about the ancients sacrificing animals and bringing plates of fruit and the produce of their fields to appease the anger of their restless gods. My passion for eating springs from a childhood not deprived of food, but deprived of good food. My mother thought cooking was a kind of slave labor that involved women having too many children. She looked upon food as a sure way to keep her family alive, and it did not occur to her until late in life that one could approach a kitchen with the same intensity as an artist nearing a canvas. To Peg Conroy, the kitchen was a place of labor, not a field of fantasy and play.

Though I grew up living along the Eastern seaboard, my mother never served fresh fish at her dinner table, even if I had caught and cleaned them myself. Since we were a Roman Catholic family (the oddest thing, by far, a human being could aspire to in the South before the Hare Krishnas turned up at the Atlanta airport), we were under a religious injunction not to eat meat on Friday. Anytime I would come into the house with a string of fish, my mother would hold her nose and say, "Get those smelly things out of my house this minute, young man."

1

My mother could not have been more upset if I had brought roadkill newly scraped off a highway into her kitchen. Perhaps Peg Conroy carried some bad experience with a fish into her adult life, like a bone lodged in her throat. Wherever her aversion to fish began, she solved the Friday problem by serving frozen fish sticks to her large, rowdy family for the approximately five hundred Fridays of my childhood. My youngest brothers thought that fish were rectangular in shape for the longest time. My brother Mike still prefers a fish stick to a salmon steak.

I did not taste fresh shrimp until I got to Beaufort, South Carolina, late in high school, yet I lived around inlets and rivers teeming with schools of shrimp swarming in their measureless fecundity. Each fresh tide brought shoals of white shrimp boiling into the creeks a hundred yards from the house where my mother heated up their frozen cousins.

But even my mother could not grow up in the South without accruing several specialties that she could render with casual mastery. She made corn bread that could not be improved upon. I can still smell her apple and peach pies cooling on the windowsills of our house on Spencer Avenue in New Bern, North Carolina. Her lemon bisque made her famous in whatever neighborhood we settled in during my much-traveled boyhood. Those she made by rote, out of a sense of duty. She took little joy from those mouthwatering recipes she had brought to her marriage. It saddens me that my mother never achieved any satisfaction from the kitchen, where she spent so much of her time dreaming of being elsewhere. I loved her grits and biscuits, and her fried chicken was so wonderful that I have spent much of my life searching for that piece of fried chicken which will provide the soul-stirring satisfaction of my mother's recipe.

But let it be said, my mother was not a gifted cook and never aspired to be one. She collected some recipes because, I think, she heard that was one of the things young wives did during the era in which she grew up. The table she set never contained surprises or those moments of ecstasy when some experiment she had wrought in her oven was brought to the table in triumph. My mother looked upon food as a necessity, not a realm of art.

When I wrote my book *The Prince of Tides,* I made the shrimper's wife, Lila Wingo, one of those Southern cooks who went to the kitchen with her passionate nature ablaze. By then, I thought about cooking the way I thought about writing. I had come to cooking by accident, and it was one of the strangest events in my life when I found myself before a stove with three daughters wandering around me fully expecting that I would feed them before I put them to bed.

When my first wife, the fetching Barbara Bolling, entered Emory University Law School, she pointed to the kitchen and told me from that day on I would be responsible for cooking the evening meal for the family. This seemed fair enough to me, but it contained the seeds of both disaster and high comedy. My mother had not taught her oldest son how to cook an egg, much less a full-bodied meal that would not cause rickets or beriberi among my feisty daughters. I have absolutely no recollection of how I kept myself alive from the time I graduated from The Citadel until 1969, when Barbara and I married. Certainly, I carry no memory of standing over a stove cooking something perfectly wonderful for dinner. Mostly I remember heating up things.

But with my first dinner in view, I drove to the Old New York Bookshop in midtown Atlanta to ask my friend Cliff Graubart for help. There was no book in the world that Cliff could not find for me and his spirit was generous and open-minded.

"I need a cookbook, Cliff," I said when I entered his store.

"Why?" Cliff asked.

"I'm in charge of feeding my family the evening meal from now on," I answered. "Barbara starts law school next week."

"I'm going to miss Barbara," Cliff said. "Starving to death is a tough way to die. And I can't sit by and let you kill your kids."

Cliff pretended to dial three numbers on his phone, then said to an imaginary speaker: "Hello, nine-one-one, I'd like to report an incident of child abuse out on Briarcliff Road."

"Very funny," I said. "You know of a good cookbook?"

Cliff thought for a moment and said, "I hear Escoffier's is good."

I walked out of Cliff's store with a copy of Auguste Escoffier's cookbook in my hand. It is not a manual I would encourage the first-time cook to turn to, but its purchase was a life-changing event. For a single year I used only recipes from Escoffier's great text. My family and friends raved about my cooking talents, and a passionate amateur was born in that kitchen on Briarcliff Road. I made the thrilling discovery that if I could read and follow directions, I could cook. If I discovered a fabulous recipe, I could prepare a terrific and praiseworthy dish. I could feed people well, and they would love me for it and sing my praises to friends and neighbors. Because of Emory Law School, I discovered an avocation as an amateur cook of some distinction, and I find that fact miraculous. The love of cooking is a portable, moving pleasure that I take with me into every house or country I enter. When other cooks ask me who taught me how to cook, I always say, without irony, "Auguste Escoffier was my first instructor." He was the hospitable maitre d' who led me by the arm and introduced me to the limitless world of cuisine. Because of him, I was a French cook before I was an American one.

I had never heard the word "stock" in my life when I opened Escoffier's cookbook, but then again, I had never heard of Escoffier either. I came upon this paragraph on the first page of his cookbook:

Indeed, stock is everything in cooking, at least in French cooking. Without it, nothing can be done. If one's stock is good, what remains of the work is easy; if, on the other hand, it is bad or merely mediocre, it is quite hopeless to expect anything approaching a satisfactory result.

"Hopeless," I thought as I read, panicking that the only stock I knew of lived in barns. I called Barbara and Cliff and a half dozen other friends. None of them could shed any light on what stock was, although Barbara told me she had used cans of chicken stock from the grocery store when she made soups. But Monsieur Escoffier mentioned nothing about cans. I set about my work. I took Escoffier to mean "If you do not use good stocks, you should not be allowed to eat."

For three days, I made stocks in my kitchen. I broke and roasted bones and had four burners on the stove burning brightly day and night. I made white stock, fish stock, brown stock, chicken stock, and veal stock. Some of the stock I turned into essences. I had made an essence before I had made a meal. I had made a glaze before I had roasted a portion of a cow or a sheep. Turning my back on glazes, I taught myself how to make "the leading warm sauces." I felt like a chemist, a magician, some sorcerer's apprentice made hauntingly alive by the luscious smells coming out of my kitchen.

Then I began to cook, and I have never stopped.

I have gravitated toward people who love to cook and eat and I have turned the art of stealing recipes into both a hobby and an art. I have lived in France and Italy and been lucky enough to eat in some of the finest restaurants in the world. Periodically, I have taken courses from cooks as varied as Nathalie Dupree and Giuliano Bugialli, but I have also learned from those I encountered along the way.

When I walked into Suzanne Williamson Pollak's kitchen on Hilton Head Island several years ago, she was fixing supper. She had her hands full and could not shake hands, but looked up, smiled, and said, "Hey, Pat. Wonderful to meet you. Why don't you make the pasta?"

On the counter was a mound of flour with three broken eggs set in its well. I had never made fresh pasta in my life, but I made it that night as Suzanne gave me directions from the stove. The directions were clear and easy to follow. We have been cooking together ever since. She is more fun to cook with than anyone I have ever met except my passel of fine and comely wives. Suzanne and I are both dedicated amateurs, but we can cook our little fannies off. We collect recipes and cookbooks, and both of us believe that the cooking of food is one of the most delightful activities a human being can do during the course of a lifetime. There is joy in the preparation of food that we share and try to spread around to those we love. Now we will try to spread the source of this joy to you. Suzanne is the great workhorse and beauty behind the recipes in this book. I provide the hot air and sense of story.

Let us take you to a restaurant on the Left Bank of Paris that I found when writing *The Lords of Discipline*. There are meals I ate in Rome while writing *The Prince of Tides* that ache in my memory. There is a shrimp dish that I ate in an elegant English restaurant that passed out Cuban cigars to all the gentlemen in the room after dinner that I can taste on my palate as I write this. There is barbecue and its variations in the South, and the subject is a holy one to me. I will write of truffles in the Dordogne Valley in France, cilantro in Bangkok, catfish in Alabama, scuppernong in South Carolina, Chinese food from my years in San Francisco, and white asparagus from the first meal my agent, Julian Bach, took me to in New York City.

I will put everything in and encourage you to make all the ingredients the freshest and the best money can buy. The first rule is this: use good stock. I am one of the few Southern boys in the history of cooking who ever delivered that instruction. And let me tell you that the world is a magical and unpredictable place when a man who has never cooked a meal in his life walks into a bookstore in Atlanta, Georgia, and leaves with Escoffier under his arm. I do not know if my novels will last or not, but Auguste Escoffier proved to me that a great cookbook can endure forever.

Now, let us begin, as I relive in my memory the fabulous things I have eaten in my life, the story of the food I have encountered along the way.

PIE DOUGH If the truth be told, I find making pie dough a daunting task. For the tomato and onion and the apple pies I make each summer, I buy frozen pie shells at the supermarket and find the results perfectly acceptable. But Suzanne Williamson Pollak is a purist about such matters, and she makes pie crust with the same ease I chop cabbage for slaw. Her pie crusts are works of art. • **MAKES 1 DOUBLE-CRUST PIE**

> 2 1/2 cups chilled all-purpose flour*
>
> 1/2 teaspoon salt
>
> 3/4 cup (1 1/2 sticks) cold unsalted butter, cut into small cubes
>
> 5 to 6 tablespoons ice water

I keep my flour in an airtight bag in the freezer so it is bug-free and always ready to use for pie dough.

1. Place the flour and salt in the bowl of a food processor fitted with a metal blade and process to combine. Add the very cold butter and process until the mixture is the size of peanuts, about 30 seconds. Drizzle in the ice water and pulse just until the dough comes together in two or three pieces. This will only take a few seconds. Do not overprocess, or the dough will be tough.

2. Transfer dough to a dry floured work surface and knead quickly (3 or 4 strokes so the butter does not get too warm). Form into two balls, one slightly larger than the other, wrap in plastic, and refrigerate. Chill for at least an hour before rolling.

INSTRUCTIONS FOR HAND MIXING

1. Sift the flour and salt into a bowl. Using a pastry blender (or two knives) cut the butter into the flour mixture until crumbly (the size of small peas).

2. Using a fork, stir in only enough water to form a dough (about

5 tablespoons). When the dough comes together in one or two pieces, transfer to a clean, dry, lightly floured work surface.

3. Knead until the flour and butter form one piece, working quickly so the butter doesn't get too warm (about 3 to 5 strokes). Form into two balls, one slightly larger than the other, wrap in plastic, and refrigerate. Chill for at least an hour before rolling.

• • •

PASTRY SECRETS

The success of pie pastry (or any pastry) depends on keeping the shortening and the flour cold and using ice-cold water.

Pastry in a pinch: When blending the butter and the flour, pinch a few crumbs together with your fingers. If the dough sticks together, you're ready to add the water. If it doesn't stick together, you have to add more shortening.

In the South, we use White Lily self-rising flour because it's the very best for pie crusts and biscuits.

Leave it alone: the less handling of the dough, the better. The pastry will be lighter and better if you don't try to smooth out every lump of butter.

All pies should be cooked in the lower portion of the oven so the bottom of the pie will cook. When making fruit pies, place a heavy-duty baking sheet in the oven while it is preheating. Place the pie on the hot baking sheet to bake; it will crisp the crust and catch the overflow.

PASTA DOUGH   The first time I met Suzanne Pollak, she led me with great efficiency through the steps that she elucidates in this recipe. She took me through each step slowly and cautioned me if the dough became too yolky or too dry because of excess flour. On the first five occasions we cooked together, I made the pasta dough until I became comfortable with the process. When I tasted the pasta that first night, it was like eating silk.

• **MAKES APPROXIMATELY 1 POUND, ENOUGH FOR 4 TO 6 SERVINGS**

3 cups unbleached all-purpose flour
3 large eggs, lightly beaten

1. Pour flour out on a clean, dry, smooth work surface and make a well in the center of the mound. Keep the sides of the well high enough and thick enough so the eggs will not leak over or through the sides of the flour wall. Slowly pour the eggs into the well.

2. While lightly beating the eggs with a fork, slowly incorporate the flour from the sides while you use your other hand to keep the sides of the well from collapsing. Using your hand, slowly sweep the flour up the sides of the well, building a thicker wall and at the same time letting a little flour fall from the top onto the eggs. You will use less than half the flour for the actual pasta dough. (If the eggs do manage to seep out beyond the wall of flour, all is not lost. Use the fork to push some flour over the puddle of eggs and scrape the mixture back into the main mass.)

3. When the mass begins to resemble dough, remove the excess flour. Wash your hands to remove extra flour.

4. Now start to knead the dough. If the dough is too sticky, add a little flour (sparingly). If there is too much flour in the pasta, the dough will dry out, becoming difficult to roll. Using the heels of your hands in an under-and-over motion, knead the dough (rotating it frequently) until it is smooth and elastic, at least 10 minutes.

5. When the dough is smooth and satiny, sprinkle it with a light dusting of flour, cover with a clean dish towel, and let it rest for half an hour. You will need the rest as well because the next step is rolling out the dough.

6. Divide the dough into three sections (or one section for every egg used) to make it more manageable when rolling. Rolling the dough by hand (instead of using a pasta machine) makes pasta that is uniquely yours because you can roll it out to the exact thickness you desire and cut it into the precise width you want.

7. Uncover the dough and knead it a few times. Using a rolling pin (preferably a pin about 20 inches long without handles, for better control), roll across the dough (back and forth) about 6 times; turn the dough 90 degrees and roll back and forth again. You want to stretch the dough to the desired thickness (about $^1/_8$ inch or less).

8. Using a sharp knife, cut the sheet of dough into strips: $^1/_{16}$ inch wide (tagliarini), $^1/_8$ inch (fettuccine), or $^1/_4$ inch (tagliatelle). Drape the noodles over a thin rod (or broom handle) to dry.

If you are serving the pasta immediately, bring a large pot of salted water to a boil and cook the noodles for less than a minute. If you decide to wait (recommended), carefully gather up the noodles and curl them into loose nests, placing them on floured baking sheets. You can let them dry for several hours or freeze for up to 2 weeks. Depending on the thickness of the noodle, the cooking time will be anywhere from 45 seconds to 3 minutes. To test for doneness, snip off the end of a pasta strand and taste.

• • •

CHICKEN STOCK   It is a rare moment in my life when I open the freezer and don't find frozen containers of chicken and beef stock. Slow simmering is necessary for a good stock, as well as the occasional skimming of the solids and proteins that bubble to the top. No fanaticism required here, but the clearer the stock, the better the cook. Never, never stir the stock. The making of stock is for poets and philosophers, dreamers and deep thinkers with a dinner party coming up populated only with people you love. **• MAKES 4 QUARTS**

Two 2½-pound chickens
2 large yellow onions, peeled and halved
3 large carrots, peeled and halved
3 whole celery stalks (with leaves), halved
Sprig of fresh thyme
1 garlic head, unpeeled and cut in half horizontally
1 teaspoon whole black peppercorns
2 teaspoons coarse or kosher salt

1. Remove giblets from the chickens. Under cool, gently running water, rinse chickens inside and out. Pat dry with paper towels.

2. Place all the ingredients in a large stockpot (at least 10 quarts). Add 5 quarts water (completely covering chickens) and bring to a boil. Simmer for 1 hour, occasionally skimming foam from water's surface with a slotted spoon.

3. Remove the chickens. Let cool slightly, pull the meat off the bones and reserve for another use. Return the chicken bones to the simmering stockpot. Depending on the stock's use, cook for another hour (a light stock) or up to 5 hours (a richer, deeper stock).

4. Strain the stock through a fine-mesh sieve (or double thickness of cheesecloth) into a large heatproof storage container with a tight-fitting lid. Discard solids. Bring stock to room temperature, cover, and refrigerate overnight. (To freeze, portion the strained stock into smaller containers.)

The stock will keep refrigerated for a week or frozen for several months. (After 8 weeks the stock begins to lose flavor.) Always skim the hardened (solid) fat from the surface of the stock before reheating.

• • •

FISH STOCK • MAKES ABOUT 1½ QUARTS

2 pounds mild, lean fish and fish trimmings (skeletons,* including
   heads and gills, removed)
1 large carrot, peeled and coarsely chopped
1 yellow onion, peeled and coarsely chopped
1 whole celery stalk (with leaves), coarsely chopped
1 cup dry white wine
1 strip lemon zest or juice of 1 lemon
Small bunch flat leaf parsley
1 teaspoon coarse or kosher salt
1 teaspoon whole black peppercorns

Do not use strong-tasting fish bones and heads such as mackerel or bluefish unless the stock will be used for a recipe featuring these fish.

1. Rinse the fish. Place the fish and vegetables in a large stockpot. Add the wine and 2 quarts cold water. Over medium-high heat, bring stock to a simmer. Use a slotted spoon to skim off foam on surface of the liquid. Add the lemon zest, parsley, salt, and peppercorns.

2. Simmer gently for 20 to 30 minutes. Depending on the stock's use, cook for another hour (a light stock) or up to 5 hours (a richer, deeper stock for gumbo and Creole dishes). Let the stock cool and strain it through a fine-mesh sieve (or double thickness of cheesecloth) into a large heatproof storage container (with a tight-fitting lid). Discard solids. Bring to room temperature, cover, and refrigerate overnight. (To freeze, portion the strained stock into smaller containers.)

The stock will keep refrigerated for a week or frozen for several months. (After 8 weeks the stock begins to lose flavor.)

• • •

BEEF STOCK
• **MAKES 3 QUARTS**

5 pounds beef bones (with a little meat still attached), cut into
   1-inch pieces by your butcher
2 large yellow onions, peeled and halved
2 carrots, peeled and halved
2 whole celery stalks (with leaves), halved
1 large ripe tomato, halved
5 garlic cloves, unpeeled
1 bay leaf
1 tablespoon whole black peppercorns

1. Preheat the oven to 450°F.

2. Put the bones in a large roasting pan and roast in preheated oven until well browned, about 30 minutes. Add the vegetables and garlic and continue roasting for another 15 minutes (roasting will caramelize the vegetables and beef, resulting in a rich, complex stock).

3. Using long tongs, transfer beef and vegetables to a large stock-pot (about 10 quarts). Add the bay leaf, peppercorns, and 4 quarts cold water (enough to cover the beef by 2 inches).

4. Over medium-high heat, slowly bring the mixture to a boil. Use a slotted spoon to skim foam from the surface of the liquid. Skim the foam frequently, being careful not to actually stir the stock. Simmer gently until the stock is deeply colored, about 5 hours. (You may have to add a little water to keep the meat and vegetables covered.)

5. Strain the stock through a fine-mesh sieve (or double thickness of cheesecloth) into a large heatproof storage container with a tight-fitting lid. Discard solids. Bring stock to room temperature, cover, and refrigerate. (To freeze, portion the strained stock into smaller containers.)

Variation Preheat oven to lowest setting, 200°F or 250°F. After bringing the stock to a boil, place the covered stockpot on the bottom rack (or floor) of the oven. Let stock simmer for 24 to 48 hours. Strain the stock, cool, and refrigerate (as above). The oven variation only applies to beef stock; neither chicken nor fish stock benefits from long simmering.

CHAPTER ONE

Nathalie Dupree

The first actual cooking teacher who took both my money and my grief for imparting culinary secrets to me was the inimitable, unclassifiable queen of the Southern kitchen, Nathalie Dupree. Though Nathalie does not know this, she is one of the few people in my life who seems more like a fictional character than a flesh-and-blood person.

When my novel *Beach Music* came out in 1995, I had included a couple of recipes in the book, and had tried to impart some of my love of Roman cuisine and the restaurants of Rome. Several journalists who write about food for newspapers interviewed me about the food angle in the novel, curious about the fact that the book's protagonist, Jack McCall, wrote cookbooks and restaurant reviews. A woman from the *Washington Post* conducted a delightful interview over the phone, and during our conversation, I mentioned that I had taken Nathalie's course in the cooking school she ran in the old Rich's department store in downtown Atlanta. The woman called Nathalie after our interview, and Nathalie tracked me down to report on the nature of their conversation.

Nathalie's voice is deep and musical and seductive. She possesses the rare ability to be both maddening and hilarious in the course of a single sentence. Her character is a shifting, ever-changing thing, and she reinvents herself all over again every couple of years. In one way, she seems the same, yet you are aware she is in the process of a complete transformation. When she tells about her life, you could swear she was speaking of a hundred women, not just one.

"Pat, darling," Nathalie said on the phone, "all my working life I've been scheming and plotting and dreaming of ways to get an interview with the food editor of the *Washington Post*. You can imagine my joy when I heard that the food editor of the *Post* had left a message on my answering machine. And I thought, Yes, it's finally happening; your prayers have been answered, Nathalie."

"That's great, Nathalie," I said, not quite knowing where she was going with this. You never know where Nathalie is going with a train of thought; you simply know that the train will not be on time, will carry many passengers, and will eventually collide with a food truck stalled somewhere down the line on damaged tracks.

"Can you imagine my disappointment when I found out that they wanted to interview me about *you*, instead of about *me*. I admit, Pat, that after I got over the initial shock, it turned suddenly to bitterness. After all, what do I possibly get out of talking about you when I could be talking about my own cookbooks? Naturally, I did not let on a word about what I was really thinking, but I did suggest, very subtly I might add, that she might want to do a feature on me and my work sometime in the future. When were you in my class, Pat?"

"In 1980," I said.

"I don't remember that. Did you really take my class? Who else was in it?"

"My wife Lenore. Jim Landon. George Lanier. A nice woman who lived on the same floor as my dad in the Darlington Apartments."

"It doesn't ring a bell for me," she said. "Was I good?"

"You were wonderful," I said.

"All my ex-students say that. It must be a gift."

"You were a great teacher."

"And sexy. I won't be happy until you tell me I was also extraordinarily sexy."

"I could barely cook I was so aroused. All the other men in the class felt the same way. It's hard to make a perfect soufflé when you're rutting."

"Pat, you know the way to a young girl's heart," Nathalie said. "But I want you to know that I'll always be perfectly furious at you for getting into the *Washington Post* food world before I did. That's my bailiwick, not yours."

"It will never happen again, Nathalie," I promised. "All your bailiwicks will be safe from poor Conroy."

When Nathalie taught her cooking class at Rich's, I learned new lessons about insouciance, style, and lack of preparation. Always, at the last minute, Nathalie's worthy assistant, Kate Almand, would move in to provide a missing utensil or bag of flour or loin of veal that Nathalie had misplaced or left in her car. The joy of watching Nathalie's cooking shows on television has always come from her artless displays of confusion and disorganization, and her sheer bravado when she actually makes a mistake. Unlike Martha Stewart, Nathalie often looks beaten up when she completes a segment of her show. She can be covered with flour up to her elbows after baking a loaf of bread, can drop her perfectly roasted capon on the kitchen floor, or can garnish her pumpkin pie with cooked rice that she meant to put in her delicious cream of carrot soup. On her television show, Nathalie has turned the culinary mistake or misstep into her signature moment.

Nathalie is always worth the price of admission and I love cooking with her. Disorder follows her around like a spaniel. There is no hum of quiet efficiency in her kitchen to intimidate me as I caramelize the onions or beat the egg whites to a stiff peak. She prides herself on being a hands-on cook, and I have seen her hands dripping with batter, red with blood, and crimson from handling baby beets. Like most good cooks, she is absolutely fearless, taking on each task with gusto. And her conversation mixes well with the mouthwatering aromas rising out of her kitchen as the meal takes shape around us. I personally do not believe Nathalie has ever enjoyed a quiet meal at home with her equally hospitable husband, the writer Jack Bass. When I knew her in Atlanta, the whole city in all its shapes, races, and classes seemed to pass by her dining room table.

She attracts friends like a magnet does iron filings. Her desire to entertain and feed people seems insatiable to me, a mark of her character as striking as her beautiful almond-shaped eyes.

On the night our class made a crown roast of pork, orange and fennel salad, turnip greens and grits, and crème brûlée for dessert, she told a story in fits and starts that ended only after she poured the dessert wine. I soon found myself looking forward to Nathalie's stories as much as I did her recipes. They ranged the world and involved famous chefs, cookbook writers of note, lovers and husbands and boyfriends of both the charming and monstrous varieties. I preferred the stories of her lovers because her voice could turn smoky and catlike as we, her students, chopped and shredded and prepared our meals according to her instructions. The story and the food comingled and exchanged properties.

I can taste neither fennel nor crème brûlée without thinking of the story she told that night. I tell it from memory, but I will try to use Nathalie's ineffable voice. She could say the word "lover" and infuse it with all the savor and forbiddenness of a Frenchwoman recalling an affair with an Italian count. "I was living in Greenwich Village in New York," she told us. "I had taken up with a dashing, utterly charming man. He turned out to be a perfect cad, but didn't they all in those days, darling? Jim, I'd slice that fennel a little thinner. It looks too much like celery when you slice it that way. Yes, perfect. He was, by far, the most sophisticated, demanding lover I had ever been involved with up to that time. He was the consummate gourmet who had eaten in the finest restaurants in the world since he was a child. Well. I decided I was going to cook him a meal that he would never forget, one that would prove my love for him, yet honor his amazing sophistication.

"I went next door to get advice from the two gay men who lived in the most spectacular apartment. They knew everybody and everything, but they were of no help that day. Greenwich Village was astir, at least the gay portion of the Village—no small share, I assure you—with the news of a gay serial killer who would not only murder his poor victims, but would then mutilate them in ghastly ways. My neighbors' hysteria rendered them useless and I heard them turn all six locks in their door as soon as I left their apartment and began the search for the most unusual meal for my lover.

"There was a little butcher shop in the East Village that sold specialty meats and could usually come up with a surprise. Pat, use a whisk to beat your eggs for the crème brûlée. You're not scrambling eggs for a country brunch. This is a French dish, dearie. Oh, where was I? Yes. The butcher had a surprise for me. He had two things in his shop he had never carried before: live escargots and testicles freshly cut from yearling calves in upper New York State. 'Mountain oysters!' I shouted in triumph, and I was sure that every snail my lover had eaten had come from a can. I paid cash for everything. I spent a fortune. But that's what you do when you're in love. You're never yourself. You are possessed. You'll do anything. George, you need to get your pork into the oven. Less fanaticism with the presentation. It's lovely, but it's still pork. And trichinosis is a fact of life. I took the mountain oysters and snails back to my apartment, then left them in the sink and ran down to buy the wine for the meal. I threw some ice on the calves' testicles because organ meat is very perishable. But I got delayed when I asked the French chef who ran a restaurant on my street about the preparation of the escargots. He had a certain dark frisson and I soon realized he was flirting with me. This made me late in my return. My lover would be arriving with roses in a few hours. I opened the door of my apartment and I'll never forget what I saw there! I've had nightmares about it more than once. The snails had conspired to effect a vast breakout. They were everywhere. On the walls, on the ceiling, trailing their slimy bodies across my copper pans, and my cookbooks. My screams of repulsion and terror resounded throughout my apartment building.

"The two dear gay men next door were the first neighbors to arrive. But the escargots did not interest them. They were transfixed by the sight of a whole bucket of male genitalia in my sink. You could not blame them. They had never seen mountain oysters, nor did they know that anyone would cook and eat them. They thought they had stumbled into the lair of the serial killer who was preying on and mutilating gay males. The snails on the walls simply added a note of horror to it all. They fled screaming down the stairs and out into the streets. The police were called.

It was an affair to remember. Pat, are you burning your greens? Good; it's sinful to burn greens. There's always a point of no return, you know.

"Did I fix my lover dinner that night? But of course. All the commotion simply made the evening more special. I served the escargots in their own shells with garlic, butter, and parsley—after I boiled and cleaned them, of course. I fried the mountain oysters, and they were superb. After dinner and cognac, my lover and I—ah, but that is personal, part of the night's mystery. There are parts of some stories that should never be told. Ah. Class, take a deep breath. Dinner is almost ready. Smell it. Breathe deeply. Now. Now."

Though Nathalie Dupree did not remember much about my presence in her class, it marked me forever. I remain her enthusiast, her evangelist, her acolyte, and her grateful student. She taught me that cooking and storytelling make the most delightful coconspirators. Either was good alone, but in communion with each other, they could rise to the level of ecstasy.

Three of Nathalie's recipes.

MELON RING WITH MINT AND HONEY-LIME DRESSING

The last time Nathalie Dupree invited me to dinner, she met me at the front door and told me with her most theatrical flourish that she felt "worse than a rabid dog or the parakeet that the proverbial cat dragged in." She is a woman of great entrances and exits, and said to me, "Pat, you must play the part of the gentleman and rescue this damsel in distress. You were my student, and you must cook the meal and save this night for me. If my guests realized I was about to begin projectile vomiting across the room, they'd just die."

"I will fix the meal gladly, Nathalie," I said, moving toward the kitchen as she moved out to the living room and the sounds of her guests in conversation. I made the meal: a standing rib roast, a simple green salad, steamed asparagus, and fresh peaches with cream and a scoop of homemade vanilla ice cream. To begin the meal, Nathalie asked, "I got a call from our good mutual friend from Atlanta, the one who's been married six times. Do you have any theories about why all her husbands have turned out to be gay?"

• **SERVES 6 TO 8**

> 2 envelopes unflavored gelatin
>
> 2 cups freshly squeezed orange juice
>
> $1/2$ cup sugar
>
> $1/2$ cup fresh lemon juice
>
> $1/4$ cup finely chopped mint leaves
>
> 1 cup melon balls (preferably a mix of cantaloupe, honeydew, and/or
>   similar kinds), plus additional (optional)
>
> **FOR THE DRESSING**
>
> 1 cup yogurt
>
> $1/4$ cup honey
>
> $1/4$ cup fresh lime juice

1. Place the gelatin, 1 cup of the orange juice, and the sugar in a small pan and heat until the gelatin and sugar are dissolved. Do not let the mixture come to a boil.

2. Remove the gelatin mixture from the heat and add the lemon juice, the remaining 1 cup orange juice, and the mint.

3. Put the pan over a bowl of ice water and stir for a few minutes until the gelatin begins to thicken. Fold in the melon balls. Pour into a 4-cup ring mold and refrigerate for at least 4 hours.

4. Unmold and fill the center with additional melon balls, if desired. To make the dressing: Mix all the ingredients together and serve with the ring and melon balls.

• • •

BAKED FISH DAUFUSKIE Nathalie baked this recipe for me in her condo in Atlanta soon after I graduated from her cooking school class. She named the dish after Daufuskie Island, where I had once taught eighteen black children in the first year of teacher integration in South Carolina. The children would often bring me gifts of deviled crab, boiled shrimp, or roasted fish their mothers sent wrapped in aluminum foil. That was the year I learned of the glory of fresh fish. "That fish was swimming yesterday evening, Mr. Conroy," Sallie Ann Robinson told me after giving me a piece of sea bass her mother had baked. Thirty-three years later, that same Sallie Ann Robinson would write her own cookbook, *Gullah Home Cooking the Daufuskie Way*, which was published in 2003 by the University of North Carolina Press. • **SERVES 4**

> 4 grouper fillets or other firm-fleshed white fish such as red snapper, sea bass, or mahimahi
> 1 medium red onion, sliced
> 1/2 cup mayonnaise
> 2 tablespoons Dijon mustard
> 1 tablespoon fresh lemon juice
> Paprika

1. Preheat oven to 350°F.

2. Put the grouper fillets in a greased baking dish and cover with sliced onion. Combine the mayonnaise, mustard, and lemon juice in a small bowl and spoon the mixture over the fish and onion. Sprinkle the top with paprika. Bake for 10 minutes per inch of thickness. Finish under the broiler for a couple of minutes to brown.

• • •

WHITE CHOCOLATE–PISTACHIO COOKIES • MAKES 50

2¼ cups all-purpose flour
1 teaspoon baking soda
½ teaspoon salt
½ pound (2 sticks) unsalted butter, softened
1 cup light brown sugar
½ cup granulated sugar
2 large eggs
1 teaspoon vanilla extract
1 cup white chocolate chips
1 cup chopped unsalted pistachios

1. Preheat oven to 350°F. Sift the flour, baking soda, and salt together.

2. In the bowl of an electric mixer, beat the butter and sugars until fluffy. Add the eggs and vanilla and blend well. Carefully add the flour mixture until well blended. Stir in chocolate and nuts by hand.

3. Drop the dough by teaspoonfuls onto an ungreased cookie sheet 2 inches apart. Bake for 10 to 15 minutes, until lightly browned. Allow to cool slightly on the sheet before removing to a wire rack to cool completely. Store in an airtight container.

CHAPTER TWO

The Pleasures of Reading Cookbooks No One Has Ever Heard Of

When I first began cooking, I had no idea that it would lead me to a forking path of minor literature that would provide me with as much reading joy as F. Scott Fitzgerald. Because I began with the astringent, no-nonsense Monsieur Escoffier, who seemed to know all things about all foods and did not suffer fools easily, it took me a long time to ease out of his authoritative embrace. In the kitchen, Escoffier is every bit as intimidating as Marcel Proust is at the writing table. What surprised me was how much pure delight I took in reading recipes I could never even think about fixing myself.

I began collecting cookbooks in a modest, desultory way. But cooking is an insidious addiction and it was many years before I realized I needed to enroll in a twelve-step program to control my passion for the ownership of cookbooks. I suffered a heart-stopping pang of pure envy when I first gazed at Nathalie Dupree's awesome cookbook collection, which sat in proud, soldierly rows in her kitchen. In Nathalie's library of food, the recipes of the entire world seemed to be jockeying for position. You could cook anything if you just owned enough of those secret-bearing texts. The sauces and salsas and sugos of the world awaited my inspection and edification if I was bold enough to purchase a serious number of these bright, ebullient books.

My beginnings were modest. After Escoffier, I started by gathering small collections of Junior League and church cookbooks from around the South. They pleased me greatly because they were such accurate reflections of their cities and towns, as authentic as fingerprints. For me, they were also compendiums of acquired wisdom and experience that offered shortcuts that I could not learn in a lifetime. One of my first purchases was a book whose title I loved, *Talk About Good!*, published by the Service League of Lafayette, Louisiana. It marked the first time I was exposed to the very usable and useful tips that experienced cooks share with one another.

> **1.** Use as little water as possible when cooking vegetables. Avoid violent boiling of most vegetables.
>
> **2.** Always add hot water, not cold, to vegetables when cooking to keep the vegetables from being tough.

A cookbook gathered by the residents of my own Fripp Island is literally chock-full of these invaluable hints that seem part folk wisdom and part residue of the observant eye all cooks develop over the course of a lifetime spent at the stove. Though I don't know why I love the authority and pungency of these kitchen aids, love them I do. Fripp Islanders supply these snappy advisories:

> **1.** A dampened paper towel or terry cloth brushed downward on a cob of corn will remove every strand of corn silk.
>
> **2.** Catsup will flow out of the bottle evenly if you first insert a drinking straw, push it to the bottom of the bottle, then remove.

You would not learn such things from the cookbooks of Julia Child, Wolfgang Puck, or Daniel Boulud, and this is not meant to be a critique of these inimitable chefs. These compilations of tips are a form of generosity and I cherish them particularly because of their anonymity. In all the small-time cookbooks I own, these clues to make your time in the kitchen richer and more efficient are never signed by their authors. They are simply proffered, bouquets tossed out to the strangers who would follow after them.

Another pleasure of the small-town or small-organization cookbook is the recipe author's personal commentary on the dish at hand. It can be as simple as "One way to a man's heart," or "The longer you keep it, the better it gets." But I look for the secret writers and dreamers who describe the special merits of their favorite snacks or meals. One such is the helpful Mrs. Arnold Rankin, who placed her recipe for Hot Sherry Cheese Dip in *Cotton Country,* a book put out by the Decatur Junior Service League in Alabama. She gives her recipe these sterling accolades: "a working girl's best friend, a bit of magic for the busy mother, a modern miracle for the I-hate-to-cook lady. There are few things this good that are really instant. This is!" That exclamation point made me a lifetime admirer of the perky Mrs. Rankin.

In the same charming cookbook, the admirable Mrs. William A. Sims composed this metaphysical advertisement for her Sweet and Sour Meatballs recipe: "The men at your party will gather like bees at a hive around your chafing dish of meatballs." The aristocratic and confident Mrs. Barrett Shelton Sr. touted her Stuffed Country Ham with this riff from her culinary trumpet: "To call this merely 'Stuffed Ham' is an injustice. 'Spectacular' is the only word to describe this ham: spectacular in appearance and taste. Trouble—perhaps—but for a buffet dinner or cocktail party mainliner, nothing could do more for your reputation as a good cook or hostess." Have you ever seen three sentences more confidently rendered by a hand so fine and sure—the disdainful dashes surrounding that intimidating "perhaps" and that bold, two-eyed colon stopping you in midstream for emphasis. A small history of the South could be composed just by studying the cadences and assuredness of position in Mrs. Barrett Shelton Sr.'s place in Decatur society. It would be paradisiacal for me to pass down a Decatur street and have the imperious

Mrs. Shelton whisper to a group of lunching friends, "Mr. Conroy's new in town, but I think he has the makings of a cocktail party mainliner."

Marian Hornsby Bowditch, the unforgettable mother of the unforgettable John Bowditch, a classmate of mine at The Citadel, wrote one of the most remarkable cookbooks I have in my possession. The entire book is written in Mrs. Bowditch's own handwriting. The recipes are free-ranging, eclectic, and brilliant. She wrote the book and dedicated it to her "four traveling gourmet sons who have called me collect from all parts of the country for recipes." It is a book of consummate genius. Every recipe seems complete and perfect unto itself—you cannot think of a single ingredient to add or subtract. The recipes were years in the composing and I have no doubt that Mrs. Bowditch is one of the finest chefs in this country. Her cookbook, *From the Kitchen at Hornsby House in Yorktown, Virginia,* is as much a treasure in its own way as *Charleston Receipts* or the early James Beard. As willful and opinionated as Escoffier himself, Mrs. Bowditch dispenses advice and precise instructions. Does she have tips? This larger-than-life woman brims over with personality, and conversation is an art form with her. Mrs. Bowditch tells you:

1. Put an oyster shell in the teakettle to prevent its becoming encrusted with lime. (How in God's name did she come up with this?)

2. Store mushrooms and string beans in a brown paper bag in the refrigerator, not in plastic.

These secrets of the trade are what I love best about those modest books that spring from the collective unconscious of churches, schools, clubs, and homes. They are bound economically and most of them are clasped together with plastic ringlets that give them the look and feel of an amateur's obsession. When I wanted to write this homage to this unpraised genre I pulled, at random, *Come and Get It!,* a cookbook put out by the Junior Welfare League of Talladega, Alabama; *Bayou Cuisine,* published by St. Stephen's Episcopal Church in Indianola, Mississippi;

and a dozen others. All are unpretentious, helpful, calming to the soul, and causing great joy to the human palate.

The only book I did not own that I quoted from was *Cotton Country*, the one from which I cheerfully quoted the ladies of Decatur, Alabama, extolling the virtues of their own recipes. A young woman named Margaret Holly who did research for me during the writing of *Beach Music* is from Decatur. I called to see if she knew those ladies I was quoting with such relish. Margaret not only knew them, she knew them exceedingly well and told me the inside scoop on the three women I had quoted. Then Margaret shocked me by proving once again that the world is closing in on itself, and that the South is the smallest geographic entity on earth.

"Pat, it's nice that you think those ladies wrote the witty little commentaries, but none of them can write that well."

"Who wrote them?"

"My mother wrote every one of them," Margaret said. "No, she had trouble with the cookies and someone else had to do those."

In the front of the book, I looked up the cookbook committee who compiled the book. At the bottom of the page I saw this notation: "Recipe Commentary—Mrs. William E. Shinn, Jr., the mother of Margaret Holly." It is one of the simple pleasures of my life that I read these unknown cookbooks, but there are certain times—like this one—when they offer me a glimpse into the magical, the purely enchanted.

COCKTAIL PECANS It is a lucky yard that hosts a pecan tree. There are several things better than a pecan pie, but not many. There are several things better than roasted, salted, and buttered pecans, but not by much. In my youth I would irritate my mother by pronouncing this as *pee-can*, which she considered redneck, and she would correct me with *puh-cahn*, which she thought more genteel. • **MAKES 1 POUND**

1 cup sugar

¾ teaspoon freshly ground nutmeg

¾ teaspoon cumin

¾ teaspoon freshly ground black pepper

¾ teaspoon cayenne pepper

1 teaspoon coarse or kosher salt

2 large egg whites

1 pound pecan halves

1. Preheat the oven to 325°F.

2. In a small bowl, stir together the sugar, nutmeg, cumin, black pepper, cayenne, and salt.

3. In another, larger bowl, whisk the egg whites until barely frothy. Add the nuts to the egg whites and turn to coat. Pour the sugar and spice mixture over the pecans and stir to coat.

4. Spread the pecans on a baking sheet and place in oven until browned, about 1 hour. Stir occasionally to prevent clumping.

5. Place the baking sheet on a rack to cool. Transfer the room-temperature nuts to an airtight container.

Warm and crisp the nuts in a preheated 350°F oven for 10 minutes before serving, if desired.

• • •

SMITHFIELD HAM SPREAD   In the South, the Smithfield ham sets the gold standard. For me, I thought the word "Smithfield" was a synonym for excellence. After the funeral of a friend in Atlanta, I heard a guest boast, "There are four hams on the table. All Smithfield. That's how much people thought about her."   • **MAKES 2½ CUPS**

    2 cups diced Smithfield ham
    ½ cup mayonnaise
    1 tablespoon sweet pickle relish
    Coarsely ground black pepper
    Thick slices country bread

1. Place the diced ham in the bowl of a food processor fitted with a metal blade and pulse until ham is roughly chopped. Add the mayonnaise and process until the ham mixture comes together. Add the sweet relish and black pepper and pulse several times to incorporate. Transfer from processor to a mixing bowl using a rubber spatula and stir the spread (with an under-and-over motion) to make sure the relish is evenly distributed.

2. Cover and refrigerate until ready to use. To serve, bring the spread to room temperature. Spread on thick slices of country bread and cut into small squares.

• • •

BENNE WAFERS

from Charleston Receipts *(collected by the Junior League of Charleston, 1950)*   • **MAKES SEVERAL DOZEN**

    2 cups all-purpose flour
    1 teaspoon salt, plus additional
    Dash of cayenne pepper

¾ cup shortening or margarine

Approximately ¼ cup ice water

1 cup toasted benne (sesame) seeds*

*To toast benne seeds, put in a heavy pan over medium heat until dark brown, being careful not to burn them.

1. Preheat oven to 300°F.

2. Mix the dry ingredients in a large bowl. Cut in the shortening and add enough of the ice water to make a dough the consistency of pie crust, then add the seeds.

3. On a dry, lightly floured surface, roll out the dough until ⅛ inch thick, then cut into small round wafers. Place wafers on a cookie sheet and bake for 20 to 30 minutes. Before removing the pan from the oven, sprinkle the wafers lightly with salt.

These may be kept in a covered tin or cracker jar. Before serving, run into a slow oven to crisp.

• • •

CRAB LOUIS

from Party Receipts *from the Junior League of Charleston*

• MAKES 2 CUPS

½ cup chili sauce

½ cup mayonnaise

1 garlic clove, minced

½ teaspoon dry mustard

1 tablespoon bottled horseradish

1 tablespoon Worcestershire sauce

¼ teaspoon Tabasco sauce

½ teaspoon salt

2 hard-boiled eggs, finely chopped

8 ounces flaked crabmeat, picked over and shells discarded

1. Combine the first eight ingredients in a medium bowl and mix well.

2. Add the eggs and crabmeat and stir gently to combine. Refrigerate for 2 to 3 hours before serving.

• • •

VIDALIA ONION DIP

from Windows *(Brenau College Alumnae Association, Gainesville, Georgia)*   • **MAKES ABOUT 5 CUPS**

2 cups finely chopped Vidalia onion

2 cups grated Swiss or Gruyère cheese

1 1/2 to 2 cups mayonnaise

crackers or toast squares

1. Preheat the oven to 325°F.

2. Mix all the ingredients together in a bowl and spread evenly in a shallow baking dish. Bake for 20 minutes. Serve with crackers or toast squares.

CHAPTER THREE

New Bern

In 1951, my mother enrolled me in St. Paul's Catholic school in the magical city of New Bern, North Carolina, where Sister Mary Maurice would teach me the useful gift of reading. Everything about New Bern seemed charged with mystery and spectacle and amusement. My mother caught a five-pound bass in the Trent River beneath the bridge, and I remember that black face rising toward the hooked worm like some behemoth out of mythology. There was a shoe store downtown where I could slide my shoes beneath an X-ray machine and study the bones of my small feet. My mother and I would mount a neighbor's stone fence and feed a speckled fawn found abandoned in the deep woods around New Bern. On the next street, a man with a scuppernong arbor with grapes cascading in green profusion told my grandfather and me to help ourselves to as many grapes as we could eat. My father taught me how to ride a bike on Spencer Avenue. Our next-door neighbors were Lebanese Catholics, the Zatoons, and their cousins, the Shapoos, lived across the street. Janet and Marilyn Shapoo were the prettiest girls in the town where Pepsi was invented. (Because I was born in Atlanta and my grandmother's property abutted the mythical Candler estate, Callanwolde, I was not allowed to switch my cola affiliation. To Peg

Conroy, drinking a Pepsi was an act of apostasy and a decision as unthinkable as a sex change operation.) Gourds as large as your head grew on vines along our backyard fence. I heard my mother sing along with Patti Page as both women celebrated Mockingbird Hill. My mother's other favorite songs that year were "How Much Is That Doggie in the Window?" and "The Tennessee Waltz." I loved the sound of my mother singing, even though it would be years before I discovered she could not carry a tune. I like to think that my mother was happy in New Bern that year; I like to think that I was.

On Sundays, we dressed up and attended St. Paul's small but pretty church. I could study the altar where my mother and father exchanged their vows. It was a city of pretty stores and distinguished houses and deep, shaded gardens where a child could lose himself in the dreaminess of games. My mother told me that New Bern was once the capital city of North Carolina and that the people who lived here had once had the courage to rise up and repel the soldiers of a British king. That is when she let me in on the secret that my countrymen were once British citizens. I did not know what Britain was or what a citizen was, but I was in first grade and wanted to know everything in the world. "The redcoats once marched down this street," my mother said with contempt, and my heart filled up with loathing of those redcoats that my mother held in such disfavor.

In school I had trouble finding my way. I discovered I could not say a word out loud because of a baffled shyness I could not control. Sister Maurice spent the year coaxing me to say anything at all to her, and it frustrated her immensely that I would not read to her from my reader or answer her questions about addition. She divided the class into three reading groups, the Eagles, the Bluebirds, and the Toads. I was placed, in great shame, among the poor Toads. I have loved all species of frog since that moment of pure mortification. When my first report card was issued, I overheard my mother tell my father, "I don't think Pat is as smart as we thought, Don."

But it was New Bern, a city enchanted with itself and the boys and girls lucky enough to be growing up on her watch, that granted me the gift of my own voice. The day after report cards came out, Sister Maurice wrote a word up on the blackboard, a new word, strange as a hieroglyph to the eyes of first graders. "Sound it out. Sound the word out. We won't go to recess until one of you sounds out this word." For two minutes, I stared at that unknown word, and I made sounds in my mind, then I raised my hand. Sister called out my name. "Radio," I said, and Sister Maurice said, "Recess time." The class stormed out into the playground. The next day she wrote another word on the blackboard, this one curlicued and laden with strange syllables. The word stared back at me as I fought against its waves and its multivoweled insolence. Three minutes and I raised my hand. "Umbrella," I said. "Recess time," the good nun said, and my classmates spilled out into the light. Sister Maurice stopped me, hugged me with great sweetness, and whispered something to me. I flew out into the sunshine, an Eagle at last.

In the school yard that same year, my father did something wonderful for me, words that do not appear often in my collected works. At recess, with the whole school watching and waiting, my father made a swift and sudden appearance in his black-winged fighter plane, the powerful and otherworldly AD. He flew so low over the playground I recognized his face. He dipped the wings of his craft as a salute to the screaming children below. He made two more passes and I kept screaming, "That's my dad. That's my dad." Then he turned his plane and headed back to Cherry Point. The high point of our life as father and son was over.

It was a time before air-conditioning, all the windows were open, and the wives all baked fresh pies and let them cool on the windowsills. Mrs. Orringer, a high-spirited Jewish woman who lived to our left in a large house that dwarfed our own, gave my sister and me free run of her garden and let us gather any blooming flowers to make bouquets for our mother. She fed us expensive chocolates made in England or Switzerland that she bought on trips to see her son in New York, who was married to one of my father's favorite singers, J. P. Morgan. It made me dream of exotic worlds where the women could call themselves J.P. My sister Carol's verbal precociousness began to assert itself about that time, and I heard her asking my mother if eating chocolate was "habit-forming."

Carol was four years old and had started constructing sentences out of the longest, most difficult words uttered by the adults around her. Often she would not have the slightest idea of what the words meant, but she threw around phrases like "the Russian Revolution" and "the bombing of Hiroshima." To me Carol seemed extraterrestrial in her verbal alacrity. None of us knew what she would say next. She was capable of saying anything and everything, a habit that has continued to this very day. An American poet grew up in the bedroom next door, and it was thrilling to see the language turn to orchids and amethysts and centipedes on her lips as she threw words all over the air in our tiny New Bern home.

My father bought one of the first television sets ever to appear on Spencer Avenue, and Carol and I would watch mesmerized for hours. I did not realize we were eyewitnesses to the early days of television because I was cocooned in a child's vision of time and had been on the planet a mere six years. Carol and I were watching the Cisco Kid and Pancho one afternoon when our parents came up behind us, and my mother said, "Would y'all like to see the Cisco Kid and Pancho tomorrow?"

"Sure," we both said.

Our parents drove us downtown to the main business street of New Bern, where we joined hundreds of parents and children who were herded into the movie theater to see those Western heroes on tour. I now know that poor Cisco and Pancho must've been on the tour from hell if they were in New Bern, but I thought it was a splendid and magical thing when I was a first grader. At the end of a screening of their film, the two Mexican cowboys made their way onstage with their gaudy costumes and outlandish hats. They drew tickets out of a hat for door prizes, and they called out my ticket number. Dad lifted me out of my seat, and I walked appalled with every eye in the theater affixed on me. I approached the two giant men on the stage, and they shook hands with me.

"Are you a good little boy?" Cisco asked me.

I have no memory of this, but my mother said I brought down the house by replying, "Si, Ceesco."

The next month, my mother walked by her two children in front of the television, and she reports that I said, "Mama, next week I'd like to meet Superman and the Lone Ranger and Tonto."

The country of first grade blends with the newfoundland of second grade, but I had to change neither teachers nor towns as Sister Maurice graduated to the second grade with me and my class, and the saltwater town of New Bern stayed the same. Each night of our childhood my mother would read books and poetry to Carol and me. I fell in love with my mother's lovely, softly accented voice. Whatever she read, Carol and I fell in love with. Though both of us bear unhealable scars from that childhood, I think both of us are writers because of it. This was the year my mother read *The Diary of Anne Frank* to her two children. As a young boy, I was caught up in the immediacy and brightness of Anne Frank's unmistakable voice. I studied photographs of Anne Frank and noted how pretty she was and how she looked exactly as I expected her to look—fresh and knowing and, this was important to me, smarter than the adults around her. I fell in love with Anne Frank and have never fallen out of love with her.

But my mother did not prepare her children for the abruptness of the diary's ending. Anne's voice went silent after the Nazis invaded her family's attic hideaway, a place I visit every time I find myself in the watery, cross-stitched city of Amsterdam.

"What happened to Anne, Mama?" I asked.

"Why'd she stop writing?" Carol asked.

And my Georgia-born mother, who did not go to college and was born into the deepest Southern poverty, began telling us about the coming of the Nazi beast, the cattle cars, the gas chambers, and the murder of six million Jews, including babies and children and the lovely Anne Frank.

I will always love and honor my mother when I think of the words she spoke to us next. "Carol Ann and Pat, listen to me. I want to raise a family that will hide Jews." And Peg Conroy repeated, "I want to raise a family that will hide Jews."

And I will always adore the spirit of my sister Carol, who asked me to walk next door to Mrs. Orringer's house on Spencer Avenue in the marvelous town of New Bern. Mrs. Orringer came to the door, dressed in grand flamboyance.

"Yes, children? What is it?"

My sister Carol looked up into Mrs. Orringer's eyes and said with a child's simplicity and ardor, "Mrs. Orringer, don't worry about anything."

"What are you talking about, child?"

"We will hide you," Carol said.

"What?" Mrs. Orringer said.

"We will hide you," Carol repeated.

She marched us into her living room and made us sit on her sofa as she called my mother next door for an explanation. We heard our mother's voice describing the reading of Anne Frank. When she got to the part about hiding Jews, Mrs. Orringer surprised us by laying the phone down in its cradle and bursting into tears. She covered us with kisses and stuffed us with chocolates from Switzerland. Before going to The Citadel, I moved twenty-three times in my nomadic, troubled boyhood, but I never had a neighbor who loved my sister and me with the passion of the generous-hearted Mrs. Orringer.

Because I was so happy there, I have never been back to New Bern, not once in my life.

GOOSEBERRY PIE   My lifelong love of pies got an upgrade when I used to take my children to spend part of the summer with my sister Carol on the North Shore of Lake Superior. My sister told me it was beautiful at the North Shore, but she did not tell me it was a spectacular landscape with rivers pouring out of the Mojave range that were wild and tumbling and so pure you could drink the water fresh in your cupped hands. The Temperance River was one of the most beautiful bodies of water in which I have ever swum. I let it take me out into Lake Superior because I was curious when the famous cold water of Superior would overwhelm the warm-watered river—I found the exact spot and was lucky to get back to the shore alive. A local fisherman told me, after I asked him why his boat lacked a life preserver, that Lake Superior killed you after fifteen minutes' submersion in its icy waters, so they had no need for life preservers on the lake.

But what my girls and I take from that summer is our love of the pies made by Minnesota women. Restaurants stretch from Duluth to the Canadian border, and every one we entered boasted homemade pies that loom large in our collective memory of those wonderful summers. It was in Minnesota that I first tasted a gooseberry pie. It is easy to make and will put you on a fast track to heaven.

The method for rolling and shaping the pie crust is the same for each recipe in this chapter.   • **SERVES 8**

    1 recipe Pie Dough (page 7)

FOR THE FILLING

    4 cups gooseberries

    3 tablespoons cornstarch

    3/4 cup plus 1 tablespoon sugar

    Pinch of salt

1. Top and tail each gooseberry by pinching off the small stems

with your fingers or clipping them with scissors. Preparing the gooseberries takes time, but this tart pie is spectacular.

2. Combine the gooseberries, cornstarch, $^3\!/_4$ cup sugar, and salt in a bowl and set aside.

3. Roll the larger piece of dough into a 12-inch circle. It is easiest to roll the dough using plastic wrap. Place a large sheet of plastic on the counter and put the dough in the center. Flatten the dough into a disk, place a second sheet of wrap on top, and roll with a wooden rolling pin. Remove the top plastic sheet and use the bottom sheet to help invert the dough into a 9-inch glass pie pan. Cover with plastic wrap and place the pie pan in the refrigerator while rolling the smaller top piece.

4. Using the same technique, roll the smaller piece of dough into a 10-inch circle. Keeping it covered with plastic wrap, put the top dough circle in the refrigerator.

5. Take the prepared pie pan out of the refrigerator and remove the plastic wrap. Transfer the gooseberries to the pie shell.

6. Remove top circle of crust from the refrigerator and lay it over the filling. Press the edges of the dough together and trim away the excess, leaving a $^1\!/_2$-inch overhang. Press the top and bottom crusts between your finger and thumb to make a decorative border.

7. Cut four slits in the top pie crust (like spokes on a wheel). Cover the pie with plastic wrap and refrigerate for 1 hour.

8. While the pie is resting in the refrigerator, place a large piece of foil on the bottom floor of the oven to catch any pie drippings.

9. Set a baking sheet on the foil. The pie pan will go directly on the baking sheet, so the bottom crust will get cooked all the way through and brown nicely. It is also easier to remove the baked pie from the oven when it is sitting on the baking sheet.

10. Preheat the oven to 425°F.

11. Remove the pie from the refrigerator and brush a little water on the pie crust, then sprinkle with the 1 tablespoon sugar.

12. Bake the pie on the baking sheet for 40 to 50 minutes, until the top crust is golden brown.

13. Cool the pie on a rack for 2 to 4 hours before cutting.

• • •

FOUR RED FRUITS PIE

• SERVES 8

1 recipe Pie Dough (page 7)

FOR THE FILLING

$^3/_4$ pound rhubarb stalks

$^1/_2$ pint red currants

$^1/_2$ pint raspberries

1 pint bing cherries, pitted

$^2/_3$ cup plus 1 tablespoon sugar

2 tablespoons all-purpose flour

$^1/_2$ lemon, juiced

Pinch of salt

1. Wash and trim the rhubarb and cut into $^1/_2$-inch pieces; you should have 2 cups. Rinse the red currants and remove the stems. Place the rhubarb, currants, raspberries, and cherries in a bowl with the $^2/_3$ cup sugar, flour, lemon juice, and salt.

2. Preheat oven to 425°F. Proceed with the dough-rolling and pie-filling instructions for Gooseberry Pie (page 40). Roll the smaller piece of dough into a 10-inch round and cut into six $1^1/_4$-inch-wide strips. Weave strips on top of filling in a lattice pattern. Pinch the edges of the strips together with the edges of the bottom crust to make a decorative border. Sprinkle with the tablespoon of sugar.

3. Place the pie on a baking sheet and bake on the bottom of the oven for 40 to 50 minutes, until the lattice crust is golden brown.

• • •

PEACH PIE Whenever I think of South Carolina peaches, I think of Dori Sanders, the novelist and cookbook author, who still sells peaches on the highway by her family farm in York County. Dori tells me that the peaches of York County are the finest-tasting in the world. I have not seen any conclusive proof that she is wrong, but I have tasted enough York County peaches to think she might be right. A ripe peach is a thing perfect unto itself, and the fruit is a tree's way of expressing devotion to sunshine. In their season, I gorge myself with fresh peaches, which always make me happy that I found South Carolina when I was a boy, or that it found me.

This peach pie is gilding the lily—the only natural way I know for peaches to taste any better than straight out of the orchard.

• SERVES 8

1 recipe Pie Dough (page 7)

FOR THE FILLING

3 pounds ripe, firm peaches (about 8 large peaches)

$^{1}/_{2}$ cup plus 1 tablespoon sugar

2 tablespoons cornstarch

2 teaspoons finely grated lemon zest

1 tablespoon freshly squeezed lemon juice

Pinch of salt

1. Peel, pit, and slice the peaches. (See page 157.)

2. In a medium bowl, stir together the $^{1}/_{2}$ cup sugar, cornstarch, lemon zest, lemon juice, and salt. Add the peaches and toss to coat them.

3. Preheat oven to 425°F. Proceed with the dough-rolling and pie-filling instructions for Gooseberry Pie (page 40). Sprinkle with the tablespoon of sugar.

4. Place pie on a baking sheet and bake on the bottom of the oven for 40 to 50 minutes, until the top crust is golden brown.

CHAPTER FOUR

A Hometown in the Low Country

Home is a damaged word, bruisable as fruit, in the cruel glossaries of the language I choose to describe the long, fearful march of my childhood. Home was a word that caught in my throat, stung like a paper cut, drew blood in its passover of my life, and hurt me in all the soft places. My longing for home was as powerful as fire in my bloodstream. I lived at twenty-three different addresses as my father moved from base to base flying the warplanes that kept our nation's airways safe. When asked where my hometown was, I answered in a complete silence that baffled strangers and embarrassed me. Because of the question, I knew it was an American's birthright to have a place name on the tip of your tongue; all I could come up with were military bases like Cherry Point, Quantico, or Camp Lejeune, vast acreages of federal property that I roamed known by the anonymous and utterly demeaning military coinage—dependent. Though I had no home, I had a grotesque father who had once—flying low, counting body parts, arms and legs and torsos as they floated in the blood-red river below him—wiped out a battalion of North Korean regulars he caught fording the Naktong River. My father made his children feel like the surviving members of that battalion, and at times we envied those slain soldiers who did not have to grow up under his savage, tyrannical rule.

Though my mother could do nothing to stem my father's cruelty, she held out great hope for her children's ardent wish to find a home. She knew of my loathing for my homeless state, and she said as she turned our station wagon onto Highway 21 and my twenty-third address since birth: "From what I understand, Beaufort, South Carolina, is a perfectly charming town, Pat. I know you hate all this moving, but this might be a place you can call home."

"I don't have a home, Mom," I answered. "I can't have one. It's too late."

"It's not too late," she said. "You're a military brat, son. Because your old man defends this country, you've got a right to claim any town in America as your hometown. Any town. It's your choice."

"I don't know a single soul in Beaufort, Mom," I said.

"It'll take some work on your part, son," she said. "You've got to earn a hometown."

I took my mother's advice to heart, and I buried myself like a wood tick into the arteries and the historical tissues of Beaufort, South Carolina. There was nothing Beaufort could do to stop my invasion of its cells. In six months, I found myself maddened with the love of this water-ringed town. The curve of the Beaufort River still remains the prettiest change of pace and direction I have ever seen a river have the innate good taste to make. The founding fathers of Beaufort agreed with me and put one of the loveliest towns in America on its high banks, and they lined Bay Street with a row of kingly mansions that look like a row of wedding cakes when viewed from the river. Within a month, I would roam the halls of Beaufort High School with classmates who lived in some of those breathtaking houses. The town had an immaculate feel of welcome to it, and I enfolded myself into its silky embrace. I have never looked back.

Most of the books I have written have been psalms and cards of pure, unalloyed praise of Beaufort, South Carolina. Before the town took me in, I had no idea that geography itself could play such a large role in the shaping of a man's fate and character. Because of the Marine Corps, I had entered at last into the country that was going to become the landscape of my entire artistic life. The great salt marsh spreading all around as far as my eye could see has remained the central image that runs throughout my work. I cannot look at a salt marsh, veined with salt creeks swollen with the moonstruck tides, without believing in God. The marsh is feminine, voluptuous when the creeks fill up with the billion-footed swarm of shrimp and blue crabs and oysters in the great rush to creation in the spring. The marsh taught me new ways that the color green could transform itself into subtle tones of gold as the seasons changed. The people in the Low Country measure the passing of the seasons not by the changing colors of the leaves of its deciduous trees but by the brightening and withering of its grand and swashbuckling salt marshes, the shining glory of the Low Country and the central metaphor of my writing life.

On the first day of school at Beaufort High School, the teacher of my life, Eugene Norris, presented himself to my junior English class. A kid on my left whispered that Gene's nickname was Cooter. The marines in my life had all carried nicknames like Bull, Wild Man, and the Great Santini, so it was a pleasure to welcome a man who was named after a water turtle. Gene Norris was the anti–Don Conroy, the antitoxin to childhood days so filled up with a screaming, out-of-control male. Gene was dapper and soft-spoken and good-humored, and in the first month, I found myself riding shotgun next to Gene as he drove me around the streets of the great cities of Charleston and Savannah, telling me the history of mansions and the names of the nearly mythical families who inhabited them. "Let's ramble," Gene would say, and we'd visit every antique store in the Low Country. During our rambles, Gene taught me to prize rarity and delicacy and craftsmanship. I learned about porcelain and coin silver and Empire furniture and Wedgwood, and I learned to recognize the furniture makers of Charleston above all others. For my mother's birthday, Gene helped me select a gift that was within my slender budget. When my mother unwrapped the celery glass that, to me, was beyond beautiful, I said with a burst of pride, "It's an antique, Mom! A real antique." That celery glass sits in my writing room today, and I cannot pass it without thinking of my pretty mother or the sweet-natured man who came into my life when I needed him the most.

The first mansion that I visited on the Point, Beaufort's historic district, was the Christenson house, where Gene rented a second-story room with a veranda and a view of the Beaufort River. While driving around the Point, Gene would tell me a story about almost every house we passed. "That house was built in the late 1700s. It's fine. Very fine. Its wooden paneling is one of the glories of South Carolina. The old woman who lives in the house across the street is just crackers and can't even tell you her first name. Over there lives a common drunk but his wife covers for him by telling everyone he's got the flu. Poor man's had the flu going on thirty years. That house is called the Castle. It's got the most beautiful staircase in Beaufort." Passing another house, Gene whispered that the family had migrated to Beaufort as carpetbaggers after the Civil War but had managed to overcome this shameful origin by becoming valuable, first-rate citizens of the town.

It was through Gene Norris that I discovered the great motherlode of story that forms the scaffolding of almost every book I have written. I had never come to a town so overripe with narrative. In the fall of that year, I saw an albino porpoise swimming in a pod in the middle of Harbor River. I learned that the white porpoise was called Carolina Snow by the locals, and that it was a sign of good luck to see her. There were black voodoo doctors who practiced their trade for great profit out on St. Helena Island. A fifteen-foot alligator had taken advantage of a spring tide to swim close to a house on the marsh and had killed a small pony before being shot to death by the man of the house. In Beaufort, there were houses still marked by wounded Union soldiers who had signed their names before facing the fearful amputations and hospitals set up in abandoned mansions. Gene showed me a boardinghouse where E. B. White had visited each year, as did Ernest Hemingway's first wife, Hadley, as had General Mark Clark of The Citadel.

On Bay Street, Gene stopped his car in front of the Verdier house and said, "On that veranda, Count Lafayette addressed the citizens of Beaufort in 1825 as he made his triumphal tour of the United States of

America." Turning on Craven Street, Gene pointed with great reverence to a two-story house and said, "That is my priest's house, the Reverend Hardy, who is charged with the care of Gene Norris's immortal soul."

"Tough job," I said. "Because you're going to hell, Mr. Norris. So is Reverend Hardy."

"Surely you aren't telling me that you Romans are so arrogant that you think we Anglicans can't go to heaven!"

"We sure are," I said. "We're that arrogant."

"I never heard such a thing," Gene said. "You papists repel me sometimes." At the next house, he paused and said, "This is the Secession House. In this house, a man named William Rhett met with a group called the fire-eaters and planned the secession of the Southern states from the Union. This is sacred territory to a Southern Civil War buff."

"Are you a Civil War buff, Mr. Norris?"

"Of course I'm a buff," he replied. "I had two granddaddies fight in the Civil War."

"Which side did they fight for?"

"My family is South Carolina born and South Carolina bred," he said.

"So they fought for the losers."

"Losers? How dare you call my distinguished ancestors losers, scalawag?" Gene thundered.

As his Buick poked along Bay Street, passing by its row of dignified mansions, Gene Norris told me of some of the great families who lived in those houses—the Fordhams, the Dowlings, the Trasks—and gave me brief histories of each family and the importance they had played in the making of the town. Stories leaked out of every windowsill and doorway we passed. On our left was the Jewish cemetery, which sent Gene into another reverie as he built his tales around the fortunes of the Lipsitz family as well as the Keyserlings and the Scheins.

I must have ridden out with Gene Norris thirty times in the two years I was at Beaufort High School, and I consider the time I spent with him as valuable as any college education could be. He taught me to value the old, to sharpen my eye for the most intricate detail, and to strengthen all the appetites upon which beauty itself fed. But most of all, Gene Norris handed me a different model of how to conduct myself as a man, show-ing me that a man could behave with sensibility and restraint and that a love of language and art could sustain him. Unlike a ride in my father's car, I never feared a backhand from my English teacher or a cuffed head or blood running down my face for displeasing the marine aviator. My father never talked to me about anything, so I discovered I loved being in a car with a man whose stories issued out in ceaseless tides. Gene Norris spoke with a storyteller's voice, and it felt like I was sitting next to Homer as he sang out in his blindness the illustrious stories of the fall of Troy. In the end, Gene Norris handed me the key to my first hometown and made it feel like the most sublime gift.

So I set a claim on Beaufort, South Carolina, the first town in America I ever called home. Though I have lived out my adult life in Atlanta, San Francisco, Paris, and Rome, it is the small town of Beaufort that still has a mortgage on my heart. All of my novels smell of the marshes, the pages wet with storm water born in the creeks that feed into the Beaufort River. I wrote the prologue to *The Prince of Tides* while living on the Via dei Forragi in Rome, aching with homesickness for Beaufort so urgently that I brought the Low Country to Italy. I can go nowhere on earth without hungering for the South Carolina Low Country. I carry its taste in my mouth, and I have smelled its fragrant marshes when I walked on a cob-bled road in Ephesus where St. Paul preached a sermon, or when I stud-ied a pyramid near Cairo, or when I contemplated the haunches of a statue of Buddha in Thailand.

I came back to Beaufort County for good in 1993 to rest my soul from the whirlwind that had become my life. I bought a house on Fripp Island, where my mother was living when she died of leukemia in 1984. When the weather is fine, I swim in the Atlantic Ocean twice a day—once in the morning, once again at sundown. One morning, I awoke and found hundreds of snowy egrets surrounding the lagoon that sits behind my house, locked in an elaborate mating ritual that contained the mysteries of dance itself. White-tailed deer roam the island in silent brown herds. From trees in my yard, ospreys hunt mullet in the lagoon. The bones of an enormous sixteen-foot alligator washed up on the island last month. A ten-foot alligator uses my yard as a highway to get to a lagoon that sits on a golf course. We have met, with some discomfort on both sides, on four occasions now.

When friends come to town, I give them my tour of Beaufort in honor of our friendship. It is, quite simply, a continuation of my rides in Gene Norris's Buick when he could not pass a house without telling me a story about the people who lived there. But now, I have added my own history to the tour. I show the houses where Robert Duvall and Blythe Danner lived while making *The Great Santini* or the houses where Barbra Streisand and Nick Nolte lived while they were filming *The Prince of Tides*. Then I show them the house where I met my first wife, Barbara, and the first house we owned, on Hancock Street, also where I wrote *The Boo, The Water Is Wide*, and the first chapters of *The Great Santini*. I have imprinted my own history into Beaufort and those stories have replaced the ones that Gene Norris told me so long ago in the amazing generosity he brought to the life of a fifteen-year-old boy. At the end of my tour, as we walk to the graves of my mother and father in the national cemetery, I tell my friends that all my novels sprang out of my father's terrible house, the front seat of Gene Norris's Buick, and the day that the town of Beaufort took me in, enfolded me into her history, and let me know in all the aching beauty of her streets and gardens that she was proud to have me call her my hometown.

SOFT-SHELL CRABS   The first time I ever heard of soft-shell crabs was when I read about the delicious crustaceans in William Warner's magisterial, Pulitzer Prize–winning book, *Beautiful Swimmers.* The people of the Chesapeake Bay and not the people of South Carolina learned the fine, patient art of catching crabs about to molt out of their old shells and into their new ones. Once these "peelers" or "busters" discard their old shells, they are among the most vulnerable creatures in the sea, and one of the most delicious.

Nothing is harder to clean than a hard-shell blue crab, and nothing is easier than a soft-shell variety. Take a pair of kitchen shears and cut off the face of the crab just behind the eyes, then lift the shell points on both sides of the crab to remove the gills or the "deadmen." These look inedible and are lined like spark plugs along the crab's abdomen. Then turn the crab over and cut away the apron on the rear end of the crab. Rinse the crab with cold water and the dinner bell soon will be struck.

I have also served soft-shell crabs with hollandaise sauce, rémoulade, and tartar sauce, with lemon and butter, and aioli, and have come up with not a single way to spoil this magnificent meal.

• SERVES 2 AS A MAIN COURSE OR 4 AS A FIRST COURSE

1/3 cup all-purpose flour

1/4 teaspoon freshly ground black pepper

1/4 teaspoon coarse or kosher salt

Pinch of smoked paprika (Spanish variety, not Hungarian)

8 soft-shell crabs, dressed

4 tablespoons unsalted butter

2 tablespoons peanut oil (or other oil suitable for frying)

2 garlic cloves, minced

1 shallot, minced

Juice of 2 lemons

2 teaspoons finely chopped fresh parsley or chives

1. Line a baking sheet with wax paper and set aside.

2. Mix the flour, pepper, salt, and paprika in a shallow dish or pie pan. Working with one at time, dredge the crabs in the mixture to coat both sides, gently shaking off excess. Transfer to prepared baking sheet, and repeat until all eight are coated.

3. In a large heavy skillet over moderate heat, melt the butter and oil until foamy. Working in several batches (depending on the size of your skillet), add the crabs to the skillet (do not overcrowd). Cook until a crisp crust forms and the crabs turn a reddish brown color, about 3 minutes per side.

4. Remove the crabs to a warm platter. Working quickly, add the garlic and shallot to the skillet and cook until lightly browned, about 2 minutes. Add the lemon juice and parsley. Bring to a boil, stirring frequently, and spoon mixture over crabs to serve.

• • •

ROASTED LEMONS

Preheat the oven to 425°F. Cut the lemons (allow $1/2$ to 1 per serving) in half and brush with olive oil. Roast, cut side up, until the surface is caramelized and the lemon is softened, 45 to 50 minutes. Squeeze the warm juice from the roasted lemons over soft-shell crabs or panfried flounder in place of tartar sauce.

PANFRIED FLOUNDER   I cannot order a flounder or sole anywhere in the world without thinking of the first native of New Orleans I ever knew well, Richie Matta. During the day he was a sergeant in the Marine Corps; at night and on weekends he was a rock star. He was mischievous, charismatic, and devil-may-care, carrying an aura of danger with him every step he took. When you were Richie Matta's friend, his loyalty and devotion to you were unshakable and not for sale. He also introduced me to the world of Cajun seasoning and food.

On a moonless summer night, in the middle of the summer, Richie took me flounder gigging at the end of Fripp Island. We put his johnboat into the Fripp inlet and he fixed a lantern that hung off the bow.

"The tide's perfect," he said as he stood and navigated over sand flats, looking much like a gondolier. We drifted over a sandbar where Richie had come across a trove of flounder. Carefully, we traded places, and I poled us across the shallow water on the starriest night of the year. Orion, the Hunter, had left us for the summer, and I longed for his return to the night sky. Richie lunged with his gig and came up with a two-pound flounder that he laid on ice in a cooler. With quick thrusts, he brought six more fish into the boat. Then he demanded that we trade places and we did so again, gingerly. I stood in the front of the boat and saw the lantern's light revealing the clean-sand bottom of the bar we were passing over. I didn't see a thing that lived or moved.

"There's nothing down there," I said to Richie.

"They're buried. Look for their shape in the sand. Look for their eyes."

It was a full two minutes before my eyes adjusted enough to follow Richie's instructions. I saw the first flounder dimpling the sand. There was a slight, odd-shaped mound in the sand, like the slightly raised women of cameos. I struck with the gig and raised my first flounder into the air.

We took in an even dozen that night. Richie was expert in all phases of outdoor life, and he made a beautifully built fire on the beach at the end of Fripp. He tossed a couple of nuggets of butter into a steel frying pan, then gutted, floured, seasoned, and filleted two of the fish. In those days I could not cook a quail's egg and took no interest in his preparations for the cooking. The stars were too brilliant and the smell of the marsh, with its aromas of salt and spartina and working tides that took the essence of the mud and marsh grass back to the sea, was something I could never get enough of. Now I am old enough to know I will never get enough of it.

Nor will I forget the delicious one-of-a-kind taste of the flounder we ate that night. The fish were not only good but cooked to perfection, and that meal remains high on the list of top ten meals I have ever eaten.

"Richie, this is fabulous. The best thing I've ever eaten," I said. "What's that taste?"

He handed me a plastic cup of white wine and said, "That's Cajun, son. That's Cajun seasoning you're tasting."

Several years ago a woman came up to me on Bay Street in Beaufort and asked me if I knew that Richie Matta had died in New Orleans. I did not and suffered that I had not done enough to keep that seminal and valuable friendship alive. But when the woman gave me such dispiriting news, the first thing I thought of was flounder.　　　　　• **SERVES 4**

Four 6- to 8-ounce flounder fillets
Coarse or kosher salt
1 $1/2$ cups all-purpose flour
2 large eggs, lightly beaten
3 cups fresh toasted bread crumbs
2 tablespoons bacon drippings
Peanut oil
Lemon wedges
Tartar sauce

1. Rinse the flounder under cool gently running water and pat dry with paper towels. Lightly salt and set aside.

2. Place flour, eggs, and bread crumbs in three large shallow bowls (pie tins work well) and arrange on work surface in that order. Dredge fillets in flour, working carefully to make sure entire surface is coated. Shake gently to remove excess. Dip fillets into eggs, again making sure surface is completely coated. Lift the fish slightly, allowing excess to drip back into the bowl. Place the fillets in bread crumbs, pressing down lightly with your fingertips so crumbs stick to the fish. Place the breaded fillets on a plate, cover with wax paper, and refrigerate for at least 1 hour before cooking.

3. Line a baking sheet with brown paper bags (cut the bags open to a single thickness and use the clean inner surface).

4. In a medium cast-iron skillet over moderately high heat, place bacon drippings and enough peanut oil to rise about $1/4$ inch above the bottom of the pan. When the fat is hot but not smoking (it will shimmer slightly), place the fillets in the skillet two at a time (overcrowding will prevent browning) and fry until a crisp, golden crust is formed, about 2 minutes per side. Learning how to adjust the heat so that the fat is hot enough to crisp bread crumbs on contact (and keep the fillets from being greasy) takes practice.

5. Using a spatula, carefully remove fillets and drain on brown paper bags to blot excess oil. Transfer to plates and serve immediately with lemon wedges and tartar sauce.

• • •

TARTAR SAUCE   I think of the highway that runs along the North Carolina coast then passes invisibly into South Carolina, following the same incursion of the Atlantic that washes up against the southern coast. It runs from Morehead City, North Carolina, down to Myrtle Beach, South Carolina, and I call it the tartar sauce corridor. It is lined with the kind of seafood restaurants where you can smell fried fish ten miles inland. They are gaudy, decorated with seagulls and buoys and shrimp nets, mobbed in the summertime and deserted and locked up in February, but all of them were born to fry things up. One is sure to be identified as an outsider or a weirdo by asking a waitress for a broiled seafood platter. These seafood restaurants are palaces of grease and monuments to the revolutionary idea that fried food tastes better than any other kind.

My lifelong affair with tartar sauce began with a plate of fried shrimp eaten in a restaurant in Morehead City when I was six years old. Tartar sauce can lift a simple fried catfish to the realms of ecstasy, turn a fried oyster into an emperor's feast, or ennoble a fried shrimp into knighthood.

Six miles from my house on Fripp Island sits the best fried food restaurant in my part of the world, and I love its tartar sauce. It is called the Shrimp Shack, and its founder and owner is the inimitable Hilda Gay Upton, who was voted Best Personality in Beaufort High School's 1959 graduating class. When my daughter Megan lived in Italy for her junior year abroad, she would write and confess that she would suffer "Shrimp Shack Attacks," even though she was eating the finest cuisine in the world. None of my family can pass the Shrimp Shack after a long absence from Fripp without stopping for one of the world-class shrimp burgers, which are one of the joys of my life.

Of course this is the place where I would share with the world the culinary secrets of making a perfect shrimp burger, but I am unable to do so because the perfidious and wily Hilda Gay Upton has refused to part with the secret recipe for her shrimp burger. I have pleaded, begged, cajoled, and all those other verbs where you really try to get something but suffer constant frustration. This has gone on for years. I've told Hilda about this cookbook, that I would praise her open-air restaurant to the skies and make hers a household name for those who prize fried and fattening foods. Hilda, an obstinate Low Country woman, whose husband is a shrimper, refuses even to tell me if there is shrimp in her "secret recipe."

Not long ago, I was returning on a flight from New York, where I had dined at Le Bernardin, Daniel's, and the Four Seasons. It is on airplanes that I read all the food magazines like *Gourmet, Bon Appétit, Food & Wine,* and *Cooking Light,* and on this occasion a magazine I was unfamiliar with called *Saveur.* While reading *Saveur* with great pleasure, I was startled to come across an article about Hilda and the Shrimp Shack. There was a photograph of Hilda, whom I have known for thirty years, and I was mildly surprised to see a middle-aged black woman named Neecie Simmons who had cooked at the Shrimp Shack since it opened. But I was flabbergasted to see the recipe for the shrimp burger that I had vainly tried to coax from Hilda for more than ten years, written down for all to see.

When my plane landed in Savannah, I headed straight for the Shrimp Shack in what once was called a beeline. I stuck my head through the small window where Hilda takes your order and your money. I held up the magazine to Neecie and said, "Hilda, I apologize; I always thought you were a white woman all these many years until I read *Saveur* magazine today on the plane."

The real Hilda said, "I knew you'd see that dadgum magazine. Only you. No one else has mentioned it."

"It was nice of you to part with your 'secret recipe' to *Saveur* magazine," I said, exaggerating the French ending.

"I didn't give them that recipe," Hilda said. "They made the thing up."

"If you don't give me that recipe before my cookbook is published, I'm going to claim I saw you out collecting roadkill to put into your secret recipe."

"A secret is a secret," she said maddeningly.

Early on a Sunday morning of this year, I was driving out on Seaside Road and was shocked to find Hilda Gay Upton shoveling long-dead possums, skunks, and raccoons into the bed of her pickup truck to form the basis of her famous secret recipe for shrimp burgers . . . she carefully brushed off the flies and maggots.

No, that's a joke. Her shrimp burgers are wonderful, and if you ever get on Highway 21, head for the beach to meet Hilda and her family and her workers. It's one of the nicest places on earth to be.

• **MAKES ABOUT 1½ CUPS**

1 cup Homemade Mayonnaise (see below)
2 tablespoons chopped fresh chives
2 tablespoons chopped fresh dill
1 shallot, finely minced
1 tablespoon capers, drained and finely chopped
2 teaspoons sweet pickle relish
2 teaspoons dry mustard
Juice of 1 lemon, strained

Combine all the ingredients in a small bowl and stir to mix well. Cover and refrigerate for at least 1 hour, preferably overnight. Taste for seasoning before serving.

• • •

Homemade Mayonnaise Let us now praise homemade mayonnaise. In her cooking class, Nathalie Dupree once made all her students make it by hand, ensuring that all of us would honor the labors of French housewives for the rest of our days. But the invention of the blender and the food processor has turned the making of mayonnaise into a matter of seconds. Here is how to do it: Drop an egg into your machine. Turn it on. Beat that sucker for five seconds. Have some vegetable or canola oil ready. Pour it in a slow stream through the feed tube. Soon, chemistry happens and magic occurs before your eyes as the egg and oil unite into something glorious. When the mixture is thick, cut the machine off. Add the juice of half a lemon or two shots of red wine vinegar. That's mayonnaise. Add a clove of garlic to it. Turn on the machine until the garlic is blended. That's aioli. Try adding some fresh herbs, and you've got herb mayonnaise. Add one-fourth cup Parmesan cheese and a couple of pinches of cayenne, and you have the fanciest, best-tasting salad dressing you've ever had.   • **MAKES ABOUT 1 CUP**

1 large egg yolk, at room temperature

1 teaspoon Dijon mustard

2 tablespoons strained fresh lemon juice

$1/4$ cup olive oil

$3/4$ cup vegetable oil

$1/4$ teaspoon sea salt

In the bowl of a food processor fitted with a metal blade, combine egg yolk, mustard, and lemon juice until smooth. Slowly drizzle in olive oil, processing until thoroughly incorporated. Add vegetable oil slowly, processing until the mixture is smooth and thick and completely emulsified. Add the salt, transfer to a storage container, and refrigerate until ready to use.

• • •

CORN PUDDING   This is comfort food, pure and simple. I think of this as a great recipe because it is easy to make and can be thrown together in a hurry when uninvited or surprise guests show up at the front door. My stepson Jason Ray, who is a chef, once brought a rock band from Birmingham to our home on Fripp Island. I walked out from my bedroom and found six young men sleeping in various stages of undress. I counted nine tattoos, but those were only the visible ones. We went to Gay's shrimp dock to buy seven pounds of shrimp. We doubled the recipe for corn pudding. The band was a hungry one, and we remember those young men for their unappeasable appetites, not their tattoos.

• **SERVES 6**

8 tablespoons (1 stick) unsalted butter

$1/4$ cup sugar

3 tablespoons all-purpose flour

$1/2$ cup evaporated milk

2 large eggs, lightly beaten

1 $^1/_2$ teaspoons baking powder

Two 10-ounce boxes frozen white corn, thawed and kernels
   blotted dry

1. Place a rack in the middle of the oven and preheat to 350°F.

2. Butter a 2-quart casserole and set aside.

3. In a medium saucepan over low heat, melt the butter. Mix together the sugar and flour and stir into the butter. Stir in the milk, eggs, and baking powder.

4. Add the corn and pour into the prepared casserole. Bake until lightly firm, about 45 minutes.

You can also add sautéed green onions, blooming chive blossoms, or a pinch of cayenne pepper.

• • •

COCONUT CAKE   I cannot say "coconut cake" without conjuring the beloved image of my beautiful aunt Helen Harper. Every time I saw her during my boyhood, I would ask her to bake me a coconut cake, and she never let me down, not once. To the Conroy children, the Harper household was a basin of permanence and stability as we rambled from base to base up and down the Southern seacoast. The Conroy family could walk into the Harper house at 945 North Hyer Street in Orlando, Florida, and nothing would have changed since the last time we had visited. The same five buck heads would stare down from the wall of the den, the same *Book of Knowledge* would be on the bookshelf in cousin Russ and Bobby's room, on the kitchen table the pepper shaker was a rooster and the saltshaker was a hen, the same unused piano stood at attention in the living room, and at seven every evening Aunt Helen would conduct a Bible reading.

On my tenth birthday, Aunt Helen made me a coconut cake and made me part of the process by having me break open a coconut with a hatchet. She invited Aunt Evelyn and Uncle Joe down from Jacksonville, and they brought the three Gillespie cousins. (Cousin Johnny had not been born yet.) It would mark the only time in my life that family members other than my own would attend one of my birthday parties. It was a joyous day, and I got to cut the cake because, as Aunt Helen said, "It's Pat's day." The coconut cake was perfect, always perfect.

• SERVES 8

FOR THE RUM SYRUP
    1/3 cup sugar
    1/4 cup coconut or plain rum

FOR THE TOASTED COCONUT
    1 cup unsweetened shredded coconut (available at health
        food stores)

FOR THE CAKE
    2 cups cake flour
    1/2 teaspoon baking powder
    1 cup sugar
    1 cup unsweetened shredded coconut
    2 large eggs
    1 cup canned coconut milk (Goya brand if possible, Leche de Coco),
        well shaken
    1/2 pound (2 sticks) unsalted butter, melted and cooled
    1 teaspoon finely grated lemon zest (1 large lemon)
    1/2 teaspoon vanilla extract

FOR THE FROSTING
    2 cups chilled heavy cream
    2 teaspoons sugar
    1 cup untoasted unsweetened shredded coconut

1. To make the syrup: In a small saucepan, combine the sugar, $\frac{1}{3}$ cup water, and the rum and heat over medium until the mixture comes to a slow boil. Continue boiling for 5 minutes. Remove from the heat and set aside until the cake is baked. (The syrup can be made one day in advance. Refrigerate until needed and reheat until almost boiling to use.)

2. To toast the coconut: Preheat the oven to 350°F. Spread the coconut on a baking sheet and toast until edges turn a light brown, 3 to 4 minutes. Toasted yet still pale shredded coconut will add another layer of flavor and a slight crunch to the frosting. Check it carefully during the toasting; coconut can burn quickly. Total toasting time should not exceed 4 minutes. Remove immediately and transfer to another (not hot) baking sheet to cool. Reserve.

3. To make the cake: Butter and flour a 9-inch round cake pan.

4. In a large bowl, sift together flour, baking powder, and sugar. Stir in the coconut.

5. In another bowl, whisk the eggs and add the coconut milk and melted butter until the mixture is smooth. Stir in lemon zest and vanilla.

6. Using a wooden spoon, mix the egg mixture into the flour until just blended.

7. Pour the batter into the prepared cake pan. Bake at 350°F until cake is golden brown and a toothpick inserted in the center comes out clean, 55 to 60 minutes.

8. Cool the cake in the pan on a rack for about 20 minutes. Invert the pan and release the cake onto a clean work surface or a cake stand. When the cake is cool, cut horizontally into two equal layers, using a serrated knife and pressing down lightly on the top of the cake as you cut. Transfer each half, cut side up, to an individual plate and prick holes in several places on the surface. Rewarm the rum syrup and brush the syrup over the cut surfaces of the cakes.

9. To make the frosting: Whip the heavy cream and sugar together until the cream is almost firm. (Do not overwhip.) Fold the untoasted coconut into the whipped cream.

10. Frost the bottom layer of cake with one-third of the coconut cream. Place the second layer on top of the coconut cream, and frost top and sides of cake with the remaining cream. Sprinkle the top and sides with toasted coconut.

CHAPTER FIVE

My First Novelist

At Beaufort High I took one course that I had to keep secret from my father at all costs. Gene Norris had talked the only writer in Beaufort County, Ann Morse, into teaching a high school class in creative writing. Mrs. Morse wrote under the name of Ann Head and admitted to me once that she never would be a distinguished writer. "But I have a few things I want to say," she said. Her list of novels included *Fair with Rain* and *Always in August*, and her first mystery, *Everybody Adored Cara*, was in galleys when we first met in a room off the library at Beaufort High. On first sight, Mrs. Morse projected a steely withholding and icy reserve that would have been off-putting to me except for the thrilling fact that she was the first novelist I'd ever met in the flesh. She looked like a woman who would not tolerate a preposition at the end of a sentence or the anarchy of a dangling participle.

"Mr. Norris has told me nice things about you, Mr. Conroy," Mrs. Morse said. "He thinks you might become a writer someday."

"How do you do it, ma'am?" I asked.

"Simple. You write. You just write. Beginning, middle, end. That's it," she said. "I made some suggestions to improve your poems and writing assignments. Mr. Norris says you got a little drunk on Thomas Wolfe last year."

"I loved him, Mrs. Morse. I couldn't help it."

"Alas and alack," she said. "If possible, don't imitate him in everything you write, Pat."

"I'll try, Mrs. Morse," I promised.

"Please do," she said. "I would like to find out what *your* voice sounds like, Pat. I had the class come into the library to read the screenplays of Ingmar Bergman. Have you ever heard of him?"

"Mr. Monte, my English teacher at Gonzaga High School, gave us extra credit if we went to see *The Virgin Spring*," I said. "I wrote a paper on it."

"This Mr. Monte must have been a special teacher," she said. "This is my personal copy. Take it home, but bring it back. I loathe people who don't return books and their tribe is legion."

"I'll bring it back next class," I offered.

"Thank you. You used the word 'poignant' in one of your poems. I dislike that word intensely. It's been greatly overused by untalented people."

"Poignant's gone, Mrs. M," I said.

"Why did you call me Mrs. M?" she said.

"I don't know," I said. "I shorten people's names. It's a bad habit."

"Mrs. M," she said coldly. "I like it. Please call me that."

Though my affliction with Thomas Wolfe was now an effervescence that lit up my prose, Mrs. M gave me assignments that showed me another way to go. She required that my adjectives actually mean something when I landed them into one of my overloaded paragraphs. She brought all six of her students news of the world of writing, read us letters from both her agent and editor, and took our efforts with high seriousness. I discovered that my lab mate in physics, Allen Ryan, was the best poet in the school by a long shot; that his sister, Terry, might have been the smartest person I'd ever met; and that a shy, unartificial girl named Joan Fewell produced work every week that was surprising, original, and offbeat. I took great delight in the work that our carefully selected class produced, and the six of us ended up filling over half the literary magazine at the end of the year. We took Mrs. M's class with the solemnity that her massive coolness seemed to require. Never once did she seem comfortable around us, her gravity and reserve forces of nature that deflected the possibility of any caprice or horseplay in her presence. She never gave the slightest sign that she was falling in love with us as we turned in our sketches, poems, and stories for her critical inspection.

Once, during basketball season, Mrs. M stopped me outside the library door and said, "Pat, where are you attending college next year?"

I blushed and said, "I don't know, Mrs. M."

"You don't know? That's absurd. Allen's already been accepted to Stanford."

"I've got to win a basketball scholarship," I said. "Otherwise I don't know if my parents can afford it."

"What nonsense. Your father's an officer in the Marine Corps," she said. "You don't come from a family of beggars. What'll you do if you don't get a scholarship?"

"I don't know, Mrs. M."

"This is preposterous. I wish to speak with your father," she said.

"I don't think that's a good idea, Mrs. M. Dad's a little different."

"I'm a graduate of Antioch College in Ohio," she said. "I think you'd flourish in such an atmosphere. It's free-spirited and bohemian."

"I wouldn't tell my father that."

"What are your parents thinking?" she said.

After basketball practice that night, I entered the car of my scowling father and he got right to the point. "Who is this Morse broad that's teaching you?"

"Mrs. M. It's an English class, Dad," I said.

"You're lying. It's a goddamn creative writing class. Did I ever give you permission to be in an artsy-fartsy class like that? Damn right, I didn't. The Morse broad started lecturing me about when we're supposed to apply for you to go to college. Like it's any of her goddamn business. Do you know what she told me? That she thought she could get you a free ride to Antioch on a creative writing scholarship. Isn't that some shit? You know what Antioch's famous for producing?"

"No, sir."

"Communists, that's what. They turn 'em out like sausages up there. It's a whole college full of fruitcakes and weirdos and pinkos. What a pushy broad. She talked to me like I was a fucking shoeshine boy and she was the Queen of fucking Sheba. Drop that course, pal. That's an order."

"Yes, sir."

"Antioch fucking communist Ohio," he said. "You can bet your sweet ass you ain't going there."

When Mrs. M drove up to the high school parking lot for the next class, I opened the door of her car and explained that my father had demanded that I drop her course. Mrs. M handed me a briefcase filled with her books and papers and we walked together toward the library.

"I must be honest, Pat," she said. "I found your father to be a dreadful man. Our conversation was not fruitful."

"You've got to catch Dad on the right day," I said defensively. "He takes some getting used to."

"He was a perfect ass," she said, and I laughed because I had never heard anyone called that in my life. "Your mother must be a saint."

"You'd like Mom a lot, Mrs. M."

"Are you going to quit my course?"

"I have to. Dad'd kill me if he knew I disobeyed him," I said.

"He told me that he was going to make you quit," Mrs. M said. "But I have come up with a plan."

"What is your plan?"

"Simplicity itself. Guerrilla warfare. I scratch you off my class roll. Yet you continue to come to class. You do all the work. If anyone asks, I will claim that you dropped the class. You do the same. We will protect each other's flanks. Our work is literature, Pat. A philistine like your father will not make us deviate from our chosen course."

"If he finds out, I'm a dead man."

"I'll call his office today to say you dropped out," she said. "I'll try to get him to reconsider. Because your father is obstinacy itself, he will refuse. It's foolproof."

"I'll do it, Mrs. M."

"One day, Pat—not now—but someday down the road when you have some distance from all this," she said, thinking, "you need to write about that guy."

After that year, Mrs. M never let me drop out of her life and wrote me carefully considered decorous letters that brought me both news of Beaufort and her career and thoughtful commentary on the poems and short stories I had published in The Citadel's literary magazine, *The Shako,* which I sent for her review. She kept her criticism upbeat and engaged and it was through her letters that I came to know the more passionate artist who simmered beneath that ice palace of a woman whose capacity for reserve seemed like a vocation. In her letters, I could translate her great fondness for me, and she let me know that she took my work with utter seriousness. She sent me a copy of Hemingway's *A Moveable Feast* when it first came out and told me that one day she and I would travel to Paris together and visit all of Hemingway's cafés and haunts. In 1979, I took that journey, but Mrs. M did not come with me.

In 1968, the first year I was teaching at Beaufort High School, Gene Norris called me at home to tell me that Ann Head Morse had died of a massive stroke at her home. Dumbstruck, I attended her funeral. I was twenty-two; it was long before I would publish a single word or reward her for the generous faith she had shown in me as a young writer. At the time of her death, Mrs. M was the only writer I actually knew by sight, and her untimely and unforeseen death robbed me of the mentor I thought would help me navigate the fearful world of American publishing. My amateurish entrance into that world was directly related to her disappearance from my life. Her remoteness now seems one of the ways that shyness can manifest itself in people who prize silence. Though I was not her type, she worked to make me her type and succeeded. I was lucky that she found me as a boy, and whenever I publish a new book, I take a rose to her headstone at St. Helena Cemetery in Beaufort and place it before her without a word, respecting her detachment as part of the bond between us. Mrs. M had a hard eye, always on the lookout for the sentimental or the maudlin, and she would disapprove of my visit. She would absolutely shudder at the rose.

ROASTED BEETS WITH BLUE CHEESE AND SHERRY
VINAIGRETTE   I have a thing for sugar beets, and I make them in a variety of ways. The recipe presented here is for those excitable moments when I wish to put on the dog. I like to roast or boil beets, chop them up with vigor until they are bite-size, then dress them with Dijon mustard, a knuckle of freshly minced garlic, and the juice of half a lemon. I've done the same using sour cream, horseradish, and lemon juice. The only flaw I find with beets is the deep magenta coloring they impart so generously to clothes and hands. Cautious cooks use rubber gloves when handling beets, but I go for several days caught red-handed by friend and foe alike.

• **SERVES 4**

FOR THE VINAIGRETTE
1 teaspoon Dijon mustard
2 tablespoons Spanish sherry vinegar
2 tablespoons olive oil
4 tablespoons grapeseed oil

6 medium beets (about 2 pounds)
Olive oil
$1/2$ cup chopped walnuts
8 ounces blue cheese, cut into small pieces

1. To make the vinaigrette: In a small bowl, whisk together the mustard and vinegar until smooth. Drizzle the oils in, drop by drop, and whisk until smooth. Reserve. Preheat the oven to 400°F.

2. Trim, scrub, and dry the beets. Place each beet in the middle of a square of aluminum foil, drizzle with olive oil, and seal the foil into an airtight packet. Place the packets on a sturdy cookie sheet and roast until tender (the tip of a paring knife will easily pierce the beet), 55 to 60 minutes. Cool on a rack until easy to handle.

3. Lower oven heat to 325°F.

4. Spread the walnuts out in a small roasting pan and toast until slightly crisp and lightly browned, about 6 minutes. (Do not over-toast.)

5. Slice the beets and arrange on four serving dishes. Evenly distribute cheese and walnuts over the portions, drizzle with vinaigrette, and serve.

• • •

OMELET FINES HERBES The well-folded omelet is the mark of a good cook. My omelets are temperamental, hit-or-miss, or suffer from slight deformities. Nathalie Dupree insisted on the eggs being stovetop for the entire journey, but I have enjoyed greater success with the broiler method. When my father was dying, I made him an elaborate omelet that took a half hour of prep work. I served it to him and he ate it with pleasure, then said, "Best scrambled eggs I ever had, pal." **• SERVES 1**

3 large eggs

1 tablespoon unsalted butter

About 1 tablespoon mixed chopped fresh herbs, such as parsley, chervil, tarragon, and chives

1. Preheat the broiler.

2. Whisk together the eggs. Set aside. Melt the butter in a pristine 8-inch nonstick pan over medium heat, swirling to distribute evenly, then pouring out any excess.

3. Place the pan over medium heat again. Pour in the whisked eggs and use a heat-resistant rubber spatula to stir the eggs as they cook. When the eggs look like they are setting (no longer wet), push down any eggs on the edges of the pan with the spatula to make sure they are even with the bottom of the pan.

4. Remove the pan from the heat and immediately place under the broiler for about 2 minutes, or until the eggs are evenly set. Sprinkle the eggs with the herbs.

5. Using a pot holder and grasping the pan with your left hand, tilt it over a serving plate, using the rubber spatula to help fold the omelet, and serve.

• • •

ASPARAGUS AND POACHED EGG SALAD WITH BACON

Asparagus with poached egg salad is notable because it is easy to make and tastes as good as anything on earth. It makes me want to sprint to the kitchen.

• SERVES 1

2 thick slices smoky bacon

1 teaspoon plus 1 tablespoon unsalted butter

1 teaspoon olive oil

1 shallot, chopped

$\frac{1}{4}$ pound medium-thin asparagus

Sea salt and freshly ground black pepper

2 large eggs

1. Cook the bacon until crisp; drain and crumble. Reserve.

2. In a medium skillet with a tight-fitting lid, heat 1 teaspoon of butter and the olive oil.

3. Add the shallot and cook until golden brown, about 3 minutes.

4. Trim and rinse the asparagus, but don't dry it (there should still be water clinging to the stalks). Add it to the skillet. Using long tongs, quickly rotate the asparagus to coat. Cover tightly and cook, turning once or twice, until the asparagus is lightly browned.

5. Season with salt and pepper and transfer to a warm serving dish (making sure to include the browned shallot).

6. Place the 1 tablespoon butter in a pristine nonstick pan over moderate heat and melt until foamy. Crack eggs into the skillet, gently swirling the whites so they spread out and fill the pan. As soon as the egg whites become cloudy—about 1 minute—lower the heat, cover, and cook until the egg whites are firm but not hard, about 2 minutes.

7. Immediately top the asparagus with the eggs, sprinkle with bacon, and serve.

• • •

LEG OF LAMB WITH ROASTED FENNEL In 1968, I took my first trip abroad and found myself at a restaurant on the outskirts of Beirut. In front of me, I found a bowlful of sheep's eyeballs, which I eyed with curiosity. Then I ate them with frightful relish. Below me was a rushing river with a pebbly bottom and a slight waterfall ahead. The owner of the restaurant pointed to a scene behind me, and I turned to watch a group of bedouins riding their camels across an aqueduct built by the Romans and a shepherd leading his sheep across the river where mythology tells us that Hercules was born. I remember thinking, I was born to see things as wonderful as this. When I turned around a leg of lamb had been put before me and my companions from a Greek cruise ship. The owner carved it into pale, juicy slices the size of playing cards. Small nuggets of garlic covered the plate, and the aroma of lamb and lemon and garlic made you believe that Hercules deserved to be born in this river. It was the finest meal I had ever eaten to that point of my life.

• **SERVES 6 TO 8 WITH LEFTOVERS**

1 leg of lamb (about 7 pounds), trimmed but still on the bone
3 sprigs fresh rosemary, coarsely chopped
Coarse or kosher salt and freshly ground black pepper
Olive oil

3 fennel bulbs, thinly sliced (6 cups)

1 red onion, thinly sliced (1 cup)

1. Bring the lamb to room temperature. Make a paste of the chopped rosemary and salt and pepper, binding it with olive oil. Rub the paste on all sides of the lamb and let it sit for 30 minutes.

2. Preheat the oven to 425°F.

3. Mix the fennel and red onion, toss lightly with olive oil (until coated but not drenched), and sprinkle with salt and pepper. Transfer to a baking pan and roast until golden brown, stirring once or twice, 20 to 25 minutes. Cool on a rack and reserve in the pan.

4. Increase the oven heat to 450°F. Adjust an oven rack to the lower portion.

5. Place the lamb in a shallow roasting dish and sear in the oven for 15 minutes.

6. Lower the heat to 350°F and roast until the internal temperature reads 130°F on an instant-read meat thermometer inserted in the thickest part of the lamb, about 1 hour.

7. Transfer the lamb to a carving board and cover with a loose tent of aluminum foil. Let rest for 10 minutes before carving. Meanwhile, return fennel and red onion to the oven to heat through. Serve the lamb garnished with warm fennel and red onion.

• • •

RATATOUILLE Ratatouille is one of those recipes I can make better than I can pronounce or spell it. When I lived in Paris, there was a shop on the rue Mouffetard that sold ratatouille by the pint, and I remember making a whole meal out of it one rainy night. In the summertime, I like to make this with fresh, peeled Beaufort tomatoes, which I consider to be the finest on earth. Ratatouille is the happiest marriage of vegetables I know of.   **• SERVES 6**

8 sprigs fresh parsley

2 sprigs fresh thyme

$\frac{1}{2}$ teaspoon fennel seeds

1 teaspoon whole black peppercorns

1 bay leaf

4 garlic cloves, smashed

4 medium yellow onions, diced

2 pounds (about 6) medium zucchini, cubed

2 pounds eggplant, cubed

4 large green bell peppers, cored, seeded, and cubed

Olive oil

Two 35-ounce cans whole tomatoes, preferably San Marzano,
    drained and diced

Coarse or kosher salt

1. Place the first six ingredients in a large square of a double thickness of cheesecloth and, using kitchen twine, tie into a bag. Set aside.

2. In a large heavy skillet, cook the onions, zucchini, eggplant, and peppers separately in small batches, using only as much olive oil as needed to prevent sticking. (The onions should be lightly browned; zucchini, eggplant, and peppers should be cooked until they begin to soften. To reduce the amount of cooking oil, toss the eggplant cubes lightly in olive oil and set them aside until ready to use.)

3. As each batch of vegetables is cooked, transfer it to a large stockpot. Then add the spice and herb bag and the tomatoes. Cover and simmer until vegetables are softened, 35 to 45 minutes.

4. Gently spoon the vegetables into a colander suspended over a large bowl. Transfer the drained vegetables to a serving bowl and return the cooking liquid to the stockpot. Reduce over medium-high heat until thick and syrupy, about 5 minutes.

5. Pour the liquid over the vegetables, season with salt, and serve at once or allow to cool to room temperature.

CHAPTER SIX

The Bill Dufford Summer

I n the summer between my junior and senior years, Bill Dufford gave me a key to the Beaufort High School gymnasium and a job as a groundskeeper for the summer. Because of some incurable wound my father suffered during the Depression, the Colonel instituted an iron-clad rule that none of his seven children could take a job that would pay them a salary. Mr. Dufford was absolutely delighted that I would move tons of dirt from one end of campus to another while refusing to take a single dime for my labor. I thought the physical work would be good for me as an athlete, and I spent the summer outdoors in the blazing heat, resodding and planting grass on every bald patch that disfigured the vast greensward of my pretty campus. Mr. Dufford also let me practice basketball in the gym the last three hours of the day before he made me close up at six.

My favorite part of each day was when Mr. Dufford drove out onto the football or baseball field where I was shoveling dirt and motioned to me to get in his car. "You sorry damned pissant," he would say. "I may not be able to pay you, but I can damn well feed you."

His red Chrysler was high-finned and flashy, and it cruised down Ribault Road like a yacht as he headed toward the business center of

Beaufort for lunch. Each day we ate at the same table at Harry's Restaurant, a town gathering place where businessmen and politicians and retirees came together—all drawn by the shaping, leavening power of gossip. Rumor was always hot to the touch and hot off the plate at Harry's. Dufford was popular with the old-timers and newcomers alike, and everyone at Harry's made an appearance at his table before he finished eating. I learned that summer that towns like Beaufort did not need novelists if they had restaurants like Harry's. Daily, I listened for the news of sicknesses and obituaries and scandals and disasters as they passed in animated conversation between men bent low over coffee and at their leisure. The whole history of the town rose and ebbed each day in the great tides of conversation, and I felt like a deep insider in the underground movements of Beaufort when that summer was over. Mr. Dufford excelled in the art of conversation and debate and the fiery give-and-take that animated the lives of workingmen. My principal was golden and eloquent and in his prime that summer. He mesmerized the movers and shakers in the town with his views on education and politics. The integration of the Beaufort schools was three years away from becoming a reality, yet its storms had already built up hurricane force, gathering at the town gates.

Harry's Restaurant also opened up the floodgates of a whole culinary world I never knew existed until that summer as Dufford told me to order anything that suited my fancy. For the first time in my life, I tasted crab cakes and shrimp salad, fried oysters and stuffed flounder. On one magical Friday, I mustered up the courage to order Roquefort cheese dressing to put on my tossed salad. I'd never tasted anything so exotic or delicious in my life. There were chowders and stews and she-crab soups and heaping, glistening salads enlivened with olives, peppers, and generous slices of cheese and meats built from scratch by Harry Chakides' Greek mother. I drank glass after glass of iced tea, sweet enough to count as dessert. Homemade biscuits and yeast rolls floated out of that kitchen, light as clouds, and the laughter of the black cooks followed the smoking bread to our table. Because of my principal, I learned how a small town worked, how it was held together by the fabulous buzz and pollination of its own most heinous or joyful stories, and I learned it while consuming the best food I had ever eaten. I would leave Harry's every day feeling as sated and gluttonous as a king. Though, in my mind, Harry's Restaurant remains a paradise of tastes and smells, it is the first sharp, fresh taste of Roquefort cheese that still leaps out as a small miracle of surprise to my immature palate.

There was another surprise at Harry's that took me over a month to ask Mr. Dufford about, but it was so incongruous and out of the order of things that I did not know how to phrase the question at first.

"Mr. Dufford," I said, "I thought that Beaufort was segregated by law."

"It is, pissant. It's not going to be for long. But you've got our all-white high school and two miles down the road, you've got the all-black Robert Smalls High School. It doesn't get more segregated than that."

"Then why's Harry's Restaurant integrated?" I asked.

"It isn't," he said. "It's against the law to serve food to black people."

"What about that man?" I said, pointing to a long, slim black man who was eating at the lunch counter.

"That's Tootie," Mr. Dufford explained. "Tootie Frutti, the kids call him. He leads all the parades at football games and the Water Festival. Sometimes he'll direct traffic at the big intersection."

"How come he can eat here? Everyone smiles and laughs when Tootie comes in. Like he's their best friend in the world. Harry feeds him lunch every day right in front of all these white folks. How come?"

"Tootie's retarded, Pat. I think pretty severely. A couple of years ago, he came in here for the first time and things got pretty quiet. Harry sat Tootie down and tried to explain to him about integration and segregation, and Tootie didn't know what Harry was talking about, so Harry said the hell with it and just brought him lunch."

Bill stared at Tootie with new awareness and said, "Come to think of it, I'll be damned. Who'd've believed it? Tootie Frutti integrated the restaurants of South Carolina, all by himself, and it didn't require a court order or a single demonstration or calling out the National Guard."

Because their impact cannot be measured, the teachers of the world drift through their praiseless days unaware of the impact and the majesty of their influence. I want to fall on my knees in gratitude whenever I conjure up the faces of those nameless men and women who spent their finest days coaxing and urging me to discover the best part of myself in the pure sunshine of learning. Because this country dishonors its teachers and humiliates them with lousy pay and a mortifying deficiency of prestige among other professions, they do not receive the gifts of gratitude that brim over in men and women like me when we remember and honor their patient, generous shaping of us into citizens of the brighter world. Bill Dufford occupies a place of highest honor among the teachers who found me directionless and yearning to become a person of consequence as I stumbled through my childhood. That summer, I took the time to study Bill as he made his way among his fellow townspeople. He attracted people with his authentic approachability, the full attention of his gaze, and the passionate authority he brought to bear on any subject that arose in Harry's. I wanted people to look at me with the admiration that those Beaufortonians showed to my high school principal. From watching Mr. Dufford, I learned that the principal of a high school is one of the central players and politicians in the life of a town. I discovered that Dufford was principal in parlous, aggravated times. The subject of integration was on everybody's minds and lips that summer of 1962. I got to watch Bill Dufford going through the painful switch from his upbringing as a Southern racist to his transformation into a Southern liberal who would play a courageous part in the integration of South Carolina schools.

"Have you ever gone to school with black kids, Pat?" he asked me at lunch one day.

"Yes, sir, I have."

"What did you think about it?" he asked.

"I never thought anything about it, Mr. Dufford," I said. "I'm Catholic. It's a sin if I believe in segregation."

"That's what they teach you? I'll be damned," he said, amazed. "What kind of sin?"

"The mortal kind. The kind where you burn in hell," I said.

"What a hell of a way to handle it," Dufford said. "Why didn't the

Protestant church think of that? Did you go to school with black kids in Washington last year?"

"Yes, sir. There weren't many in Gonzaga, but every class had some."

"So what did you think? Did you get to know any of them personally?"

"Louie Jones was in my class," I said. "He was a great guy."

"What kind of student was he? Could Louie Jones keep up with the rest of the class? Was he a troublemaker? How'd he get along with the other kids?" Mr. Dufford said, fixing me with his fully engaged gaze.

"Louie was the smartest kid in the class, Mr. Dufford," I said. "Maybe Mike Higgins was as smart. But everyone liked Louie. He was elected secretary of my homeroom. You'd've loved Louie Jones, Mr. Dufford. He was your kind of kid."

"It's coming," Dufford said. "It's coming, and it's coming soon and I don't think anyone in this whole damn state is ready for it."

"Are you ready for it, Mr. Dufford?" I said, the first time I remember teasing Bill Dufford. He looked at me oddly, then said, "You sorry damn little pissant, you're damn right I'm ready for it. I've been thinking about this a lot lately, Pat. I'm Southern to the bone and was raised to defend the Southern way and I've done it my whole life. I've defended segregation my entire life, until lately. I think of segregation and then I think of words like 'justice' and 'freedom' and 'liberty.' I think of the Declaration of Independence and the U.S. Constitution. I think of the teachings of Jesus Christ. See where I'm going with this, Pat?"

"Yes, sir," I said.

"If people in this restaurant heard what I just said to you, I'd be fired tomorrow," he said. "Could you have brought Louie Jones home to your house? To eat dinner? To spend the night?"

"Yes, sir. Everybody's welcome at our house," I said.

"Have you ever used the word 'nigger'?" he said. "And I want an honest answer."

"When I was five, I used it and my mother heard me. I thought she was going to beat me to death. She wore my fanny out with a switch."

"Why'd she beat you?"

"Said she was raised colored. That her folks were poorer than all the black families around them. She said the black families brought food to her house during the Depression. Said she'd let us be anything but white trash. She doesn't tolerate white trash."

"Your mother sounds like a hell of a woman," he said.

"Mom's something," I said.

I spent that summer so full of joy I never wanted it to end. I moved dirt in wheelbarrows and planted and cut grass with my principal coming out to help me in the fields. Dufford loved physical labor and the outdoors and sweating in the man-eating Beaufort sun. I would hitchhike the ten miles into town early each morning, receive my assignments from Mr. Dufford, work hard until lunch at Harry's, finish my work in the afternoon, then hit the gym at three, where I would spend three hours trying to turn myself into the best basketball player in the state. My ambitions exceeded my talent by a long shot but I didn't know that then, and I drove myself to the point of collapse each day. I worked on going to my left all summer, and during one of those hours each day I would only dribble with my left hand and only throw up left-handed hook shots off the drive. I invented dribbling and passing drills for myself, and I played imaginary games from start to finish in my head. Those imaginary games, populated by a whole nation of made-up players, were my first attempts at writing short stories, and all the games ended the same way, with me in a heroic, winner-take-all, last-second shot on a drive down the lane with my invisible enemies closing the lane down around me. Hard labor, great food, basketball—I had everything—the best summer of my life.

CRAB CAKES   Somewhere, lost in the high alps of *Beach Music*, the narrator, Jack McCall, evidently gives out his recipe for crab cakes to someone. So when I sign books in faraway cities, people often ask me about that recipe for crab cakes, and I write it out for them. I think I make the best crab cakes and shrimp salad in the world, and I will take on all comers.

I became so connected to the crab cake during the *Beach Music* tour that I was invited on the *Good Morning America* show to cook crab cakes for Charlie Gibson. I love everything about Charlie Gibson except the time I have to get up for the show. It is usually five in the morning, and my habits are such that years go by when I never see the planet at five in the morning. But, for the crab cake session, they forced me to rise at 4 A.M. so I could prove to a staff member that I could actually cook a crab cake. I learned this only when I got to the studio and was met by the staffer herself, a pretty, self-confident woman dressed in a chef's apron.

"Do you really know how to cook a crab cake?" she asked. "If you can't, I'll show you how to do it."

"I'm from the coast of South Carolina," I said. "In the summer I set a crab pot every day."

"But can you cook a crab cake?" She pointed to three containers of picked blue crabmeat.

I washed my hands thoroughly and began to pick over the crab, removing all shell fragments and ligaments.

"Why are you doing that?" the young woman asked me. "No one's going to eat them."

"Then I will eat them," I said. "This is beautiful crabmeat."

"Ah!" she said. "Why don't you use any breading, like sodacrackers?"

"If I wanted soda crackers, I would eat a soda cracker. I like crab, just crab."

If memory serves me right, I used a scallion that day instead of the snipped chives in the recipe below, and I tossed in some capers and chopped red pepper for effect.

I gave the young woman one to taste; she said, "This is delicious!"

So I went live on TV across the nation, where my only surprise was that Charlie Gibson peppered me with so many questions I discovered I could not cook and talk at the same time. Charlie is animated and cheerful in the early-morning hours, and he asked questions about every phase of the assemblage of the proper, well-schooled crab cake. When the ordeal was over, I was exhausted, but edified when a charge of cameramen who descended like vultures for the carcass of a possum devoured those crab cakes in the time it took to do one commercial.

One of them said, "No one is hungrier than cameramen who work the morning shows. No one."

And the pretty young woman who made me prove that I knew my way around crabmeat? I did not get her name at five in the morning. I was channel-grazing years later when I saw her on the Food Network, and I recognized her immediately. Whenever I see Sara Moulton on her wonderful cooking show, I always think of crab. • **MAKES 8**

1 pound lump crabmeat, picked over and cleaned, with all shell fragments removed

1 egg white, lightly beaten (until just foamy, not stiff)

1 tablespoon all-purpose flour

2 tablespoons finely snipped fresh chives

1 teaspoon freshly ground black pepper

$1/4$ teaspoon cayenne pepper

2 teaspoons coarse or kosher salt

3 tablespoons unsalted butter

2 teaspoons peanut oil

Lemon wedges

1. Place the cleaned crabmeat in a medium mixing bowl. Pour the egg white over crabmeat slowly, stopping occasionally to mix it through. When the crabmeat has absorbed the egg white and feels slightly sticky to the touch, sift the flour over crabmeat and sprinkle the chives, black pepper, cayenne, and 1 teaspoon of the salt evenly over the top. Lift the crabmeat from the bottom of the bowl, turning it over gently, to mix the ingredients without overhandling.

2. Separate the crabmeat into 8 equal portions and gently roll each between the flattened palms of your hands to form loose balls. Flatten slightly and transfer to a plate. Sprinkle both sides liberally with the remaining 1 teaspoon salt and refrigerate for at least 1 hour before cooking.

3. Line a baking pan with paper towels. Fry the crab cakes in two batches to ensure a crisp crust. Using a small (8-inch) heavy skillet that conducts heat well, melt half the butter and oil together until the mixture is foamy and begins to brown. Carefully place the crab cakes in the hot fat and fry until a crust forms, turning only once, about 2 minutes per side. (The fat should be sizzling hot, enabling a crisp crust to form before the crab absorbs the cooking fat. This is the Southern secret to perfect crab cakes.) A small pastry spatula (with a thin tongue) will make lifting and turning the delicate crab cakes a lot easier. Remove the crab cakes and drain in the prepared pan. Cover loosely with aluminum foil to keep warm while you make the second batch.

4. Carefully pour off the cooking fat from the first batch, wipe out the pan, and return it to the heat. Prepare the second batch of crab cakes using the remaining butter and oil.

5. Serve hot with lemon wedges.

• • •

SHRIMP SALAD

• **SERVES 4 AS A FIRST COURSE OR SANDWICH FILLING, 2 AS A LIGHT LUNCH**

1 pound large (21–25 count) shrimp, peeled and deveined
2 tablespoons mayonnaise
2 tablespoons sour cream

1 tablespoon finely minced fresh tarragon

1 teaspoon fresh lemon juice

1 teaspoon tarragon vinegar

$^1/_4$ cup finely diced celery

$^1/_4$ cup finely minced scallions

1 teaspoon coarse or kosher salt

$^1/_2$ teaspoon freshly ground white pepper

1. In a medium stockpot over high heat, bring 4 quarts abundantly salted water to a rolling boil. Add the shrimp and cook until just pink, about 3 minutes. Immediately transfer to a colander and run under cool water to stop the shrimp from cooking any further (only takes several seconds; shrimp should still be slightly warm when dressed). Shake the colander to drain any excess water.

2. In a small bowl, mix together mayonnaise, sour cream, and tarragon. Set aside.

3. In a medium mixing bowl, toss the warm shrimp with the lemon juice and vinegar. Stir in the celery and scallions. Add the mayonnaise mixture, salt, and pepper and toss to coat. Cover and refrigerate until ready to serve. Taste to correct seasoning.

• • •

SWEET POTATO ROLLS   • MAKES 24

1 package ($^1/_4$ ounce) dry yeast

$^1/_4$ cup warm water

1 tablespoon sugar

1 teaspoon coarse or kosher salt

2 large eggs

8 tablespoons (1 stick) unsalted butter, melted

$^1/_2$ cup milk

1$^1/_2$ cups mashed cooked sweet potato

4 to 5 cups all-purpose flour (depends on moisture of sweet potato)

Cornmeal

1. Place yeast, warm water, and sugar in the work bowl of a standing mixer and let the combination stand until it becomes foamy, about 5 minutes. Using the paddle attachment, add salt and then beat in the eggs, melted butter, milk, and mashed sweet potato until thoroughly combined.

2. Begin adding the flour, 1 cup at a time, up to 4 cups, reserving the remaining cup. (The rolls will taste better if the dough remains slightly sticky, pulling away from the sides of the bowl without becoming too dry.) Transfer the dough to a large mixing bowl and cover. Let rise in a warm place until doubled in size, about 1 hour. (Alternatively, cover the bowl with plastic wrap and place in the refrigerator for several hours or overnight.)

3. Lightly flour a clean, dry work surface and transfer the dough to it by inverting the bowl. (This will deflate the dough as well.) Using an under-and-over kneading motion, punch down the dough, continuing to knead until smooth, about 2 minutes. Add the remaining flour, 1 tablespoon at a time, if the dough is too sticky to knead.

4. Preheat the oven to 400°F.

5. Sprinkle cornmeal on several baking sheets and set aside.

6. Using a serrated knife, separate the dough into halves, then quarters, and then eighths. Cut each eighth into three pieces. Press each piece of dough with the heel of your hand in a circular motion, forming a ball. Transfer the rolls to the prepared pans, cover with a dish towel, and let rise until doubled in size, 1 to 2 hours, or cover with plastic wrap and let rise in refrigerator overnight. Bake for about 20 minutes. To test for doneness, tap the bottom of a roll. It should sound hollow.

INSTRUCTIONS FOR HAND MIXING

1. Place the yeast, warm water, and sugar in a large stainless steel

bowl and let stand until foamy, about 5 minutes. Add salt to yeast mixture along with the eggs, melted butter, milk, and mashed sweet potato. Using a large wooden spoon, beat until thoroughly combined.

2. Beat in flour, 1 cup at a time. Each additional cup makes the dough harder to beat, so this will take concentration and elbow grease. When the dough begins to form a ball, transfer it from the bowl to the work surface and start kneading, adding flour as needed, until the dough forms a smooth ball but is still sticky to the touch.

3. Let rise and bake as above.

• • •

CHEDDAR CHEESE AND SAUSAGE BISCUITS

• MAKES 18

3 cups self-rising flour (preferably White Lily)

2 teaspoons baking powder

$1/4$ teaspoon baking soda

$1/4$ teaspoon coarse or kosher salt

7 ounces sharp cheddar cheese, coarsely grated

2 teaspoons freshly ground black pepper

8 tablespoons (1 stick) cold unsalted butter, cut into small pieces

$1 1/4$ cups buttermilk

3 tablespoons finely chopped andouille sausage, sautéed until crisp, and drained

1. Preheat the oven to 450°F. Place rack in middle of oven.

2. Sift the flour, baking powder, baking soda, and salt together into a large bowl. Stir in the grated cheese (reserve 2 tablespoons for the topping) and black pepper. Add the butter pieces to the flour and cut it into the flour with two knives (or with your fingers), moving quickly before the butter gets soft. When butter is the size of peas, pour in the buttermilk, add the sausage, and stir with a wooden spoon just until the dough is in one piece. If the dough is overworked, the biscuits will be tough. (That's why making biscuits by hand is the secret to light, fluffy, melt-in-your mouth biscuits. Overhandling, especially by using a processor or standing mixer, creates tough biscuits.)

3. Turn the dough onto a lightly floured, dry work surface. With a wooden rolling pin, roll the dough into a rectangle at least $1/2$ inch thick. Use a biscuit cutter (or the open end of a glass) to cut rounds of dough. Gently push the dough out of the biscuit cutter and place on an ungreased cookie sheet. The scraps of dough can be gathered and rolled again one more time. (If not baking biscuits immediately, cover with plastic wrap and refrigerate for several hours or overnight.)

4. Sprinkle the biscuits with the reserved grated cheese and bake for 15 to 18 minutes, until the biscuits have risen and the tops are lightly browned. Serve hot.

• • •

SUMMER CHOWDER

• **SERVES 4 AS A MAIN COURSE OR 8 AS A FIRST COURSE**

6 slices smoky bacon, coarsely chopped (about 1 cup)

1 cup minced red onion

$1/4$ cup finely diced celery

3 cups fresh corn kernels (about 5 ears)

3 cups whole milk

$1/2$ pound new red potatoes, washed but not peeled and cut into
$1/4$-inch cubes

$1/2$ cup heavy cream

1 teaspoon Tabasco sauce

2 tablespoons snipped fresh chives

1 pound sea scallops, rinsed and patted dry

Coarse or kosher salt and freshly ground white pepper

1. In a medium stockpot over moderate heat, cook the bacon until the fat is rendered and bacon is almost crisp, 5 to 8 minutes. Using a slotted spoon, remove the bacon and reserve. Drain off all but 2 tablespoons bacon fat, reserving the extra in a small bowl for later use.

2. Reduce the heat to low, add the onion and celery to stockpot, and cook in the bacon drippings, stirring occasionally, until the vegetables begin to soften, 12 to 15 minutes. As the vegetables begin to exude their moisture, use a wooden spoon to scrape up any browned bits clinging to the bottom of the stockpot.

3. Using a food processor fitted with a metal blade, puree 1 cup of the corn kernels with 1 cup of the milk. Add to the stockpot and stir well. Add the remaining corn and milk and the potatoes, stirring to combine. Lower the heat and cook until the potatoes and corn are tender, about 35 minutes.

4. Stir in the reserved bacon, heavy cream, Tabasco, and chives and simmer until chowder thickens, another 3 to 5 minutes.

5. While the chowder is thickening, place the reserved bacon fat in a small heavy skillet over high heat. When the fat is hot, sear the scallops until golden brown on each side but still slightly opaque in the center, about 2 minutes on the first side and 1 minute on the other.

6. Season the chowder with coarse salt and ground white pepper to taste. Ladle into deep bowls and float scallops in the center. Serve immediately.

• • •

BREAKFAST SHRIMP AND GRITS During the summer before my father died, his friends and family gathered in Beaufort and Fripp Island to say goodbye to him. After the Marine Corps, my father's life became rich in friendship; his personality bloomed when he did not have to face the world as a professional tough guy. I grew up not hearing Don Conroy say a single funny thing, and it startled me to find out that he could be hilarious. He is the only father in the history of American letters who considered it his just due to sign copies of his oldest son's latest book. Starting with *The Great Santini*, he signed with me at his side in at least six American cities. When other writers asked me why I allowed this incursion, I explained that my father and I had to search for ways to say we loved each other without saying the words.

When the visitors swarmed out to Fripp that last summer, my job was to feed everybody lunch and dinner. I own a huge dining room table that was once used as a library table at Cambridge University, and I have fed up to thirty people on it. That summer I averaged twenty diners a shift. My father would always ask, "What's the chow tonight, son?"

"What would you like, Dad?"

"Everybody loves your shrimp and grits. Everybody loves your shrimp salad. They like that Spanish soup you make. Gashippo."

"Gazpacho, Dad."

"Yeah, that stuff."

"Dad, isn't it odd for a Chicago boy to be asking for grits?" I asked.

"I've always had an ability to grow, son," he answered. "To enlarge my boundaries. You always missed that about me."

"Sure did."

"Colonel Pinkston and his bride are coming tonight. So shrimp and grits is the order of the day."

As I spent that summer at the stove, I became proficient enough to make shrimp and grits and shrimp salad blindfolded. Cooking is most sublime when it is creative and playful. I sometimes put a little flour in the leftover bacon grease, made a dark roux (being careful not to burn it), and then poured in a cup of water to make a thin but luscious gravy. I substituted red onions, Vidalia onions, scallions, and even garlic when I didn't have shallots. But I do that with every recipe I have in my possession. A recipe is a suggestion, a field guide and a road map; it is not totalitarian in nature—except when you are baking. My overwrought, disorganized nature does not serve me well when I am baking a pie or cake. Baking is a high branch of chemistry and woe to the home cook who does not follow the homemaker's recipe with absolute precision. But recipes like shrimp and grits and shrimp salad invite experimentation. That following winter, I prepared oysters and grits for Dad, and he claimed to like them better than he did the shrimp.

Toward the end of the summer, my father asked me to bring him the phone, and I did. He was trying to get some friends of his from the Marine Corps to come down for Labor Day weekend. He surprised me by saying, "Pat'll feed you like a king. That's a promise. My kid's fed everybody this summer. Man, it's been a loaves and fishes scene down here."

My childhood was brutal, unforgivable, and long. But I watched my father change after he discovered how much I loathed that childhood. I could tell he loved that I fed his family and friends and him. By the end of his life, my father had become proficient at telling his children he loved us, and he never once had to say the words. **• SERVES 4**

> 1 cup coarse white grits
> 2 thick slices country bacon, cut into matchsticks (about $^1/_2$ cup)
> 1 small shallot, finely minced
> 2 tablespoons unsalted butter
> 1 pound shrimp, peeled and deveined
> 1 teaspoon strained fresh lemon juice
> Coarse or kosher salt
> 2 to 3 drops Tabasco sauce

1. Slow-cook the grits according to the package directions. (This will take about 60 minutes.) Set aside.

2. Place a medium, heavy skillet over moderate heat. When the pan is hot, add the bacon and cook until the fat is rendered and bacon is crisp, 5 to 8 minutes. Using a slotted spoon, remove the bacon and reserve in a small bowl, keeping the pan as is, fat and all. (This can be done in advance . Do not cook the shrimp until the grits are ready and resting.)

3. In a low oven, warm four heatproof serving plates.

4. Return the skillet with the bacon fat to moderate heat. Add the shallot and cook until soft but not colored. Add butter and when it's melted, add shrimp, cooking until just pink, about 3 minutes. Add lemon juice and a pinch of salt and toss to coat.

5. Spoon about $^1/_2$ cup steaming grits into the middle of each warm plate. Using a slotted spoon, place shrimp on top of the grits. Add reserved bacon and Tabasco to the pan juices, swirling the skillet for a few seconds to create a thin sauce. Pour over the shrimp and grits.

• • •

GUMBO A gumbo is another handy dish to know when you are required to feed the multitudes at family reunions, Super Bowl parties, and tailgating at football games. I made a variation of this recipe for three straight Super Bowls and two New Year's Day parties when I lived on Maddox Drive in Ansley Park, the prettiest place in Atlanta. I made it once for the crowd that swarmed my house during my father's last summer. At the end of the cooking time, I also added oysters with the shrimp and crabmeat and crawdads, when I could get them, and I served it in large bowls over rice. The payoff for this recipe is the moans of pure pleasure from your guests as they take in the aromas and begin eating this dish. There is no great beast of an appetite out there that this recipe cannot sate.

This recipe came to me from Julia Anderson, a local artist, and we didn't change it a lick. It was perfect. **• SERVES 8**

$^1/_3$ cup vegetable oil

$^1/_3$ cup all-purpose flour

1 whole chicken

1 large onion, peeled and quartered

1 cup diced celery, plus leafy tops of 1 bunch celery

1 bay leaf

2 tablespoons coarse or kosher salt

$1/4$ cup olive oil

1 cup diced green bell pepper

1 cup diced red onion

1 teaspoon red peppe flakes, or to taste

$1/2$ teaspoon freshly ground white pepper, or to taste

$1/2$ teaspoon freshly ground black pepper, or to taste

$3/4$ teaspoon gumbo filé

$3/4$ teaspoon dried thyme, or 1 $1/2$ tablespoons chopped fresh thyme

6 garlic cloves, finely minced

$1/2$ pound bacon, coarsely chopped

1 pound smoked andouille sausage, cut into $1/4$-inch-thick slices

One 16-ounce can tomato purée

1 pound large shrimp, peeled and deveined

1 pound picked crabmeat (optional)

The first step to making gumbo is to get all the ingredients ready. Once you are set up to cook, this dish goes together quickly.

1. Place oil and flour in a small saucepan over medium heat and whisk to combine. Cook, whisking constantly, until the mixture turns a dark caramel color and begins to smell like toasted almonds. This is called a roux and it will take about 15 minutes to produce a smooth paste that will not only thicken your gumbo but lend a deep, rich color. Transfer the roux to a small bowl and let cool to room temperature. When the roux is cooled, drain the excess oil. (This can be done in advance and refrigerated for no more than 24 hours.)

2. Place the chicken, onion, celery tops, and bay leaf in a large stockpot. Cover chicken with water, add the salt, and bring to a boil over medium-high heat. Reduce the heat and simmer until the chicken is tender and the water is infused with flavor, about 60 minutes. Remove the chicken and let it cool. Strain the stock and reserve. (You'll need at least $4^1/2$ cups.) When chicken is cool enough to handle, strip the meat from the bones and shred into bite-size pieces.

3. Wipe out the stockpot and return it to medium-high heat. Warm the olive oil and add the green pepper, diced celery, and red onion. Cook, stirring occasionally, until the vegetables begin to soften and color lightly on the edges, 12 to 15 minutes. Combine the red, white, and black pepper, the filé, and thyme together in a small bowl and sprinkle evenly over the vegetable mixture. Cook, stirring constantly, until the vegetables are well coated, about 8 minutes. When the spices are cooked, mix in the garlic, cooking for another 3 minutes.

4. Heat the stock in a saucepan over medium heat. Whisk $1/4$ cup of the stock into the roux until it forms a smooth paste. Add it to the stockpot along with the shredded chicken and the remaining stock, stirring well to combine. Bring the mixture to a boil, lower the heat, and simmer for 60 minutes, stirring occasionally.

5. While the gumbo is simmering, cook the bacon in a heavy skillet until the fat is rendered and the bacon is crisp, 5 to 8 minutes. Add the andouille sausage and stir to coat with the bacon drippings. Reserve.

6. After the gumbo has simmered for 60 minutes, add the tomato purée and bacon and sausage mixture. Take 1 cup of the hot gumbo liquid out and deglaze the bacon pan. (Deglazing means to return the pan to the heat, add the liquid, and bring it to a boil while stirring and scraping the bottom and sides of the pan to loosen any browned bits.) Add these pan juices to the gumbo and continue simmering until the gumbo is slightly thickened, about another 30 minutes. (This recipe can be prepared in advance up to this point.)

7. Stir in shrimp and crabmeat (if using), cooking only until the shrimp are pink, about 10 minutes.

● ● ●

ICED FRUIT TEA

4 tea bags

1 lemon

1 orange, sliced, plus more for garnish

$1/2$ pint strawberries or raspberries, plus more for garnish

1 cup cubed fresh pineapple, plus more for garnish

1. Place the tea bags in a large heatproof pitcher. Using a vegetable peeler or small paring knife, remove the rind from the lemon, being careful not to include any of the bitter white pith. Cut into strips and reserve. Juice the lemon and reserve.

2. In a kettle, bring 10 cups fresh, cold water to a rolling boil. Pour over tea bags and let steep for 10 to 15 minutes, depending on your preference. Remove the tea bags and discard. Add the lemon rind, lemon juice, and other fruits. Refrigerate overnight.

3. Strain the fruit from the tea and discard. Pour the tea over ice cubes and garnish with a pineapple cube, an orange slice, or a strawberry.

• • •

ROQUEFORT DRESSING   In the summer of 1962, I first tasted Roquefort cheese dressing at Harry's Restaurant on Bay Street in Beaufort. Nothing had tasted so rich or wonderful to me; I had never heard of Roquefort cheese in my life; no Roquefort ever set foot into the Conroy household as I was growing up. Harry's salad dressing had a body and an elegance I had never tasted on a salad. It was the first time I realized that something as simple as lettuce could be raised to sacramental levels by something as simple as a sauce.

For years I have begged Harry Chakides for the recipe for his Roquefort dressing. Harry is a Citadel man, and I had a crush on his wife,

Jane, when I was in high school. (Girls of Beaufort—a confession—I had a crush on all of you.) But Harry joins other secretive Beaufortonians who hoard their recipes and refuse to share them with me for the appreciation of the larger world. In every decade I have begged Harry for the recipe, but he will not deliver this pillar of his Greek family heritage. One thing is certain: this dressing cannot be called Roquefort cheese dressing unless the provenance of the cheese you use is Roquefort, France. If not, it is called blue cheese dressing. • **MAKES ABOUT 2 CUPS**

$^1/_4$ cup strained fresh lemon juice (1 lemon)

$^3/_4$ cup olive oil

$^3/_4$ pound Roquefort, at room temperature

6 tablespoons buttermilk

1 teaspoon Worcestershire sauce (or more depending on your preference; start slow, you can always add more)

$^1/_2$ teaspoon coarse or kosher salt

1 teaspoon freshly ground black pepper

In a medium mixing bowl, stir together lemon juice and olive oil. Use a wooden spoon to mix in the cheese until you have a thick, lumpy texture. Blend in the buttermilk, Worcestershire, salt, and pepper with a few quick strokes. Cover and refrigerate until ready to use.

CHAPTER SEVEN

A Recipe Is a Story . . .

My love of story has been insatiable since I was a young boy and growing up in the story-haunted South with fighter pilots engaging in faux dogfights over the Atlantic. I can remember falling asleep as my Grandmother Stanny told me about safaris in Tanganyika, belly dancers in Lebanon, and the illegal ivory markets of Hong Kong. My mother, who was no stranger to wildlife, collected poisonous snakes and once told me that a copperhead I caught her for Mother's Day when she was pregnant with my brother Jim was the most thoughtful present she had ever received. In Kissimmee, Florida, long before Disney World, a mandrill grabbed my arm and refused to let go until my mother and Aunt Helen fought the ape off. "Thank God it was not a great ape," my mother said in the retelling. My great-grandfather on my father's side, J. B. Hunt, was a sea captain who claimed he brought salmon to the Great Lakes. He also said a painter named Francis Millet rented a room from him and paid his rent with his paintings years before Millet went down with the *Titanic,* and every Good Friday in Anniston, Alabama, my Uncle Cicero walked with a wooden cross to commemorate the Passion of Jesus. It was a source of great pride to my mother's family, shame to her, and wonder to me. A poet grew up in the bedroom next to mine, and when she was five, my sister came up after dinner and said to me, "Our parents are both crazy. Both nuts."

"No, no, Carol Ann," I said. "Don't say that. That's our mom and dad."

"I've been watching how families act on TV shows," she said. "Our family is nuts. You'll see. You'll see."

Stories have always hunted me down, jumped out at me from the shadows, stalked me and sought me out, grabbed me by the shirtsleeves, and demanded my full attention. I've led a life chock-full of stories, and I know now that you have to be shifty and vigilant and ready to receive their incoming fire. Sometimes it takes the passage of years to reveal their actual meaning or import. They disguise themselves with masks, disfigurements, chimeras, and Trojan horses.

When I write, I wait for the sudden appearance of signs and portents in the air, always on the lookout for secret messages encoded in graffiti or heralds disguised as strangers in the club cars of trains. A bright encounter with twins, a brother and sister, on a morning flight to Rome changed the entire configuration of the Wingo family in *The Prince of Tides.* The wife of a former mayor of Mobile, Alabama, took me out to her yard overlooking Mobile Bay and told me the story of her three-year-old daughter who could not sleep in the heat of the summer. The mother brought the girl out to the end of the dock to watch the sunset, then turned and saw the moon rising out of the east. As the sun disappeared, accompanied by radiant clouds along the horizon, the moon kept rising, pale gold, then pale silver, then a deeper silver, with the child spinning to see both the sun and the moon. When it was over, to her mother's delight, she said, "Oh, Mama—do it again!"

I told the mayor's wife at that instant, "Madam, consider that story stolen." The story fills the prologue of *The Prince of Tides* with just the right spillage of light, and it anchors the last chapter with the sudden coming of darkness. Alertness is a requirement of the writing life, staying nimble on your feet, open to the stories that will rise up and flower around you while you are walking your dog on the beach or taking the kids to soccer practice. The great stories often make their approach with misdirection, camouflage, or smoke screens to hide their passage through your life. Once when I was a boy, I witnessed an angry father ricochet a basketball off the back of his son's head after the kid had beaten him in a game of horse. That image was lost to me for twenty years when I wrote a chapter about Ben Meecham defeating his fighter pilot father in a one-on-one game early in *The Great Santini.* I needed a scene of unendurable humiliation for the son, then I recalled that man bouncing that basketball off that lost boy's head. As the Great Santini followed his son Ben into the house, he taunted him all the way to his room, mimicking again and again that terrible father who had followed me out of time to present me with a story which had all the immediacy, power, and cruelty to demonstrate what Ben Meecham's life felt like at that very moment he had beaten his father in a game for the first time. Ironically, my father and I would witness the filming of that alarming scene and watch as Robert Duvall and Michael O'Keefe would play it to perfection while Blythe Danner looked on in horror in the film version of *The Great Santini.* A diminutive older woman who was on the set that day approached my father with some trepidation and asked, "How often did you and Pat play games like that, Colonel?"

My father stared down at her and then deadpanned, "Every day, madam. Every single day." And another story was born.

But sometimes stories hide themselves from writers like trolls under bridges. Then the writers of the world must keep their bodies attuned for the sudden appearance of the story that is powerful enough to change their novels and their lives. They must train themselves to recognize the divine moment when a great story reveals itself. I know dozens of Southern writers who followed the murder trial of socialite Jim Williams in Savannah, Georgia, but it was the stranger from away, John Berendt, who saw the incredible richness of the story and blended it together with the bizarre and magical atmosphere of the city itself in his book *Midnight in the Garden of Good and Evil.* The story can be living beside you or locked in the house next door or delivering your mail. The gift of the writer is recognition—the awareness when the story has introduced itself to you.

I grew up in the house where a man who called himself the Great Santini initiated a reign of terror that was to last for twenty-one years. I carried my deep hatred of him inside me because I thought he would kill me if I ever let it spill out. I never felt safe a single day of my disgraceful, anxious childhood.

In 1975, I was finishing my first novel, *The Great Santini*, in a farmhouse in Dunwoody, Georgia, provided to me by the great Houghton Mifflin book rep Norman Berg. For two months I wrote at a furious pace, then came to the last chapter and hit an impassable wall—I lacked all imagination about how I would end the book, or to put it in other words, I ran out of story. That night I had a startling dream that took me back to a funeral at Cherry Point, North Carolina. A friend's father had crashed his plane during maneuvers over the ocean. I remember my friend and his sister and mother weeping as they followed his coffin out of the church, and I remembered shocking my third-grade heart by thinking that I'd be the happiest boy on earth if my father's plane crashed.

I awoke the next morning, and I had my story. I said aloud: "I'm going to kill the son of a bitch."

I drove to the Darlington Apartments on Peachtree Street, where my father lived in a one-bedroom pied-à-terre. My parents were not fully aware of what I was up to in writing *The Great Santini*, but then again, neither was I. The week before I had caught my father, in flagrante, with a strange woman after he had forgotten that he had invited me over to watch a basketball game that same night. A better man would have quietly closed the door and never mentioned the intrusion, but I howled with laughter. As Dad and his lady friend hid under the sheets, I marched to the bookshelf, pulled down Dad's Bible, dusted it off, and read Dad and his lovebird the Ten Commandments out of Exodus with great relish and showmanship.

My father was still petulant over the encounter when I knocked at his door. Dad said, "Thanks for knocking this time, jocko."

"Good to see you, Romeo," I said. "I need to ask you some questions about flying an airplane."

"You came to the right place, pal," he said.

"I told you I was writing a book based on a Marine Corps family?"

"Anybody I know?"

"Nope, total fiction. But at the end of the book I need to kill my pilot. I can't have him just flying through the air and have his plane explode. It ain't artful, Dad. I need suspense. I need danger. I need excitement. Then I'm going to kill the bastard."

"Bad idea, son," he said.

"Why?"

"It'll screw up the sequel."

"Let's start, Dad," I said. "I don't know one thing about flying. I don't know if you turn on a key, if you have four on the floor—not zip."

"You came to the right guy," my father said, beginning our afternoon together. "Let's make it a night flight. I used to have to get four hours of flight time at night every month."

"I didn't know that."

"Let's put it in Key West. I loved flying out of Key West. Make it 0330, which would put me in Beaufort at about, say, 0520. We'll fly the bird at thirty-two thousand feet. Flying is the most amazing thing a human being can do. No one loved it more than your old man."

"Keep it going, Dad," I said, writing. Dad shifted his wooden chair around so he was facing me, straddling the chair like a detective questioning a criminal he loathes. But Dad reached out over the chair's back and grabbed the stick with his left hand. For the rest of this imaginary flight, he would control that throttle with his left hand. He was the fighter pilot and he was in control. I wrote as fast as I could as he described that night flight over Florida.

My father's face became transformed as his eyes wandered over the gauges in his imaginary cockpit. He described the lights of Orlando, then the lights of Jacksonville, and on his right, the great abyss of darkness that was the Atlantic. Closing fast on Savannah, my father reached for a phantom radio and said, "Atlanta Center. Marine 657 over Brunswick at flight level three-two-zero. Requesting a Tacon approach to Beaufort. Over."

Then, in a different voice, Dad spoke as the voice of the anonymous controller in Atlanta. "Roger. Six-five-seven is cleared to the Sand Dollar intersection for Tacon approach. Contact Beaufort approach control on 325–0 at this time."

My father switched frequencies and called the Beaufort tower, pressing the radio near his mouth. "Beaufort approach, Marine 657 inbound. Sand Dollar intersection for Tacon approach. Flight level three-two-zero."

"Roger," the air station controller said, and my father surprised me by using a different voice than the Atlanta controller. "You are cleared to approach altitude. Report leaving three-two-zero."

I had entered a world of my father's that was a complete mystery to me and where I had never ventured before. Every word he uttered I took down, every number, and I could feel the tension build in the cockpit between us. Then I looked up at my father, whose intensity and concentration were in perfect congruence, and I said, "Dad, now you got to help me kill the guy. We've got to kill the pilot."

My father looked up and pointed his finger to something he could see, but I could not. "Right there, son. High on the left of the instrument panel—the fire warning light."

"Is that bad?" I asked, writing furiously.

Dad looked at me as though I was a moron, then said, "It could ruin your whole day." He made an involuntary movement with his right hand to his face that I didn't understand.

"Why'd you do that, Dad?" I asked.

"I'm pulling up my oxygen mask to check for smoke. Any smoke in this cockpit and I'm outta here, pal."

"No smoke, Dad. No smoke at all," I said. "Is there anything else I can add to make this flight more difficult?"

"Fog," he said. "A pain in the ass. Hell, I can't bring this plane in from this direction."

"Why not?" I asked as I wrote.

"Too many civilians if I bring it in this way. Got to go around."

"Who cares about civilians if your plane's on fire?"

My father glared at me with contempt and said, "Fighter pilots do, pal. Part of the code."

"Oh, I see. Good code. Now, Dad, something bad's got to happen to this airplane."

"Okay. I've started this bird down the slope, my boards are out, I'm ready for anything."

Then something shifted radically in the nature of both the interview and the history of this mythical flight taking place on a wooden chair in my father's cramped apartment. His left arm jumped and he had trouble controlling the stick as he reached for the radio and said in a measured voice, "Mayday. Mayday. Six-five-seven. I'm in the soup at two thousand. Have severe engine vibration and oven temp. Am going to guard channel and squawking emergency. Out."

"What's guard channel?" I asked, writing.

"It'll put me on every radar screen on the East Coast," he said as he fought the stick, his left arm fighting against the convulsions taking place deep inside his aircraft.

He reached for the radio again, every nerve in my father's body alert with the mortal danger of the situation. "Six-five-seven is out of five thousand feet at ten miles. Unable to contact GCA. Request a straight-in approach. Give me full lights. Losing power and engine vibration severe. Tower. Engine explosion. Cockpit lights out. I can see the runway."

Dad replaced the radio and then took the stick to fight it with both hands. I looked up and saw that he was sweating profusely and fighting against that fighter jet with every skill he could summon from a lifetime of flying. Both arms were shaking with the death of that fictional plane. My father took me by complete surprise by looking me straight in the eyes and snarling through tightened, grim lips: "I can bring it in."

"What?" I said, looking at him.

"I can bring this bird in, pal," he said. "I've done it before and I can do it again."

"Sorry, Dad. This is for the book. You've got to die."

"I'm not letting you crash a twenty-million-dollar airplane just for your goddamn book," he said. "It's a waste of taxpayers' money."

"It's not a real plane, Dad," I said. "You're sitting in a chair."

"Then let me turn it starboard. I'm too near civilians again. I'm not going to let you kill any civilians on my watch."

"Turn it starboard, Colonel. No civilians die."

"I want to die on land," he said. "I never wanted to dump a bird in water. I know a place. A tomato field. I'll take her in there."

"Take her in there, Dad."

He took her in, and we both fell back exhausted in our chairs. I thought I knew every story of my father's, and I had hated every one of them. He was the worst father I had ever seen, and I have not been shy about proclaiming that. But, until that day, I had no idea I was being raised by one of the goddamnest fighter pilots in the history of the Marine Corps. My father and I looked at each other, and I believe we both realized we had just completed our first great day as father and son. There would be many, many more, but this was the day my father took me into his life as a Marine Corps aviator and did me the high honor of asking me to be his wingman, at last.

"Let me take you to the Colonnade for dinner," I said, mentioning my father's favorite restaurant. "You earned it, Colonel."

"I need to take a shower," he said. His shirt was soaked with sweat, and so was mine.

My father had just delivered me of the last chapters of my new novel by offering me a great story. I could reward him with food, because it is my most religious belief that a recipe is just a story that ends with a good meal.

Honeymoon: The Romance of Umbria

"Tell about Italy," my wife says, her voice sugared with her deep Alabama accent. "Tell me what you loved the most."

I tell her two stories: In the house I once rented on the Via dei Foraggi in Rome, my landlord stood beneath a painting of St. Sebastian.

I asked the man, "This house I'm renting, is it very old?"

"No, no, no, no," he said quickly. "You Americans love the old things, but this house is not even five hundred years."

Stunned, I said, "It was built before Columbus set sail."

"Yes," my landlord said. "But you don't understand. In Rome, she is a baby."

That is how Italy taught me about time.

Then I tell my wife of the morning I left Rome to return to the South to help my mother fight the cancer that would soon kill her. I walked to the small piazza where my family did its shopping to say goodbye. My infant daughter, Susannah, was radiant in her stroller, and everyone in the piazza knew *la famiglia americana* was leaving their city forever. When I rolled Susannah to the center of the piazza, all the shopkeepers boiled out onto the cobblestones. One woman scooped Susannah into her arms and cried out, "You cannot take Susannah *tutta panna* from us. She was born here. She is a *romanina*. She belongs to Rome!"

The women passed the baby back and forth, smothering her with tearful kisses. Adele, the vegetable lady, in a mournful, ancient voice, said through tears, "We did not do our jobs. We did not love your family enough. If we had done our jobs better, you could never leave us. You would be Romans forever."

Then the wine man handed me a bottle of Frascati for the journey, and the cheese lady cut off an enormous wedge of Parmigiano-Reggiano. Sausages and loaves of bread, *pizza bianca*, fragrant mozzarella, bunches of grapes and olives: every shopkeeper in that piazza came forward bearing gifts, generous as the Magi.

I always compare this completely unexpected scene with the time I was moving to Rome and shopped in Atlanta's Kroger for the last time. For ten years I had shopped there and nowhere else in my hometown. I did not know the name or face of a single sourpuss employee in that store, and not one knew mine.

That is how Italy taught me about being alive.

After I told my wife these two stories, she said, "A honeymoon in Italy. It has a ring to it, Southern boy."

Since I met Cassandra King of Pinckard, Alabama, daughter of a peanut farmer who once walked from Alabama to Miami looking for work during the Depression, I am finally living the life I think I was meant to live. I had no idea that a man in his fifties could fall in love with a woman in her fifties and that they could teach each other things about love and ecstasy and wonder, things I have tried to infuse in the secret corners of my novels but have rarely encountered in real life. Because our nation is stupid and Hollywood is coarse, there is no one to tell us of the deep and extraordinary beauty of older women. I now see them all around me and am filled with a fierce joy that one of them has come to live in my house.

The president of the College of Charleston, Alex Sanders, married us in the gardens surrounding his lovely eighteenth-century mansion, where John James Audubon once taught a class in ornithology. My father had just died, and our children from various marriages over the course of our sloppily lived lives were visiting our island house for their summertime breaks. There was no time even to think about a honeymoon. Our lives were busy, disjointed, American. No one told my generation that none of our children would ever grow up, that they would be forever discontented, underemployed, and woebegone. We share seven children and six grandchildren between us, and our hands are constantly full. Still, Sandra deserved a honeymoon, and we began a long dialogue about where it should be.

It amazed me that she had never seen the Pacific Ocean and, though she had traveled to London twice, had never drifted over to continental Europe, where our language is put out to pasture. Not to have traveled widely seemed unlucky to me, but not to have seen Italy was heartbreaking. My own heart has been shaped like a boot since I lived in the city of Rome for three years in the faraway eighties. If you cannot find happiness in Italy, I told Sandra, then I do not think you can find it in Eden.

We plan our honeymoon in Umbria, a part of Italy where I have never spent a night, and on the flight over, I fear I have erred greatly, perhaps tragically. I tell my new wife I should have taken her to Venice, that gondola-blessed city that looks as if it were carved by swans from ice. If not Venice, then immovable, Tiber-cut Rome, which I could walk through blindfolded; I know those beloved and noisy streets so well. Then there is the incomparable Amalfi coast. And how could I leave out Florence or unknowable Siena or the Alpine majesty of Lake Como? Then I relax and put my trust in the simple mystery that Italy has never let me down, never refused to lay its dazzling treasures at my feet.

You go to Tuscany because you must; you go to Umbria because you can. It is the province in Italy you travel to when you want the country itself to enter the pores of your skin after you have grown weary with sites and endless churches and surly crowds moving through the taut, sovereign air of museums. Umbria is Italy turned inward, its prayer to itself.

We stay at the Palazzo Terranova, a sublime eighteenth-century restoration, recently opened, that looks like the castle you always hoped Cinderella got to live in with the prince. A British couple, Sarah and

Johnny Townsend, run the palazzo, which I predict will soon be famous all over the world. Above the hotel, a footpath cut into the crest of the mountain by the Etruscans themselves winds its way to a small hill town three miles away. The walk is breathtaking. Sandra and I tell each other we are in the best place in the world to be on a honeymoon.

The view from our room, which looks down on time-shaped olive groves, three lakes nestled like freshwater pearls in the landscape, and a ruin that makes the vineyards near the village of Ronti seem noble and necessary, appears as an untroubled dream that one mountain had of many others, as though time itself could come to rest in these valleys.

Since Sandra has never seen an olive tree, we walk the precipitous road that winds its way from the palazzo to the village. Halfway down the mountain, we hear a car coming from behind at warp speed. I turn to Sandra and say, "I haven't told you about Italian drivers yet, have I?"

"Better do it quick," she says, and suddenly the small car is over the blind ridge that separates us. Sandra and I hug an outcropping of rock. The driver sees us and squeals to a dramatic stop. The woman who brought our breakfast that morning, Piera Menardi, leaps out of the car: "Oh, Mister Johnny and Miss Sarah will not like that I have killed two of our guests. This is for sure."

Earlier that morning, I observed a scene that made me fall madly in love with the richly good-humored Piera. To get a recalcitrant worker to help her with some heavy lifting, she pulled out a picture of herself in a bikini on an Adriatic beach in 1967. She showed him the picture. It is almost a pleasure to be run off the road by such a woman thirty-two years later, her beauty still a pleasant, inmost thing.

Piera drives off, imperiling every living creature she encounters, and we descend toward the olive groves and approach a marvelous ruin of a farming village where remnants of tobacco-curing sheds remind us both of our own roots in the Deep South. I gaze at olive trees hundreds of years old, loving the silver-headed shimmer of their wind-tossed branches, and think, What is more beautiful or useful than an olive tree? What is prettier than a bowl of green olives or the molten green of the first pressing of extra virgin olive oil looking, in cut-glass cruets, like liquid jade? For a souvenir of our honeymoon, we take a single small branch as both memento and pledge to each other, then walk back to the hotel, perched above us like a bird of prey the color of fire.

The next day, the hotel's chef, Patrizio Cesarini, offers to give us a tour of his hometown, Città di Castello. As we board the chef's little Fiat, I tell Sandra that she is lucky she has relatives who are native to Talladega, Alabama, where one of the most famous NASCAR racetracks is located, for she is about to feel like a NASCAR racer herself.

Then Patrizio is off, careening down the mountain at such a precipitous rate it makes Piera look like a high school driving instructor. We travel at cheetahlike speeds even through small medieval alleyways. When he hits the autostrada, it simply feels like space travel. When we reach Patrizio's hometown, Sandra, ashen and shaken, says that she thinks she has never traveled at such speed, even in an airplane. I say, "He was slow. Wait until we ride with a Calabrian. They get faster as you move south in Italy."

Patrizio now walks us languorously through the ancient, hidden-away parts of his town, leading the way in a happy bracelet of *"ciaos,"* for he knows almost everyone he passes. When I ask him to tell us the differences, if there are any, between Umbrians and Tuscans, he answers cheerfully, "It is very easy. We are the best. They are the worst," admirably summing up why we are at the tail end of the bloodiest, most chillingly fratricidal century in the history of mankind.

Once we reach the market, Patrizio moves through it like a perfumer gathering wildflowers in a bee-struck field. Sandra moves through it with the astonished, mouthwatering appreciation of a rookie in the folkways of Italy.

At an outdoor *salumeria,* Patrizio orders prosciutto for the meal that night. "See the motion," he tells us as a young man cuts razor-thin slices from the top of the cured ham. "That is called 'playing the violin.' It is very difficult to master. I have mastered it." The young man lifts a piece of meat in the air to let us see the sunlight flow through it like some odd and flawless merger of paper and flesh.

We wander from stall to stall, the food so fresh that the smell of the earth itself is the strongest, most assertive odor in the marketplace until we pass the store that specializes in the sale of local white truffles. The odor of truffles is as distinctive as the giveaway scent of marijuana. It enlarges the air around itself and gives you some idea of what a tree must smell like to itself. I have never quite forgiven American forests for their shameless inability to produce truffles. When I see Patrizio enter the shop and purchase a small, knobby truffle for that night's pasta, I want to kiss him on the lips but hesitate for fear the gesture may be misinterpreted.

It is a pleasure to watch a Southern farm girl wander about an Italian food market, surrounded by the abundance taken from the countryside. I follow as Patrizio and Sandra inspect great albino-faced cauliflowers, egg-plant displays that look like a rack of bowling balls, porcini mushrooms the size of kittens, the cool anise-smelling fennels that always look like failed cacti to me, and the mounds of huge, brilliantly yellow peppers that make their space look like the entrance to a gold mine. Blood oranges from Sicily are sliced open to reveal exactly what shade of dripping scarlet is inside. When I reach to taste a sprig of mint, a fierce old Italian woman, who probably was part of the crowd that murdered Mussolini, slaps my hand firmly and wags a gnarled finger at me. Her finger looks truffly, which somehow pleases me.

Sandra tastes grapes, arugula, oregano, spring onions, plum tomatoes, each time turning to me and shaking her head. I do not have to ask what she is thinking. It is this: Food tastes better in Italy than anywhere else in the world.

As we leave this deep-throated market, its musk a nosegay of aromas, we pause at the fishmonger's, where Patrizio studies a tank of slithering freshwater eels netted that same morning from Lake Trasimeno. More amazing still, the woman behind the counter prods one of the oceangoing crustaceans that the Italians call *canocchie,* tasty creatures that appear to be a cross between a shrimp and a praying mantis. She prods it again, and it moves—in landlocked Umbria, it moves. Among Italians, the love of freshness is a form of both spontaneity and discipline.

But bold Patrizio is in a hurry now, and he marches us past an ancient tower that is made of stacked stone with no cement at all. It is called the Torre Rotonda and is the pride of Città di Castello. Patrizio tells me that he feels as if he owns the tower. He does now, but Sandra and I know that the Torre Rotonda will wait him out and one day reclaim its title from Patrizio. We *"ciao"* our way back through the old city, then rocket our way back into the green hills of Umbria for what will be a fantastic meal. My wife, in utter terror, does not open her eyes a single time on the trip back to the hotel.

Over the next few days, Sandra and I drift through hill towns we had never heard of. In the lentil-happy town of Monterchi, Italy reaches up, striking quick as an adder, and grabs us by the throat. In what looks like a minor chapel serving a monastery across the street, we encounter Piero della Francesca's breathtaking painting *Madonna del Parto,* the famous "Pregnant Madonna." I had read about it in art history books but could not believe such a masterpiece had not been relocated to one of the grander Italian cities. It is the most serene portrait of Mary I have ever seen, granting new meaning to the very idea of serenity. Its discovery, in the tomb of a nobleman a long time after its rendering, has brought pride and joy and many art lovers to this town. Six hundred years later, the painting still shimmers with the genius of the artist. As I stand before it, I think of what it must have been like to be a man of genius, godstruck in his native Umbria, painting a portrait of the woman he considered the mother of God, carrying that God inside her. This is what art should be.

"This," I say to my wife, "is your honeymoon gift."

From our hotel, we walk along the Etruscan ridge to an exquisite hill town called Monte Santa Maria Tiberina and try to put the unstressed, unpurchasable beauty of this place into words. Both of us are novelists and believe that words can do anything. The stones from which the town's houses are built have had their color bled out from them by time itself. Sandra says that the town is so lovely, its residents should be allowed to make only music boxes or perfume bottles. When it begins to rain, we seek shelter in Oscari, the only bar or store in town. Oscari himself, a man of grace and elegance, serves us cappuccino. Preparing it, he looks like a priest at Mass. There are pictures of his son, a soccer star, on the walls; the taste of that cappuccino—*perfetto*. That taste is Italy in a cup, my honeymoon in a cup, at Oscari in a hill town in the rain.

We have come to our last hill town, and our honeymoon nears its end in a piazza in the gemlike town of Citerna. We have said the things to each other that we needed to say, made all the promises we needed to make. But we stand overlooking a valley with farmhouses and palazzi of infinite age staring coldly back at us. This town seems conceived by waterless Venetians driven out of their city and forced to seek refuge in the hills. The colors of the stones puzzle because age has formed them and we have no equivalent in our American vocabulary to name them, our culture is still so new and shiny. These stones are the color of bruised fruit, I start to say, or the shade of some rough white wine. But another house is darker, an amber bracelet perhaps, and others are the shade of palominos or horseshoe crabs. I catch myself writing in my head again instead of living in the moment of sunset in the Umbrian hills on the last day of the first honeymoon I have ever taken.

In that piazza in Citerna, our honeymoon ended, and our accidental life together had its Umbrian beginning.

FAVA BEANS AND PECORINO   • SERVES 4

2 pounds fresh unshelled fava beans (as young as possible)
Olive oil
Juice of 1 lemon (or 1 Roasted Lemon, page 51)
Coarse or kosher salt and freshly ground black pepper
8 ounces Pecorino, cut into small pieces (approximately the size of
    the favas)

1. Shell the beans; you should have about 2 cups. Blanch the beans
in a pot of boiling water to loosen their skins, about 1 minute. Drain
in a colander. The beans should slip right out of their skins.

2. Transfer the beans to a mixing bowl and drizzle with a little
olive oil. Add the lemon juice and toss with salt and pepper to taste.
Fold the Pecorino cheese into the fava beans and serve.

• • •

PORK AND ROSEMARY RAGÙ   My passion for all things Italian
began with my two Italian roommates my sophomore year at The
Citadel, Bo Marks and Mike Devito. The name Marks inspires no special
vision of Italy, but Bo's immigrant grandparents carried the surname
Miercovincici ("mark of the winemakers") to the gatekeepers on Ellis
Island. They entered into Manhattan with the Americanized moniker
Marks. Mike Devito considered that this capitulation to the authorities
brought great shame to Bo's family, who should have insisted on the right
to keep their Italian name. Through them I would find myself immersed
in the lives of two Italian-American families. Bo-Pig and Mike-Swine
had learned that none of the other freshmen in "R" company wanted to
room with me, so they came to my room after exams to invite me to room
with them our sophomore year. They embraced me and called me
"paisan." I had no idea what a paisan was, but I knew I wanted to be one.

Of course, Mike-Swine and Bo-Pig were the models for Mark Santoro and Pig Pignetti in my novel *The Lords of Discipline.*

From the first week of school until the last, Bo-Pig received packages of Italian food from his girlfriend and her family. The ethereal Phyllis Parise came from a family that still remained true to the Old World and the old ways, and their gifts of food were prodigal. In my childhood, my mother had served up Velveeta and whatever cheese came with the frozen macaroni, and, of course, the cheese of cottage. I was ill-prepared for the arrival of Gorgonzola, five or six varieties of goat cheese (I didn't know there was such a thing as goat cheese; hell, I didn't know there was such a thing as goat's milk), provolone, and the divine Parmigiano-Reggiano. There was an inexhaustible supply of hard sausages and pepperonis, cans of tuna drenched in olive oil, anchovies, and packages of Parodi cigars. What amazed me was that these gift packages were meant for "the room," all of us, and not just Bo-Pig. In the first month, I received a letter from Phyllis thanking me for taking such good care of her fiancé. During the second month, Phyllis's mother wrote me a letter thanking me for the same thing. Before Christmas, Phyllis's father wrote me a letter promising to teach me how to make a pizza if I ever got up to his pizza shop in Greensburg, Pennsylvania. I had a soft spot for the whole Parise family long before I ever met them.

• MAKES 8 CUPS, ENOUGH FOR 2 TO 3 POUNDS PASTA

2 tablespoons olive oil

8 large garlic cloves, roughly chopped

8 sprigs fresh rosemary

One 3$\frac{1}{2}$- to 4-pound pork bone-in rib roast, ribs removed and tied
onto a roast

1 red onion, roughly chopped (about 2 cups)

One 35-ounce can whole tomatoes, preferably San Marzano

2 pounds pasta (preferably pappardelle), cooked

Freshly grated Parmigiano-Reggiano

1. In a large skillet over moderate heat, warm the olive oil. Add the garlic and rosemary and sauté until the rosemary needles sizzle and turn crisp and the garlic is golden, 2 to 3 minutes. Remove and reserve.

2. In the same pan, sear the pork in the hot flavored oil, turning it occasionally, until all sides are nicely browned, 5 to 7 minutes. Transfer to a large stockpot and set aside.

3. Add the onion to the flavored oil and cook, stirring occasionally, until browned (adding more oil sparingly if the pan is too dry), about 3 minutes. Crush the tomatoes with your hands and add, with their juice, stirring to scrape up any browned bits of pork stuck to the bottom of the pan. Transfer the tomato mixture to the stockpot and bring to a low boil over medium heat. Cover the pot, lower the heat, and simmer until the pork is tender enough to shred (when scraped with a fork), about 2 hours.

4. Cool the pork in the tomato sauce. (The cooled pork roast and sauce can be transferred to a storage container and refrigerated overnight. Wrap and store the garlic and rosemary separately.)

5. Remove the pork from the tomato sauce and reserve. In a food processor fitted with a metal blade, process half the tomato sauce with the fried garlic cloves and rosemary needles (discarding stalks) until somewhat smooth. Stir the puréed sauce back into the pot with the rest of the tomato sauce. The goal is a sauce with a rough, chunky character.

6. Shred the pork and strip the meat from the bones. Discard the bones. Chop the meat finely by hand, not in a food processor, and stir it into the tomato sauce. Heat and serve over pasta, passing the cheese on the side.

• • •

WILD MUSHROOM SAUCE   During Easter holiday of my sophomore year at The Citadel, I traveled to Greensburg, Pennsylvania, to visit
Bo-Pig's family. They lived in a suite atop the Hotel Greensburg, but we
would spend most of our time in Greensburg at the home of the Parise
family, where Bo's charming fiancée, Phyllis, resided. When I walked into
the Parise house, my induction as a full-fledged member of the Italian
household had taken place without my knowledge. Phyllis hugged me
and kissed me on both cheeks, as did her mother, father, and grandparents.

The family led us into the dining room, where a huge celebratory meal
was in progress. What I came to love when I lived in Rome, I came to love in
the Parise household that Easter week—a freewheeling, rollicking love of
family and friends and a great simplicity, yet complete integrity, when it
came to the preparation and eating of food. The table glistened with bowls
of olives and pickles, and an array of the cheeses was lined up on a sideboard.

The grandfather eyed me with a discriminating and unnerving dis-
cernment before pronouncing, "*Irlandese.*"

"*Sì, Irlandesi,*" Phyllis said. "Irish."

The grandfather handed me a bowl of olives and said, "*Mangia, Irlandese.*" I ate the olive, but the pit surprised me, and after I ate around it, I
didn't know what to do with it. I sat immobilized with every eye in the
room observing me. The grandfather lifted a relish plate to my lips and I
deposited the pit on the plate to cheers. The grandfather said, "*Buono.*"

Phyllis nodded, and I said, "*Buono.*"

He cut me a piece of cheese and said, "*Mangia.*"

I ate the cheese and said, "*Buono.*"

He said, "*E Italiano.* Provolone."

When the pasta dish arrived at the table, the grandfather said to me,
"Pappardelle. No spaghetti. Pappardelle," opening up the mysteries and
the shapes that Italian pasta could assume, all of them glorious.

The whole week was like that, the grandfather leading me on an idyllic
voyage through the pronunciation and devouring of splendid food. In the afternoon, Bo and Phyllis would slip away to be alone, and I would go over to

her parents' mom-and-pop pizza shop. Mr. Parise put me into an apron and taught me how to make pizza dough. "It's easy. You just do it," he explained.

By the end of the day, they were selling the pizzas I was making from scratch, which pleased me enormously. The Parises brought me out and introduced me to the woman who had purchased my first pizza. In my exuberance, I kissed her hand, thinking it was the Italian way. The woman was Irish, and she looked at me like I was nuts.

• MAKES 6 CUPS, ENOUGH FOR 2 TO 3 POUNDS PASTA

3 ounces dried wild mushrooms (look for an Italian mix, heavy on the porcini and easy on Asian mushrooms like shiitakes, or use just porcini)

4 cups boiling water

$1/2$ cup dry vermouth

3 tablespoons olive oil

1 pound cremini mushrooms, cleaned, stemmed, and thinly sliced

1 teaspoon coarse or kosher salt

$1/2$ teaspoon freshly ground black pepper

1 heaping tablespoon chopped fresh rosemary

1 garlic clove, finely minced

One 35-ounce can whole tomatoes, preferably San Marzano, broken up into small pieces, with their juice

Pinch of sugar

2 pounds pasta (preferably pappardelle), cooked

1. Place the dried wild mushrooms in a bowl and cover with the boiling water. Let soak until softened, at least 30 minutes. Remove the mushrooms with a slotted spoon and strain liquid through a double thickness of cheesecloth, reserving $1^1/2$ cups. Mix the reserved liquid with vermouth.

2. In a small saucepan over moderate heat, bring the liquid to a boil, then reduce the heat and simmer until reduced by half. Finely chop the softened mushrooms and set aside. (This can be done in the food processor, but do not pulverize them.)

3. In a medium stockpot over moderately high heat, heat the olive oil until hot but not smoking. (A drop of water should sizzle immediately upon contact when dropped in the oil.) Add the cremini mushrooms and cook until golden brown, stirring occasionally, 5 to 7 minutes. Lower the heat, sprinkle with salt, pepper, rosemary, and garlic; and cook for another 2 minutes, stirring frequently.

4. Add the chopped dried mushrooms and the mushroom broth, stirring as the liquids simmer to scrape up any browned bits from the bottom of the pot. Cook until slightly reduced, stirring frequently, about 2 minutes. Stir in the tomatoes with their juice, add the sugar, and simmer over low heat until thickened, about 25 minutes. Serve with the pasta.

• • •

QUICK PAPPARDELLE WITH PANCETTA AND CHESTNUTS

• SERVES 4

1 pound pappardelle

1 cup diced pancetta

1 cup chopped roasted chestnuts

1 $\frac{1}{2}$ cups heavy cream

2 fresh sage leaves

Freshly ground black pepper

Freshly grated Parmigiano-Reggiano

1. Cook pappardelle according to package directions in abundantly salted water.

2. Brown the pancetta in a medium skillet. Remove and reserve. Heat the chopped chestnuts in the cooking fat. Add the heavy cream and the fresh sage leaves. Reduce slightly before returning the pancetta to the pan. Add black pepper to taste.

3. Drain the pasta and add to the skillet, stirring gently to coat the noodles. Transfer to a warm plate and sprinkle with Parmigiano-Reggiano.

• • •

QUICK PAPPARDELLE WITH BLACK TRUFFLE SAUCE

• SERVES 4

1 pound pappardelle

8 tablespoons (1 stick) unsalted butter

1 cup (4 ounces) mascarpone

1 medium fresh black truffle

1 cup freshly grated Parmigiano-Reggiano, plus additional

1. Cook pappardelle according to package directions in abundantly salted water.

2. Melt the butter and mascarpone together in a medium skillet over low heat. Shave the truffle into the butter mixture, giving it a minute to perfume the sauce, and sprinkle in the Parmigiano-Reggiano, gently shaking the pan to incorporate.

3. Drain the pasta and add to the skillet, stirring gently to coat the noodles. Transfer to a warm plate and sprinkle with additional Parmigiano-Reggiano.

• • •

SUGARED BLOOD ORANGES

Slice the blood oranges as thinly as possible and spread out on a platter. Sprinkle them with raw, or turbinado, sugar and let them sit at room temperature until the sugar dissolves. Serve with biscotti and gelato.

The skin on real Italian blood oranges is typically very fragile and therefore difficult to peel without damaging the fruit. Leaving the skin on the orange makes it easier to pick up the slices with your fingers or a fork.

CHAPTER NINE

Travel: Tuscany and Rome

The irresistible desire to travel is known in my family as being "Jasper-blooded." The idea of voyage, of breaking out into the unknown, of those unappeasable dreams of the road, is central to the identity of my family, but is also nonetheless profoundly troubling and distrusted. There are those among us who live in the South our whole lives and rarely venture very far from the places we were born. Then there are the others, like me, who are Jasper-blooded.

My grandfather Jasper Catlett Peek was a restless, godstruck man who roamed around the small towns of the South selling Bibles and cutting hair. It was said he could not bear to stay in a place for more than three months at a time. "Jasper could never stay put," my grandmother once told me. "But he never had much imagination about traveling; he only traveled the South." But if any of us move away from our hometowns, take a job in a distant city, or marry boys and girls from "away," it is always blamed on Jasper. He was the first holy man of the open road our family produced, and he looked forward to the journey more than the arrival. Such figures define families.

My grandmother did not lack imagination and she never sold a Bible in her life. Margaret Nolen Stanton, Jasper's wife, circumnavigated the globe three times by ship, sending back commemorative postcards from Madagascar, Hong Kong, Egypt, India—from everywhere. As a boy, these postcards were the first travel literature I ever read. Her handwriting, unintelligible as Arabic, seemed congruent with the exotica she described. She posted them with exotic stamps, as strange and luminous as the cities she celebrated in the hurried prose-poems she wrote from along the shipping lanes of the world. My grandmother traveled to be amazed, transformed, and to build up a reserve and bright ordnance of memories for her old age. She was the first philosopher of travel our family produced, and I became an acolyte of that philosophy.

When I was thirteen, my grandmother took me aside and announced to me that she had studied me carefully and that I was destined to be the real traveler among her grandchildren. She then described the most wonderful thing she had ever seen in her journeys around the world. In the Atlantic, off the coast of Africa, at dusk, a sea monster had surfaced near her ship. She told me the rest of our family had laughed at her when she described this miraculous experience, but she knew I would not. She proceeded to describe her monster with such precision, vitality, and even affection that, to this day, I believe in the existence of the fabulous unnamed creatures navigating the darkest streams and currents of the oceans. And I believe they appear to special people who find the proof of God and the reason for travel in the wildest ecstasies of the sacred imagination.

As an advocate of my grandmother's philosophy, I have traveled to twenty-five countries and have plans to visit fifty more. She passed her inextinguishable curiosity on to me, and I am a changeling because of the urgency of her love affair with the world. My ex-wife Lenore and I once rented an exquisite house in the center of Rome. Our terrace overlooked Capitoline Hill, the Campidoglio, and the northern section of the Roman Forum. I would have liked to bring my grandmother there and shown her the view from that terrace.

I would have shown her this: in the summer, in the opaline light of late afternoon, the city is the color of pale bruises and softly spoiled fruit. The history of the Western world rises up in the wordless articulation of ruins. I have watched friends grow mute as the light dispersed behind the palms and cedars, and the cats began to move out of the caverns that led to the buried city beneath Rome. In Rome, I learned that with every step I took, I was walking on the remains of empire. The proper study of Europe is impermanence; dust and stone are the true vassals of time. There is such a thing as too much beauty and too much history. There is even such a thing as too much travel, and thus I will add to my grand-mother's philosophy. But first, I must explain why to her. She is part of the change.

Several decades ago, in the Villa la Massa outside of Florence, Lenore and I decided we would not live in Rome for more than two years. The decision was a complicated and painful one, and we needed the ambience of the Massa, our favorite hotel, to make that decision.

On the appointed day we walked through the Uffizi Gallery looking at Renaissance art. Lenore's face was like that of one of those mysterious, sensual women who stood in radiant attendance to those leaf-crowned goddesses in Botticelli's paintings. Later, at the perfect hotel, which had a view of the water, Lenore and I watched the fishermen on the Arno cast-ing for trout as we dressed for dinner.

We then went down to the bar for a glass of wine. At the Massa, they know that there must be private, well-lit places to write letters and to observe other guests. There must be places to talk about how you want to live the rest of your life. The bar is an elegant room on the river side of the hotel, intimate and charming, where the gold-leaf wallpaper and candlelight turned Lenore's face into something less than gold and some-thing more. The bar itself is centrally recessed, the Arno like a side altar in an unpraised cathedral. It gleams with marble and the bold, glossy images of heraldry. The bartender worked on a crossword puzzle between fixing drinks for the guests. Elegantly, he presided over his well-appointed fiefdom, and there was no drink he couldn't make. He was never rushed because the Villa la Massa inspired a wish that time would come to a complete stop and a moment of grace would last forever.

Our wine was there. It was there at that moment. It was white and cold, a pale Chianti from the hills above Siena. The bottle sat beside pink roses, arranged in a crystal vase. When the wine was finished, my wife's lipstick was on the glass, and thirty minutes of our lives were over. My mother was very ill, my grandmother had had a stroke, and Lenore and I had decided that there was too much of America in us to become permanent expatriates.

The bartender was half-finished with the crossword puzzle when we approached the bar. He was stuck on three or four words as we departed. You left the bar and the roses and hoped the bartender completed the puzzle, because you had just sat and thought about the puzzle of time passing, of mortality, of human choice, and you wished you were smart enough to invent some explanation or to write a perfect poem that ended with the print of Lenore's lips on the wineglass. Our lives are longer but as fragile as roses. There are always three or four words in our lives we can never articulate. They are always the three or four words that would solve the puzzle. But on that night, Lenore and I solved part of it: we were going home, we said. My grandmother had left out an important part of her philosophy. I knew she would always travel, but I never thought she might leave me.

On the terrace overlooking the Forum, I tried to write my grandmother a love letter. I tried to give her a summing-up, a bedazzled inventory of all I had seen and learned while living in Europe. She was recovering from her stroke in a nursing home in Jacksonville, Florida, and I wanted my letter to be perfect.

I told her about the previous summer, about renting an old farmhouse in France, in the town of Meyrals in the Dordogne Valley, and about taking her great-grandchildren into the prehistoric caves of Font-de-Gaume. I had bored my older daughters senseless by force-marching them through the major museums of Europe. But standing in half-light before the paintings and carvings thirty thousand years old, I watched the eyes of my daughters change as they studied the delicate etchings of mammoth and deer. In the cold and darkness of those caverns, we watched the movement of the silent, immemorial herds of bison that in their passage across the stone express something ineffable and fine about the human spirit. I had taken my children to the dawn of creation and shown them the first immaculate urge toward godhead and art. In the intimacy of those caves, I heard the breathing of my children, the soft voices of their astonishment, and I knew I had changed their lives forever.

But those images reminded me of something else, and it took me a while to make the connection. They conjured up images of those post-cards my grandmother had sent me from around the world that I would study in the privacy of my room: the lionesses of Kenya, the elephants of Tanganyika, the cobras of Bengal. Those postcards, faded and yellow now, were my introduction into the bright world of travel, fantasy, and art. In this perfect letter I would tell my grandmother this.

But no. No, sweet Margaret Stanton, there are no perfect letters to frail and wonderful grandmothers. The gratitude is in the emulation; the joy is always in the voyage, the setting out. You and my grandfather pre-sented me with the wanderer's gift. I have been true to it; I have not abused it.

And something else: it came to me like a postcard or a painting on a cavern wall. When I heard of your stroke, I thought about living in the world without you and I felt the air grow still and the light change. Then I saw him for the first time and understood at last. I saw your sea mon-ster, kindly and serene, mythic and loving, rise out of the Gulf Stream and swim casually toward the shores of Jacksonville, toward his old friend and traveler. I hope that when he comes, you will be ready with all your bags packed. I hope for you that this last voyage through dreams and seas is the best of all.

When it is my turn, old traveler, after I have directed my grandchil-dren to some of the fabulous places of the earth that you urged me to visit, send him softly to me. I'll be easy for any well-traveled beast to rec-ognize.

I'm your grandson.

The grateful one.

The Jasper-blooded one.

RIBOLLITA   A Tuscan reboiled minestrone soup that is thickened with bread and made the day before it is to be served.   • **SERVES 6**

8 ounces dried cannellini beans or Great Northern beans

1 slice (about 2 ounces) pancetta or prosciutto

$1/2$ cup olive oil

1 large red onion, thinly sliced

2 carrots, scraped and diced

3 celery stalks, diced

1 medium potato, peeled and diced

$1/2$ small head savoy cabbage, shredded

1 small bunch Swiss chard, cleaned, trimmed, and roughly chopped

1 cup canned whole tomatoes, preferably San Marzano, broken up
   into pieces, with their juice

Rind from 1-pound piece Parmigiano-Reggiano, scraped clean, plus
   freshly grated Parmigiano-Reggiano

6 cups Beef Stock (page 13) or Chicken Stock (page 11)

Coarse or kosher salt and freshly ground black pepper

12 thick slices day-old Tuscan bread

1. Soak the dried beans overnight in a bowl of cold water. The next day, drain the beans, transfer them to a large saucepan, and cover with cold water (the level of the water should rise 2 inches above the beans). Add the pancetta and bring the beans to a boil to partially cook them, about 15 minutes.

2. In a stockpot large enough to hold all the ingredients, heat the olive oil over medium-low heat and cook the onion until pale but not browned. Add the carrots, celery, and potato, stirring a few times and cooking the vegetable mixture until slightly softened, about 15 minutes. Add the cabbage, chard, and tomatoes.

3. Drain the beans and transfer to the stockpot. Add the Parmigiano-Reggiano rind and enough stock to cover the vegetables by about 3 inches. Slowly simmer until the vegetables are soft and the flavors marry, about 1 hour. Taste for salt and pepper.

4. Tear large chunks from the bread slices and place in the soup. Bring the soup to a boil for about 1 minute, using a wooden spoon to stir the soup and break up the bread. Cool to room temperature, transfer to a storage container, and refrigerate overnight. (The soup will thicken.)

5. Reheat the soup and ladle into bowls. Sprinkle with grated Parmigiano-Reggiano cheese, passing extra cheese on the side.

• • •

BEEFSTEAK FLORENTINE FOR TWO   If you are ever lucky enough to find yourself in Tuscany, make sure you order a *bistecca alla fiorentina*. The Tuscans raise a breed of cattle called the Chianina that tastes more flavorful than any cow with a Texas accent. At the Villa la Massa outside of Florence, I ordered the *bistecca alla fiorentina* while I watched the sunset over the Arno River as a fly fisherman made the sunlight lash about on the river. It was a perfect scene and a perfect meal, and eaten with complete joy in a perfect country.   **• SERVES 2**

> 2 teaspoons coarse or kosher salt
>
> 1 teaspoon freshly ground black pepper
>
> 1 teaspoon granulated garlic
>
> Olive oil (only enough to moisten the spices)
>
> T-bone or porterhouse steak, approximately 2$\frac{1}{2}$ pounds and
>   2$\frac{1}{2}$ inches thick
>
> Lemon wedges or balsamic vinegar

1. Mix the spices together and add the olive oil drop by drop until a paste forms. Rub the paste on both sides of the steak. (Use sparingly; excess paste will sit on the surface and make the meat mushy.) Wrap in plastic and refrigerate for at least 2 hours.

2. Light a hot fire in a charcoal grill or preheat a gas grill to medium-high. Place the steak on the grill, cover, and cook until done: 6 to 8 minutes per side for rare, 7 to 9 per side for medium rare.

3. Transfer the steak to a cutting board and let it rest for about 10 minutes to let the natural juices redistribute. Using a knife with a thin sharp blade, cut the meat away from the bone. Carve each section of the steak into thick slices and reassemble around the bone on a serving platter. Serve with lemon wedges or balsamic vinegar for drizzling.

• • •

PIZZA BIANCA   If the wind was coming off the Campo de' Fiori when you woke up in Rome, you could smell the pizza bianca coming from the ovens of the bakery at the far side of the Campo, where the flower ladies were arranging lilies and the olive man was moving his cart into position. At the other end of the Campo, the fish were being laid out like playing cards on shaved ice and the garlic man was yelling at an early-bird *turista* that he was not open for business until he had his *caffe* and his pizza bianca. The pizza bianca came out of those ovens hot to the touch and you bought it when it could still warm your hands on a cold day. It had no mozzarella on it, no garlic, and no basil. What I remember, though, is salt, and never has salt and dough and yeast tasted better than when I walked down an obscure alleyway near the Campo and partook of that simple Roman pleasure. In Rome the simplest things were always the best. We jazz our recipe up with mozzarella and basil, making it more Neapolitan than Roman. Both are divine.

• MAKES ONE 12-INCH PIZZA

1 package ($1/4$ ounce) dry yeast
$1/2$ cup plus $1/4$ cup warm water
$1 3/4$ cups plus 2 tablespoons unbleached all-purpose flour
$3/4$ teaspoon coarse or kosher salt

Several garlic heads

2 tablespoons olive oil

1 pound fresh mozzarella, cut into thin slices

Several fresh basil, leaves torn into thin strips

1. Stir the yeast into the $^{1}/_{4}$ cup water and let stand for 10 minutes.

2. Mix the flour and salt together. Pour the $^{1}/_{2}$ cup water into the yeast mixture. Add the flour and mix well with a wooden spoon, a food processor, or a standing mixer until the dough comes together and is smooth and elastic. Place the dough in a large bowl, cover with a damp dish towel, and put in a warm place away from drafts. Let the dough rise until doubled in size, about 2 hours. Punch the dough down by turning it out onto the counter and kneading it with the palm of your hand once or twice. Put the dough back in the same bowl and let it rise for another hour. The dough is now ready for shaping.

3. On a lightly floured, clean, dry surface, roll the dough out into a rough circle. Rotate and turn the dough, adding flour if the dough sticks to the work surface. Roll the dough until it is about 12 inches in diameter. (If the dough becomes difficult to roll, let it rest for a few minutes before continuing.)

4. Preheat the oven to 300°F.

5. Separate the garlic cloves and toss them in the olive oil. Place the cloves in a roasting pan and bake until soft and aromatic, about 1 hour. Peel the cloves (the skins should easily slip off) and transfer to a mixing bowl. Smash the cloves with the back of a wooden spoon to make a paste. Set aside.

6. Adjust the oven temperature to 450°F.

7. Spread the roasted garlic paste over the prepared pizza dough. Cover with slices of fresh mozzarella. Bake in the lower third of the oven (or better still, on the oven floor) for 15 minutes, until the rim is golden and the cheese is lightly browned. Remove from the oven and garnish with strips of fresh basil. Serve hot.

...

SCOTTIGLIA In Siena, that most mysterious and storied city, with its mélange of oddly named and competitive wards that strive against one another during a horse race called the Palio (one of the wards is called Bruco, "the Caterpillar"), I first tasted the divine *Scottiglia*. I personally believe that *Scottiglia* made in Tuscany tastes better than it does anywhere else in the world, but that is only a personal belief.

• SERVES 4 TO 6

3 tablespoons olive oil

2^1/2 pounds beef short ribs (about 5 ribs, cut flanken style)

^{1}/2 pound pork shoulder, cut into 2-inch cubes

^{1}/2 pound veal shoulder, cut into 2-inch cubes

One 2^1/2-pound rabbit, cut by your butcher into 6 pieces: front legs, back legs, and split saddle

^{1}/2 cup diced carrot

^{1}/2 cup diced celery

3 shallots, coarsely chopped

2 garlic cloves, minced

2 cups red wine

3 cups Chicken Stock (page 11)

1 tablespoon chopped fresh sage

1 tablespoon chopped fresh thyme

1 small dried red chile

1 cup canned whole tomatoes, preferably San Marzano, broken up into small pieces and drained

Coarse or kosher salt and freshly ground black pepper

Grilled Tuscan bread, rubbed with cut garlic cloves

1. Preheat the oven to 375°F.

2. In a large Dutch oven over high heat, heat the oil until hot but not smoking. Brown, remove, and reserve meats separately, in the

order listed. Add the carrot and celery to the pot and cook, stirring frequently, until they begin to color on the edges, about 3 minutes (adding more oil sparingly, if necessary). Remove and reserve with the browned rabbit (or whatever meat will be the last addition to the stew).

3. Add the shallots and garlic to the pot and quickly stir to wilt. Add the red wine and stir, letting the liquid bubble up and loosen any browned bits stuck to the bottom of the pot. Adjust the heat slightly lower and add the stock, sage, thyme, chile, and tomatoes. Let simmer for several minutes.

4. Add the beef short ribs, pork, and veal. When the cooking liquid returns to a simmer, cover and immediately transfer pot to the oven for 1 hour. Remove the pot from the oven to add the rabbit, carrot, and celery, then return the pot to the oven until the beef short rib meat is tender and falling off the bone and the rabbit is cooked through, about 45 minutes.

5. Season the stew with salt and pepper and serve over grilled bread.

Timing and cooking method in this Tuscan dish of mixed meat stew (also called cacciucco di carne*) vary from kitchen to kitchen depending on the meat used, as well as on whether it is on or off the bone. (The more meat on the bone, the better the stew.)*

Brown and reserve the meat separately and add to the stew in order of toughness to tenderness (cooking time required). In this particular version, the short ribs, pork, and veal go first, then the rabbit.

• • •

BAKED TOMATOES WITH RICE

4 medium tomatoes, about $1/2$ pound each

2 tablespoons olive oil

2 shallots, finely chopped

$1/4$ cup finely chopped red bell pepper

2 cups rice cooked in chicken stock

2 tablespoons finely chopped flat-leaf parsley

Coarse or kosher salt and freshly ground black pepper

1. Preheat the oven to 350°F.

2. Lightly oil a baking dish just large enough to hold the tomatoes snugly.

3. Cut off the "cap" (a thin slice) from the top of each tomato and spoon out the pulp (being careful not to tear the walls). Reserve $3/4$ cup of the pulp and discard remainder or save for another use. Invert the tomatoes on a paper towel–lined baking sheet to drain.

4. In a large skillet, heat the oil over moderate high heat. Add the shallots and red pepper, cooking quickly until the edges begin to color, 2 to 3 minutes. Add the reserved tomato pulp and reduce over medium heat until thickened, 4 to 6 minutes.

5. Stir in the rice and cook until the tomato is absorbed and the flavors marry, about 3 minutes. Sprinkle in the parsley, season with salt and pepper, and remove from the heat.

6. When the mixture has cooled slightly, spoon the rice into the hollowed-out tomatoes and place in prepared baking dish.

7. Bake until heated through, 12 to 15 minutes. Check frequently, as overcooking will cause the tomatoes to split and fall apart. Serve 1 tomato per person.

• • •

SPAGHETTI CARBONARA   My landlord in Rome, Spiro Rascovic, told me of the widespread starvation throughout the city during World War II before the American army swept in from the south and liberated it. His brother, Savo, was on the brink of dying when Spiro walked out into the piazza as an American jeep entered it by a side street and drove straight toward the group of men with whom Spiro was standing. A striking American named Dan Wickersham stood up and shouted, "Does anyone speak English here?" Spiro's hand shot up and he said, "I do, sir." Captain Wickersham motioned for Spiro to get in the jeep.

They drove to headquarters just south of Rome, and when Wickersham led Spiro through a mess tent, Spiro almost fainted at the smell of food. They passed a corporal grilling steaks, and Spiro stopped Captain Wickersham and said, "Please, my brother and I have not eaten for days." Wickersham grabbed six uncooked steaks and gave them to Spiro, who told me, all those years later, "The great Captain Wickersham saved the life of my brother and me."

Later, Spiro admitted to me that he rented the house to my family only because I reminded him of the great Dan Wickersham.

Spaghetti Carbonara was born at the same time that Wickersham was liberating Rome. My neighbors at the Piazza Farnese told me that the army of liberation brought eggs and bacon into Roman restaurants and asked the chefs to make them a pasta sauce. The Romans quickly adapted the ingredients into this delicious recipe, and my family often dined at a restaurant near the bakery and the olive man in the Campo de' Fiori with "Carbonara" in its name. The Romans use pork jowl, but pork jowl is hard to come by in America. I normally use pancetta, but the finest grades of bacon work well.

• SERVES 4 AS A MAIN COURSE OR 6 AS A FIRST COURSE

    1 pound thick-sliced bacon, chopped

    1 pound spaghetti

    4 large eggs

    2 teaspoons freshly ground black pepper

1 cup plus 2 tablespons freshly grated Parmigiano-Reggiano or
   Pecorino

1. In a large heavy skillet over medium heat, cook the chopped bacon until crisp. Remove the bacon and reserve, saving the bacon drippings separately.

2. Cook the spaghetti according to package directions in abundantly salted boiling water. While the spaghetti is cooking, beat the eggs, pepper, and 2 tablespoons cheese together in a bowl.

3. When spaghetti is al dente, drain thoroughly and return to the pot. Toss with about 1 tablespoon of the bacon drippings (all the noodles should be coated).

4. Place the pasta in a warm serving bowl, add the egg mixture, and toss quickly. Add the reserved bacon and 1 cup grated cheese and toss again.

5. Serve at once, passing more cheese and the pepper grinder at the table.

CHAPTER TEN

Letter from Rome

In the early eighties, I brought my family to live in Italy based on an ill-conceived theory I have about the effects of expatriation on writing. I've always thought that writers should spend part of their lives testing themselves in the crucibles of alien cultures. As a Southern writer I've worried that my prose would smell too much of okra and sweet potatoes, that my vision would begin and end along the drifting, surreal avenues of small Southern towns, and that all my novels would be summed up in the phrase "the night the hogs ate Willie in South Carolina." For a long time I've looked on Europe as a kind of finishing school for writers, a place for me to replenish exhausted metaphors and to refresh my dimming imagination before I sat down to write a new novel. What I didn't know but learned fast is that living abroad is Europe's revenge for our ancestors' migrating to the United States.

We chose Italy because of the weather and because Italians seemed as friendly as Southerners. My mother raised a grinning child with a congenital need to be around other smiling people. We rented a house outside Rome in a compound surrounding a castle called Largo Olgiata. We moved to ancient Rome to reside in a modern villa built in 1971. Our house was made up of rhomboids and trapezoids and had all the warmth of a Rubik's cube. But the house was authentically Italian, and we did without electricity, gas, telephone, heat, and water at various unbearably lengthy intervals during our time there. If something worked in Italy, it was considered accidental and temporary, and rather amusing.

Instead of writing deathless, flowing prose, I spent much of my time apologizing to my children for brutally uprooting them from the emerald city, Atlanta, and transporting them to Europe. Moving will never be easy for children, and no child will ever make it easy on his or her parents. I showed them the Alps, castles, medieval towns, the Sistine Chapel, the mustard crops of Dijon, the lake country of Italy, and all the glories of the Uffizi Palace, and they fixed me with their wounded, kidnapped eyes and wailed they would much rather be at Six Flags Over Georgia. High in a snow-glistening Alpine pass I heard one of the children whisper, "This is okay, but I like Stone Mountain a lot better."

But the South was deeply in them. The fall we lived in Rome, Lenore and I took the children to Florence as a reward for not once mentioning Atlanta during a blissful three-hour period. We stayed at the exquisite hotel Villa la Massa, in Bagno a Ripoli, a converted palazzo overlooking the Arno River. The Villa la Massa was my candidate for the perfect hotel, with a splendid restaurant, a discreet staff, grapes ripening in the arbors, and a German shepherd named Otto who was multilingual and could say "good morning" in four languages. There was a small chapel in the garden, a bar with gold-leaf wallpaper overlooking the river, and brimming fishponds. The goldfish, wary of the resident cats, swished along the bottom like animated bullion. A perfect hotel can seduce even children, and I watched each of them solemnly sign the leather-bound guest book in the hotel's sitting room. When I signed the book as we left, I read my daughter's note. She had loved the hotel but was holding fast to her identity. The note read: Megan Conroy, Atlanta, Georgia. *How 'Bout Them Dawgs?*

Yet education is a secret and indefinable thing, and I watched the effects of travel on my children, who changed, despite their allegiance to Atlanta. I had a feeling the sediments of Rome were going to rest in the hidden sills of their memories for years to come. While in Rome, they went to dinner with an Italian countess who had attended bullfights with Ernest Hemingway; drifted silently beside the tombs of popes; went to parties with their schoolmates, Soorig, Dariush, Atubia, and Jean-Franco; ate octopus ("It tastes like a tire, Dad"), prosciutto, *finocchio* (fennel), and a dozen different varieties of olives and olive oils; tasted wine from almost every district in Italy; sledded in the Apennines with a writer who had written five novels; and lit votive candles in every church along the Corso in Rome. (They prayed they would soon return to Atlanta.) I no longer told them that they'd someday regret not getting more out of the Roman years. Rome did its work quietly on all of us, and there was nothing we could do about it except be grateful.

My youngest daughter, Susannah Ansley, was born on December 7 at Salvator Mundi International Hospital in Rome. I became the first Southern writer I've ever known who's the father of an Italian citizen. She was delivered by cesarean section in the city where Julius Caesar drew his first breath by the same method more than two thousand years ago. When Sister Magdolena emerged from the operating room she carried an inert bundle in her arms and passed me without saying a word or nodding in my direction. Her face was covered with a gauze mask and the baby, ominously silent, lay still beneath a white blanket that covered her face. I trailed after Sister Magdolena until she came to a small chapel. She entered, held the child aloft, and genuflected before a crucifix.

"Sister," I asked, "I hate to bother you, but can I ask you a question?"

"*Sì*," she answered through gauze.

"Is this my baby?"

"*Sì*."

"Sister Magdolena, is the baby alive?"

"*Sì*. Big. Molto grande. Tre kilos, sette cento."

"Can I see the baby?"

"No, *signore*. You have many germs in the mouth."

I could have lived in Italy for a hundred years and never known the true weight of *tre kilos, sette cento*. Later, an American friend with a calculator informed me that Susannah weighed eight pounds, three ounces. I called my mother that night and told her that the family had produced another Roman. My mother was born in Rome, Georgia, and the binding of the two Romes provided a pure associative joy.

When she was old enough to understand, and we were back in the South, I told Susannah about Rome and her first days on earth and the friends who came to see her in the hospital. I told her why we went to Rome and how the city changed us forever. That is the singular gift of travel: it changes you because it gives you more to celebrate, to cherish, and to remember. I told Susannah how Italy changed me and changed how I looked at the world. It made me confront the essence of my being Southern. It had nothing to do with geography; it had everything to do with my own personal view of the world.

When I refer to myself as Southern, I am talking about the part of myself that is most deeply human and deeply feeling. It is the part of me that connects most intimately and cordially with the family of humankind. There are qualities of grace and friendship and courtesy that will always seem essentially Southern to me, no matter where I encounter them on the road. Then I told my daughter that I never appreciated the South until I left it for the first time. And that the reason you travel is to find out who you really are and what you really believe. I came to understand that the country of Italy produced Michelangelo, da Vinci, Dante, Garibaldi, and most significantly, for the history of my family, because of accident and writing and a need for definition, a pretty black-haired Roman named Susannah Ansley Conroy.

ITALIAN SAUSAGE WITH CRISPY SWEET POTATOES AND WILTED BROCCOLI RABE

• SERVES 4

3 large sweet potatoes (about 3 pounds), peeled and sliced into
   $1/4$-inch medallions
Olive oil
1 lemon, halved
Coarse or kosher salt and coarsely ground black pepper
3 pounds hot Italian sausage (in one piece)
Two 1 $1/2$-pound bunches broccoli rabe, trimmed, washed, dried, and
   cut into 1-inch pieces

1. Preheat the oven to 400°F.

2. Toss the sweet potato slices with olive oil until lightly coated (do not drench). Add the juice of half a lemon and salt and pepper to taste. Divide and transfer to two baking pans. (Overcrowding will prevent the potatoes from browning.) Roast until golden brown, about 20 minutes, turning the slices over halfway through. Set aside.

3. Lower the oven temperature to 350°F.

4. Loosely coil the sausage into a large ovenproof skillet (packing it too tightly will prevent the sausage from cooking evenly). Prick the casing with a fork or the tip of a sharp paring knife (you want the sausage to provide cooking liquid for the broccoli rabe) and place the skillet in the oven until the sausage is cooked through, 20 to 25 minutes. Transfer the sausage to a cutting board and loosely cover with aluminum foil.

5. Return the potatoes to the oven.

6. Transfer the hot skillet (be careful; the handle will also be hot) to the top of the stove over moderate heat and bring the sausage cooking liquid to a low simmer. Immediately add the broccoli rabe (this must be done slowly because the skillet will be very full until the broccoli rabe begins to wilt), squeeze the remaining half a lemon over the greens, and cook until crisp-tender, about 3 minutes. Transfer to serving dishes.

7. Cut the sausage into serving-size pieces and place on top of the greens. Tuck the warm potato medallions alongside and serve immediately.

• • •

ROASTED FIGS WITH FRASCATI ZABAGLIONE When my daughter was born in Rome, Italy, on December 7, 1981, I sent telegrams to the United States to the houses of Bo Marks and Mike Devito. The telegrams said, "The first true Italian has been born to our room, and her name is Susannah Ansley Conroy." For one week, until I registered her with the *questora*, Susannah was an Italian citizen, and I rejoiced in that sweet fact. I was the first to father an Italian child in the history of the Conroy family, and all the surprises and astonishments and switchbacks of fate and history lay contained in the joy of her birth.

While living in Italy, I grew familiar with all the small-change bigotries that the Italians from different regions have for one another. When I told an elegant Milanese businessman that I lived in Rome he sneered and said, "Africa," summing up the northern Italians' contempt for those in the south. I remembered Bo-Pig and Mike-Swine warning me about the provenance of each other's families when we roomed together at The Citadel.

Mike would mutter darkly about Bo, "You cannot trust Bo-Pig. He is Siciliano."

"He's what?" I'd ask.

"A Sicilian. They are the scum of Italy."

"Wake up, boy. You're an American now."

"Some things never change," Mike said. "Blood is blood."

"Where are your people from?"

"Northern Italy. I came from aristocrats," said Mike.

Later Bo-Pig would take me aside and say, "You can't trust Mike, paisan."

"Why not?"

"His family is from northern Italy."

When I returned to America, Mike and I went out to Gene and Gabe's Restaurant in Atlanta. We talked about my long-ago weekend in Greensburg and the pleasure of getting to know Phyllis Parise and her family.

"The reason you liked the Parise family so much is because they are from northern Italy like my family," Mike said.

"Where in northern Italy are they from?" I asked.

"Naples," said Mike with pride and could not understand why I roared with laughter. Naples, of course, is the very heart and soul of southern Italy.

• SERVES 6

24 Black Mission figs

ZABAGLIONE SAUCE

6 egg yolks

$\frac{1}{2}$ cup sugar

Pinch of salt

1 cup Frascati wine

1 cup heavy cream

2 teaspoons freshly ground white pepper

1. Preheat the oven to 400°F.

2. Place the figs on a jelly roll pan or in a shallow cooking dish to maximize browning (do not crowd the figs because they will steam instead of roast).

3. Roast the figs until soft, 5 to 8 minutes. Remove the pan to a rack and cool to room temperature.

4. To make the sauce: Fill a heatproof bowl (large enough to hold the bowl with the zabaglione) with ice and reserve.

5. Simmer water in the bottom of a double boiler.

6. Place the egg yolks in a stainless steel mixing bowl and whisk in the sugar, salt, and Frascati. Suspend the egg mixture bowl over the simmering water (the bowl should not touch the water) and whisk rapidly (to incorporate as much air as possible) until the egg mixture is thick and pale yellow, 8 to 10 minutes. (The mixture should not boil.)

7. Nestle the zabaglione bowl into the bowl filled with ice and continue whisking until the zabaglione is cold.

8. Whip the cream and fold it into the zabaglione. This can now be refrigerated until ready to serve.

9. When the figs are room temperature, transfer them to large balloon-shaped wineglasses, 4 per glass. Fold the white pepper into the zabaglione and spoon the sauce over the figs to serve.

• • •

SQUASH BLOSSOMS THREE WAYS When I was living in Rome, the Jewish ghetto was very near our house on Via dei Foraggi. The restaurants of the ghetto, like all of the other restaurants in the city, were wonderful, but their specialties of stuffed fried zucchini blossoms and fried artichokes were both ambrosial. In the first summer Suzanne Pollak and I were planning this cookbook (that was ten years ago—Suzanne's a quick study, but she soon found that her partner moved like a glacier through the high mountain passes), Suzanne discovered a farmer who brought her twenty zucchini blossoms he had picked from his garden that morning. Since I am a devotee of the great Italian cookbook writer Marcella Hazan, I knew that the male blossoms were the only ones good enough to eat. The male blossoms grow on stems, while the female blossoms are attached to the zucchini and are too mealy for Marcella's refined palate.

All afternoon, Suzanne and I thought up new stuffings for zucchini blossoms, then fried them in peanut oil. The three recipes that follow were the best we came up with. Incidentally, in her masterful book *Essentials of Classic Italian Cooking*, Marcella dips the blossoms in a *pastella*, a flour and water batter, then fries them without stuffing. In the ghetto of Rome, they stuff them with magnificent and tasty ingredients. Like all glorious fried things, they should be eaten while hot to the touch.

Fried Squash Blossoms

• SERVES 6 AS AN APPETIZER

12 open squash or zucchini blossoms
$2/3$ cup all-purpose flour
$1/4$ teaspoon sweet smoked paprika
Peanut oil
Sea salt

1. Line a baking sheet with brown paper bags and set aside.

2. Rinse the blossoms, gently checking to make sure there are no bugs inside.

3. Pour 1 cup cold water in a pie pan or shallow bowl. Sift the flour and paprika into the pan, whisking constantly to prevent any lumps.

4. Add enough oil to a heavy frying pan to come about $3/4$ inch up the sides of the pan. Heat the oil over medium-high heat until almost smoking. Working with one at a time, use tongs to dip each blossom in the batter, letting the excess drip back into the pan. Slip 2 or 3 batter-covered blossoms (as many as will comfortably fit in the frying pan) in the hot oil and cook until golden brown, turning only once, about 2 minutes total.

5. Transfer the fried blossoms to the prepared baking sheet to drain. Sprinkle with salt and serve piping hot.

Stuffed Squash Blossoms 1

• SERVES 6 AS AN APPETIZER

12 open squash or zucchini blossoms
$2/3$ cup all-purpose flour
$1/4$ teaspoon sweet smoked paprika

12 small pieces (about $^1\!/_8$ pound) Manchego cheese, about $^1\!/_4$ inch
thick and 1 inch long
2 thin slices Serrano ham, cut into 12 pieces
Peanut oil
Sea salt

1. Line a baking sheet with brown paper bags and set aside.

2. Rinse the blossoms, gently checking to make sure there are no bugs inside.

3. Pour 1 cup cold water in a pie pan or shallow bowl. Sift the flour and paprika into the pan, whisking constantly to prevent any lumps. Set aside.

4. Insert a piece of cheese and a piece of ham into each open blossom. Carefully twist the ends of the blossoms to close them.

5. Add enough oil to a heavy frying pan to come about $^3\!/_4$ inch up the side of the pan. Heat the oil over medium-high heat until almost smoking. Working with one at a time, use tongs to dip each blossom in the batter, letting the excess drip back into the pan. Slip 2 or 3 blossoms (as many as will comfortably fit in the frying pan) in the hot oil and fry, turning once, until the blossoms are golden brown and the cheese is melted, 2 to 3 minutes.

6. Transfer the fried blossoms to the paper bags to drain. Sprinkle with sea salt and serve.

Stuffed Squash Blossoms 2   • **SERVES 6 AS AN APPETIZER**

12 open squash or zucchini blossoms
$^2\!/_3$ cup all-purpose flour
$^1\!/_4$ teaspoon sweet smoked paprika
12 small pieces (about $^1\!/_8$ pound) fresh mozzarella, about $^1\!/_4$
inch thick and 1 inch long
12 Sicilian (green) olives, pitted and quartered

Peanut oil

Sea salt

1. Line a baking sheet with clean brown paper bags and set aside.

2. Rinse the blossoms, gently checking to make sure there are no bugs inside.

3. Pour 1 cup cold water in a pie pan or shallow bowl. Sift the flour and paprika into the pan, whisking constantly to prevent any lumps. Set aside.

4. Insert a piece of cheese and 4 olive quarters into each open blossom. Carefully twist the ends of the blossoms to close them.

5. Add enough oil to a heavy frying pan to come about $^3/_4$ inch up the sides of the pan. Heat the oil over medium-high heat until almost smoking. Working with one at a time, use tongs to dip each blossom in the batter, letting the excess drip back into the pan. Slip 2 or 3 blossoms (as many as will comfortably fit in the frying pan) in the hot oil and fry, turning once, until blossoms are golden brown and cheese is melted, 2 to 3 minutes.

6. Transfer the fried blossoms to the paper bags to drain. Sprinkle with sea salt and serve.

• • •

SALTIMBOCCA ALLA ROMANA   If you are a beginning cook, Saltimbocca alla Romana is a dish you should incorporate into your repertoire immediately. It is simple, easy to prepare, and magnificent. In Italian, *saltimbocca* means "to jump in the mouth," a fond acknowledgment of its wonderful taste.   **• SERVES 4**

Eight 3- to 4-ounce veal scallops

8 thin slices prosciutto, skin rind removed

8 fresh sage leaves

About ⅓ cup all-purpose flour

4 tablespoons (½ stick) unsalted butter

1 cup dry white wine

Coarse or kosher salt and freshly ground white pepper

1. Lightly pound the veal scallops until they are of an even thickness. Place a piece of prosciutto over each scallop and top with a sage leaf. Use a wooden toothpick (threaded in and out like a needle) to secure the layers. Lightly dredge in flour.

2. In a heavy skillet over moderate heat, melt 3 tablespoons of butter until foamy. Add the prepared veal scallops and cook until browned, about 2 minutes per side, being careful not to crowd the pan. Cook in batches, if necessary. Remove to a warm platter and cover loosely with aluminum foil.

3. Turn the heat to high and melt the remaining 1 tablespoon butter. Quickly deglaze the skillet with the wine, bringing the liquid to a rapid boil while scraping up any browned bits from the bottom of the pan. Let the pan sauce reduce until slightly syrupy, about 3 minutes. Add salt and pepper to taste.

4. Transfer the veal to serving plates and spoon the sauce over to serve.

CHAPTER ELEVEN

Italian Waiter

On a hillside street curving off the hind flank of the Borghese gardens, an Italian waiter taught me what it is to perfectly dress a salad. When he took our orders he was unmannerly and dyspeptic, rare qualities in that magnificent, white-jacketed tribe. He acted as though we held some timeless grudge against him because we insisted on ordering a meal in his restaurant. But his mood did not deflect from the perfection of the bruschetta or the *bucatini all'Amatriciana* that came out of the kitchen.

However, the waiter's distemper could not hide the artistry that was native to his species when he brought out three *insalata mistas* for me and my companions. The salads were perfectly composed of curly chicory and escarole with a green and welcome addition of field lettuce and a shy appearance of arugula. The waiter took the salads to a dressing table, where his movements slowed and his work turned sacramental. Surprising me, he turned a salt grinder a single time onto a plate, and the salt snowed down in a soft hail. Then he squeezed the freshest lemon onto that plate, which was ivory white. Slowly, he dissolved the salt by whisking a fork through the lemon juice. When satisfied that the salt had disappeared, he poured a parsimonious amount of red wine vinegar and incorporated that with great care. Afterward, he filled the plate with bright green extra virgin olive oil that looked like it had been harvested from a field of emeralds, again working the fork until the dressing appeared right to him. Then, with an acrobatic move that I advise no one else to emulate, he tilted the plate and dressed the first salad, shifted the dressing to the second salad without spilling a drop, and then moved to the third, his instincts guiding him every step of the way. When he finished, he tossed the three salads in their individual plates and brought them to the table. Each salad glistened like a gemstone. I lifted the salad to my mouth and realized I had never tasted—really tasted—a salad before. The greens were so fresh that they must have rested in fields that very morning; the olive oil was rich and fresh and perfectly complemented by the bite of lemon and vinegar. The salt was a breath of itself, a sea breeze hidden in the salad. I was dining on the mother of all salads, and my mouth could not have been happier. Putting my fork down, I applauded the waiter, but he was disdainful of praise, sniffed, and returned to the kitchen. It was the first and last time in Rome that I would see a salad dressing composed on a dinner plate.

In Italy, the usual order of business is salt, a carefully chosen extra virgin olive oil, and a good red wine vinegar. As far as I can tell, the use of balsamic vinegar in salads is an American fad. Maybe it is used in Modena, where the vinegar is born, but I never got to Modena. The Italians are resolute and athletic when it comes to tossing their salads, and they insist that all ingredients merge. In Italy, the oil is king, queen, and everything when the subject is *insalata mista*.

BRUSCHETTA   Bruschetta is Italian comfort food of a high order, but now that I think about it, the entire cuisine of Italy is based on comfort food. The toasted rustic bread sandpapers the garlic into small, fragrant bits when you rub the bread as it comes out of the oven. I've made bruschetta with fresh mozzarella and homemade tapenade, also with arugula, and with great passion when Beaufort's summer tomatoes come into season.   • SERVES 4

> 1 round loaf hearty rustic-style bread, cut into $1/2$-inch slices (each
>   slice cut in half, depending on the diameter of the bread)
> 4 garlic cloves, halved
> Olive oil
> 6 ripe Roma tomatoes, cut into slices
> Coarse or kosher salt and freshly ground black pepper

1. Preheat the oven to 350°F. Place the bread slices directly on the oven rack and toast until lightly browned on both sides, about 3 minutes.

2. Quickly remove toasted bread and rub the cut side of a garlic clove on one side of each slice. Transfer to serving plates, drizzle lightly with olive oil, and top with sliced tomatoes. Sprinkle with salt and pepper and serve immediately.

• • •

BUCATINI ALL'AMATRICIANA   In my travels around the world, I have never seen the word "amatriciana" without its being introduced first by its brother pasta, the thick, tube-shaped bucatini. This is a fast, delicious meal that is both easy to make and sexy. The two small red chiles provide the heat that gathers all the flavors of this dish in its arms. Like pasta carbonara, this recipe is claimed by the Romans, its provenance being the Roman town of Amatrice.   • SERVES 4

2 tablespoons olive oil

1 tablespoon unsalted butter

$1/2$ cup finely chopped onion

$1/3$ pound pancetta, cut into $1/4$-inch slices, then into $1/4$-inch strips

$2^{1}/2$ cups canned whole tomatoes, preferably San Marzano, drained
   and diced

2 small red chiles, crushed

Coarse or kosher salt

1 pound dried bucatini

Freshly grated Parmigiano-Reggiano

1. In a large skillet over moderate heat, melt the olive oil and butter together until slightly foamy. Add the onion and cook until lightly colored, about 8 minutes. Add the pancetta and cook, stirring frequently, until the fat on the pancetta is slightly translucent, about 2 minutes.

2. Add the tomatoes, chiles, and a pinch of salt. Adjust the heat to bring the mixture to a low simmer and cook, uncovered, until thickened, 20 to 25 minutes.

3. Meanwhile, in a large pot of abundantly salted water, cook the pasta according to package directions until al dente. Drain in a colander, but do not rinse.

4. Add the pasta to the sauce and toss. Immediately transfer to serving plates. Sprinkle with grated cheese and serve, passing extra cheese on the side.

• • •

INSALATA MISTA (MIXED LETTUCES AND GREENS)

• SERVES 4 AS A FIRST COURSE

4 handfuls mixed young lettuces and greens
$1/4$ cup extra virgin olive oil
Sea salt
1 tablespoon red wine vinegar
Freshly ground black pepper

1. Inspect the lettuces. Remove any brown or old leaves.

2. Wash the lettuces in a sink filled with cool water. Dry in a salad spinner. If not completely dry, pat with paper towels. Place the lettuces in a salad bowl and set aside.

3. Combine the oil and salt to taste in a small bowl and whisk with a fork to dissolve the salt. Add a small amount of the vinegar. Taste the dressing, then dip a leaf in the dressing and taste again. If the lettuces are young, they may not need all the vinegar.

4. Toss the lettuces with enough dressing to coat well and distribute the salad among serving plates. Offer freshly ground black pepper at the table.

CHAPTER TWELVE

Eugene Walter of Mobile

When I moved to Rome, Italy, in 1981, I did not expect to meet the large number of American Southerners who had ventured to Rome in their youth and never gone back to their homeland. They popped up everywhere and in strange contexts. The word "expatriate" took on a dark, smoky luster that it had never had before for me. To find the courage to give up everything that had made your childhood either immemorial or unbearable was a vanity of freedom I had never encountered. As an adult, I found myself so haunted by my parents and my geography that I have spent a lifetime trying to write my way out of my addiction to their memory. The American expatriate I had expected to meet in Italy, certainly; the Southerner, never. I thought all unhappy Southerners migrated to New York. Never did it occur to me that for some of them, New York was just a stop-off point where they made their flight connections to distant points on the globe.

During the whole first year in Rome many of those disaffected Southerners I met said, "What a shame you missed Eugene Walter. A magnificent Southerner. More like a Renaissance man than a sad-sack Alabamian. A novelist. A poet. An actor. He was in Fellini's *8 ½*, you know.

A songwriter. A translator. An Air Force cryptographer living in the Aleutians during the war. A famed gardener. And the best cook in Rome."

That I had missed the best cook in Rome caused me great anguish and keen regret. What was remarkable was that I rarely met a single American who had not known Eugene Walter and could not share a tale about this garrulous and perfectly whimsical enchanter. Rome had soured for him when the Red Brigades began to set off bombs in his neighborhood and to kidnap policemen he knew by name who were guarding the headquarters of the Communist Party and the Christian Democrats, both of which were a block from his garden apartment. As for timing, my family and I passed Eugene almost in midair over the Atlantic. As we began our first day in Rome, he ended his last. Eugene returned to his roots in Mobile, Alabama, where he would live out the rest of his artful and overachieving life. Because I listened so ardently to the plainsong of his nearly inconsolable friends, I always felt that I had missed one of the great opportunities of my life by not getting to sit at the feet of Eugene Walter.

"The food you missed," Alfred de Rocca, the composer, would say, shaking his head sadly. "The meals were simply magnificent, spread out like works of art."

The great artist Zev, whose artworks seemed painted with peacock tails and the dreams of preoccupied children, told me, "Eugene Walter was a walking civilization. He could do anything and knew everything. The conversation you missed! He didn't just *talk*. It was never just *talk*. It was grand opera."

I could not pass a restaurant without being told by some new friends that they had dined on *that* terrace with Eugene or walked along the path of *that* park or sat in the shadows of *that* ruin talking to Eugene Walter about Camus or Sartre or Genet, all of whom Eugene Walter had known and entertained and fed. I met more Italians who were in love with the whole state of Alabama just because Eugene Walter had sprung so fully formed and elegant from that Deep South state. Many Italians were fully prepared to like me because they knew my native state of Georgia was contiguous to the one that had produced the incomparable Eugene Walter. His footsteps were numerous and broad and just by tracing them through his abandoned Rome, I realized the part expatriates play in defining the American spirit to their host countries. More than all the diplomats I met abroad, Eugene spread the joy and honor and wonder of being American and represented the essence of our finest selves as he told his incomparable stories and wove his tantalizing web during his Roman years.

I never saw Eugene Walter in Rome, but I felt his presence keenly. When my family returned to America after two years in Italy, I placed a call to him in Mobile and sent pleasant greetings and a hundred *"ciao*s" from a diverse and fervent group of friends from Trastevere to Parioli.

"You must come to meet me at once," Eugene said, after I had delivered the message from his Roman life. "There's friendship waiting here for you in Mobile. Time is swift and glorious friendship is one of the few condiments that makes life both sweet and sour. What sign are you?"

"Scorpio," I answered.

"How dreadful. But it cannot be helped. I'll do the best I can to like you. Though I can't promise a thing. You are a large man with a weak voice, aren't you?"

"Yes," I said.

"Your family is not much, I would guess. Good solid peasant stock, but nothing to write home about."

"Exactly."

"Call your travel agent this moment," Eugene Walter said to me. "I know destiny when I hear her precious heartbeat."

I followed the call of destiny's precious heartbeat the following summer and found myself embracing Eugene Walter as though we had known each other for many years. He walked me through the dining room of a very fine restaurant where he was well-known. Every eye was on him. He was wild-haired and fixed you with dark, piercing eyes. His voice was honeyed and piping and his pronunciation was precise as befitted the actor and the linguist he was. He sounded like Nero with lines written by Truman Capote.

"Let us get something straight between us," Eugene said as we took our seats and the busboy filled our water glasses. "Your mother misnamed you. She was a frittery, vain woman who did not take the trouble to get your name right. You have never been a Pat and never will. It's a name for other people of no consequence. I will think of a name for you."

"Thank you," I said.

"No need to thank me. That'll come due when I find the exactly right name for you. Naming is one of the most important things. Ah! It's coming to me. I've got it. It's perfect. Do you want to hear what you should've been called all your life?"

"Yes," I said. "I guess."

"Lyon," Eugene said. "L-Y-O-N. You are Lyon and will always remain Lyon to me."

And so I did. Each time I called to check in with him in Mobile from that day on, Eugene Walter would say, "Greetings, Lyon. You evade me because you know you should be here in Mobile, living across the street from me, sitting at my knee and writing down every word I utter. It troubles you, Lyon. You could be my Boswell. Instead you are vegetating in a perfectly empty and licentious life in Atlanta, the whore of Georgia. Do you know the oldest thing I've ever seen in Atlanta is a traffic light or maybe a half pound of rat-trap cheese? You belong to the ancient places, Lyon. You are an Etruscan and that is both your honorific and your tragedy."

In the restaurant that night, Eugene took the pepper shaker, unscrewed the cap, and poured the pepper into an ashtray on our table. When the waiter appeared, Eugene said, "Take this and flush it down the toilet of the men's room. It is dead dust and has no relationship to the sacred pods of real black pepper. This has the taste of talcum or black sand formed on volcanic beaches. Freshly ground pepper has volatile, tempestuous oils which only last about an hour after grinding. This oil is an aid to digestion. It also cleanses the blood, like garlic or cognac. Rid us of this sawdust, good man. What sign are you?"

"Sagittarius," the young man answered, removing the offending ashtray filled with the discredited pepper.

"Splendid," Eugene said. "Sagittarians are the blown kisses of the

Zodiac, sweet-natured but peppery, like old-fashioned nasturtiums, not the sickly aromatic hybrids of today's tacky gardens."

I was in Mobile with my lawyer, Jim Landon, and we were staying with his sister, Sue Beard, in an area of the city near Spring Hill College. Eugene insisted that he would cook lunch for Jim and me the very next day, but he warned me that we should come prepared for chaos and surprise. Those were two watchwords of Eugene's life that he shared with me whenever I saw him in Mobile. He took the idea of whimsicality to almost absurd heights. Jim and I entered the shabby foyer of a nineteenth-century house that Eugene was "renting for a song and the utter prestige of having me lease such a déclassé abode."

The cats that moved throughout the house were named with boisterous, T. S. Eliot flair. Boxes, piled to the ceiling, still bore the name of an Italian shipping company. Eugene brought an insouciance to the science of disorder. Jim and I cleaned off a sofa as Eugene served us a glass of red wine.

Jim Landon possesses one of the most spectacular visual memories of anyone I have ever known. This lunch took place in Mobile eighteen years ago, yet when I called Jim at his law office at Jones, Day in Atlanta, he began speaking of it in precise detail.

"Eugene served us on beautiful Capodimonte china, although I do not think the word 'china' is correct. It is simpler than that. Very elegant. Let's say plates. Yes, that will do fine. His wineglasses were thick, unwieldy, the provenance, I would venture, Woolworth's. The tablecloth was lovely and I first guessed mohair, but upon further examination, I ventured it was cat hair. He served us barbecued chicken with a barbecue sauce I can taste to this day, taste but cannot duplicate. Pat, do you remember the orange slices floating in it, mustard and vinegar and we just raved about it? Then a perfectly composed salad, dressed with balsamic vinegar and extra virgin olive oil. We peeled our own oranges for dessert. You mangled yours of course. I cut my peel very precisely in one continuous piece that sprang back into its original shape when I laid it upon my Capodimonte plate. Afterward, he served us a demitasse of strong Italian espresso. Then he gave us each a teaspoon of sugar moistened perfectly with Angostura bitters."

"No wonder people think I'm a redneck, Jim," I said. "I never think about moistening sugar with Angostura bitters."

"That is only the beginning of the thing, Conroy," Jim said. "I must take my leave now. I have real paying clients who actually require my legal services. 'Capodimonte,' I believe you will discover, means 'at the head of the mountain.' "

Eugene Walter sent me a paperback copy of his cookbook when it was published in November of 1982. He had titled it with a baroque Eugene Walter–like flourish, *Delectable Dishes from Termite Hall: Rare and Unusual Recipes.* I read the book from cover to cover the day I received it, and it remains one of my favorite cookbooks in a collection that has grown into a fairly extensive library. There is not a recipe in the entire book that does not shine with a ray or two of Eugene's strange, piquant life. On every page, his complaints and prejudices about food and life spill out, staining the napery and the carpets with his vinegary opinions about everything. I have not come across a bad recipe in the book, and certainly not a dull one. It was Eugene who told me that as a cookbook writer he was always trying to disguise the fact that "my real job is to be a philosopher king or a prince of elves. If it has magic, Lyon, look for my footprints nearby. Promise me that, Lyon. Always."

But always is never long enough and it is a word that runs out of time the way that life does. When I heard about his death in Mobile, I took down his first novel, *The Untidy Pilgrim,* from the shelf. I turned to the first sentence of the first page because I wanted the essence of the man to enter the room where I stood grateful to have known and loved him: "Down in Mobile they're all crazy, because the Gulf Coast is the kingdom of monkeys, the land of clowns, ghosts, and musicians and Mobile is sweet lunacy's county seat."

Ciao, maestro. Whenever I feel magic in my life, I will look for your footprints. That is a promise, Eugene Walter, a promise from Lyon.

TUNA AU POIVRE   Before I leave the glorious subject of Eugene Walter, I would like to quote from a small diatribe he sounded in his quirky cookbook *Delectable Dishes from Termite Hall.* Please note his obsession with freshly ground pepper; the next six recipes pay fine homage to that lordly obsession. At the beginning of chapter 6, Eugene Walter writes about the Salad Question: "A barbarous movement has swept America in the three decades that I lived in Europe, a movement as barbarous as that sullen minority which calls itself the Moral Majority, as barbarous as plastic plates and glasses, as barbarous as synthetic cheeses or the crap-glop salad dressings, as barbarous as restaurants claiming to be first class but lacking a pepper mill." Eugene rants for another couple of pages about how Americans are like huns because they eat their salads before the first course, not after it like Europeans do. In Mobile, they give out an annual Eugene Walter prize to a writer of note, and the splendid T. R. Pearson received the award in 2004. A wonderful book called *Milking the Moon* came out in 2001 in which Eugene Walter tells his life story to Katherine Clark. What an impish, pixilated, and original man! *Ciao* again, maestro, your Lyon will honor you for all time.

• SERVES 4

$^{1}/_{4}$ cup coarse or kosher salt
$^{1}/_{2}$ cup whole black peppercorns, coarsely cracked
4 bluefin tuna steaks ($^{1}/_{2}$ pound each)
Vegetable oil

1. Combine the salt and cracked pepper in a shallow baking dish and press the tuna into the mixture, covering both sides of each steak.

2. In a large nonstick skillet, pour enough oil to submerge (and thereby cook) the tuna. Heat the oil over moderately high heat until hot but not smoking and sear the tuna until a crust forms. Using a long-handled slotted spatula or tongs, turn the tuna only once: 3 minutes total cooking time for rare, 4 minutes for medium rare.

• • •

PEPPERED NEW POTATOES

• SERVES 4

1³/4 pounds small red new potatoes (about 24)
3 tablespoons unsalted butter
Coarse or kosher salt and coarsely ground tricolor pepper

1. Wash the potatoes, but do not dry. Peel a ring around the center of each potato. In a pot large enough to hold the potatoes in a single layer, melt the butter over medium-high heat until foamy and almost browned. Place the wet potatoes in the pot and cover tightly.

2. In about 3 minutes, the potatoes will start to sputter. Holding the lid in place, shake the pot to crisp all sides of the potatoes. Continue to shake the pot frequently until the potatoes are browned on the outside and tender inside (the tip of a knife or fork should slide in easily), 15 to 18 minutes. Season with salt and abundant coarsely ground tricolor pepper.

• • •

PEPPERED PEACHES   Adapted from one of Lee Bailey's ground-breaking books, *Country Weekends*. Peppered peaches are the right combination of sweet heat to pair with grilled or roasted meats.

• SERVES 12

6 large peaches, ripe but not mushy (will yield to gentle pressure
   without bruising)
¹/4 cup fresh lemon juice (1 lemon)
1¹/2 tablespoons sugar
1 teaspoon coarse or kosher salt
Coarsely ground black, white, and cayenne pepper

1. To peel the peaches: Place 2 trays ice cubes in a bowl with 2 cups cold water and set aside. Cut an X in the end (not the stem end) of each peach. Using a slotted spoon, lower the peach into a pot of boiling water until the skin loosens, about 2 minutes. Transfer to the ice bath and cool, about 3 minutes. The skin should slip off easily.

2. Cut each peach in half around the seam and remove the pit. Transfer peach halves to a large platter, pit side up. Brush with lemon juice and dust with the sugar and salt. Sprinkle with pepper. Do not refrigerate before serving.

• • •

BLACK PEPPER AND PISTACHIO TRUFFLES

• MAKES ABOUT 60

3 cups unsalted, uncolored shelled pistachios
1 pound best-quality semisweet chocolate (like Sharffen Berger), coarsely chopped
1 cup heavy cream
1 vanilla bean, split lengthwise, seeds scraped out and saved
1 1/2 teaspoons freshly ground black pepper
1 tablespoon Frangelico (hazelnut liqueur)
1 pound best-quality dark chocolate, coarsely chopped

1. Preheat the oven to 325°F.

2. Spread the pistachios on a shallow baking sheet and toast in the oven, 8 to 10 minutes. When cool enough to handle (but still warm), transfer the nuts to the center of a clean kitchen towel. Gather the ends together to form a loose bag and vigorously rub the towel between your hands to remove the skins. Transfer the nuts to a cutting board and finely chop. Set aside.

3. In a double boiler over hot water (simmering, not boiling), melt the semisweet chocolate, stirring occasionally until smooth.

Stir in $\frac{1}{2}$ cup of the chopped pistachios. In another saucepan over moderate heat, bring the heavy cream, vanilla (pod and seeds), and pepper to a low boil. Remove the vanilla pod, stir in the Frangelico, and immediately pour hot mixture over the melted chocolate. Whisk gently to combine and pour into a 9-inch round cake pan. Freeze for at least 30 minutes.

4. When the mixture has set, use a teaspoon (or melon ball scoop) to scrape the chocolate into small balls (irregularly shaped is okay; this misshapen appearance is behind the confection's name "truffle," after the earthy and expensive fungus). Place the truffles on a baking sheet and refrigerate until ready for dipping. (The recipe can be done in advance up to this point. Cover the truffles with plastic wrap and refrigerate for up to 24 hours.)

5. To dip and roll the truffles: Melt the dark chocolate in a double boiler over hot but not boiling water. Stir occasionally until smooth. Divide the remaining chopped pistachios into two bowls.

6. When the truffles are set, working with a few at a time (and leaving the rest refrigerated), use two forks to dip and roll each truffle in the melted chocolate. (The chocolate should be warm to the touch, but not too hot. If the chocolate "slips" off the ball instead of coating it, the chocolate is too hot. Adjust heat.) Roll quickly, tapping the fork on the side of the pot to remove excess. Immediately place the coated truffle in a bowl of pistachios and roll, pressing down gently to coat the entire surface. Do several more (leaving the coated truffles in the bowl) and then place the bowl in the refrigerator. Let the truffles harden for several minutes before transferring them to a plate. Repeat with the remaining truffles (rotating the bowls of nuts to keep a steady work rhythm going). Refrigerate until ready to serve. (Or freeze in zippered bags for up to 4 weeks.)

• • •

BLACK PEPPER AND PEAR TARTE TATIN   • SERVES 8

1 recipe Pie Dough (page 7); you will end up using only about three-
    quarters of the dough
6 Bartlett or Bosc pears (about 3 pounds)
Juice of 1 lemon, strained
8 tablespoons (1 stick) unsalted butter
1/2 cup sugar
1 vanilla bean, split lengthwise, seeds scraped out and saved
1/2 teaspoon freshly ground black pepper
2 tablespoons heavy cream

Use a copper tart pan or a 9-inch skillet with a nonstick surface and ovenproof handle.

1. Preheat the oven to 400°F.

2. On a lightly floured surface, roll out one round of pastry slightly larger than the surface of the skillet, about 12 inches. Place the pastry round on a baking sheet and chill until needed.

3. Peel, core, and quarter the pears. Place in a large mixing bowl and toss with lemon juice.

4. In a nonstick skillet over medium-high heat, melt the butter and sugar, stirring frequently, until a golden caramel color. Stir in the vanilla bean scrapings and black pepper. Add the heavy cream and continue cooking and stirring for about 2 minutes. Tightly arrange the pears in the pan with their narrow points facing toward the center of the pan and 4 or 5 slices in the middle of the pan. (It is best to crowd the pears into the pan because as they release moisture, they will shrink.) Cover and cook until pears are translucent, about 20 minutes. Cool.

5. Gently lay the pastry over the pears. Tuck edges of pastry under the pears. (This does not have to be perfect: tarte Tatin is a rustic tart.) Refrigerate for 15 minutes. Transfer to the oven and bake until the pastry is golden and crisp, about 30 minutes.

6. Allow the tart to cool on a rack for 10 minutes. Place a serving platter (with a large enough diameter to extend at least 2 inches beyond the rim of the skillet) upside down over the skillet. Holding the platter firmly against the rim of the skillet, quickly flip the pan, gently easing the tart onto the platter. If some of the pears fall off the serving platter while being flipped, rearrange them on the pastry in the same pattern. Serve hot.

• • •

PEPPERY TEA
• MAKES 8 CUPS

4 teaspoons black tea leaves
One 2-inch piece ginger, peeled
1 small piece crystallized ginger
1 cinnamon stick
10 whole cloves
10 cardamom seeds
1 tablespoon whole black peppercorns
1 long strip orange zest
8 thin orange slices

1. Bring 9 cups cold water to a boil. As soon as the water comes to a boil, take the pot off the heat and add all the ingredients except the orange slices. Steep for 8 to 10 minutes.

2. Place an orange slice in the bottom of each cup and pour tea.

• • •

CAPICOLA

Buy a smoked pork butt (get a soft one that has a lot of fat in it) and remove the casing. Mix 1 cup salt (make sure it's iodized) and $^1/_4$ cup red pepper flakes together, pressing the smoked pork butt in the mixture until all sides are well coated. Wrap the peppered pork butt in white paper towels and secure tightly with rubber bands. Refrigerate (the dampness from the meat will wet the spices and turn the paper towels slightly reddish) until the meat feels hard and the paper towels are dry, about 6 weeks.

MADAGASCAR GREEN PEPPERCORN BUTTER

For each stick (8 tablespoons) of butter, you'll need 1 tablespoon drained Madagascar green peppercorns (canned and preserved in brine), 1 tablespoon finely minced shallot, and 1 tablespoon finely minced fresh parsley. Soften the butter to room temperature. Mash the peppercorns with the back of a spoon. Fold the shallot and parsley into the butter. Refrigerate or freeze. Bring to room temperature before using on fish or meat.

PARMIGIANO-REGGIANO CARPACCIO

The presentation of this dish is similar to carpaccio, with the taste balanced among the saltiness of the cheese, the sweetness of the olive oil, and the bite of the pepper. Using a cheese shaver, cut long, thin strips of Parmigiano-Reggiano by dragging the blade across the face of a wedge of cheese. Place the strips on a plate (plain white, if possible, so the cheese appears translucent), drizzle with olive oil, and sprinkle with lots of coarsely ground black pepper. Serve with toasted Tuscan bread on the side.

CHAPTER THIRTEEN

Southerner in Paris

In the late spring of 1979, I was coming to the end of my time in Paris, and I could feel *The Lords of Discipline* moving toward completion. I would walk the city at night paying homage to writers who had lived there before me. I paid homage to Proust at his grave in Père Lachaise Cemetery, tipping my hat to Héloïse and Abelard, and paid my dues to the excesses of my rock-and-roll generation by spending ten minutes at the grave of Jim Morrison of the Doors. I found the shop that had once housed Sylvia Beach's famous bookstore, Shakespeare & Company, where every English-speaking writer in the world seemed to have landed, but where James Joyce would come for gossip, sustenance, pocket money, and the companionship of a woman who thought he was the greatest novelist on earth. I spent a morning at Victor Hugo's house and walked past the hotel where Oscar Wilde had died and ate frequent dinners at Le Polidor, the cheap and unpretentious restaurant where every writer who passed through Paris had eaten dinner. Walking across the Luxembourg Gardens, I would stop at the doorway where Gertrude Stein and her companion, Alice B. Toklas, had kept an apartment, where Picasso and Matisse and Hemingway and Fitzgerald had come to pay homage.

Paris is a city of words and a secret city of words not written. Signs on buildings give away the names of unknown authors who once lived between those walls. You cannot take a step in Paris without walking on the footprints of a thousand artists and writers who have come before you. It excites every cell in your body; it unnerves you that you are adding your voice to the great simmering bouillon of all the writers who have come before you as the great city and time turn their blind careless eyes toward you. There, at the Deux Magots, Sartre sat with his hand on Simone de Beauvoir and his walleye lingering on an actress coming out of the powder room. Baudelaire got drunk in that tavern and Jean Cocteau ate a dozen oysters at the window of that café in the corner, and Mary McCarthy is living on the third floor of that building at this very moment. The light in her office is on.

But for me, Paris has always been the city of Ernest Hemingway since I first read *A Moveable Feast* in my sophomore year at The Citadel. That book took me over like a fever. Hemingway captured all the romance and wistfulness of both the city and the writing life. He made me want to sit in Parisian cafés, smoking Gitanes, taking notes for stories in embryo, reading *Le Monde* while sipping a café au lait and thumbing through a paperback edition of *Madame Bovary*. Now that I had done all this I was getting ready to leave Paris, and the thought of it almost killed me, because I realized I had taken a great chance by following my editor and his wife on his sabbatical year to Europe. I could feel that I had changed my whole life because of it. After reading *A Moveable Feast*, I had promised myself that I would one day live and write in Paris, and I had kept that promise and come to the city with a spirit of adventure that is rare for me. But I had written the last chapter of *The Lords of Discipline*, and my remaining time in the city was short.

From the time of my arrival, I had made pilgrimages to the places and houses, parks and apartments that Hemingway mentioned in his book. John and Susan Galassi stayed at a charming hotel across the street from where Ernest and Hadley Hemingway had rented an apartment above a sawmill at 74 rue Cardinal Lemoine. I would wander for hours amid the prodigious human traffic that made its way down the rue Mouffetard to the Place Contrescarpe, past booths overflowing with vegetables, groaning with massive white heads of cauliflower, rivers of mâche and asparagus and cabbages from the countryside. The *charcutier* with his trays of sausages and offal sang behind his counter as I passed live chickens in their boxes and the iced-down shrimp and oysters driven over from the coast. The strong smell of cheeses and the bakeries perfuming the streets with the brown aromas of croissants and pastries that made you salivate when you caught their sweet scents in the scrimmage of odors that fought for your attention as you made your way in crowds down that fine, unruly street.

I passed by the tobacconist and the man who sold horseflesh and the one who sold only artichokes and the onion lady who was just before the olive man whose whole existence centered on the presence of olives in France. I headed down the street slowly, Hemingway-besotted, as I tried to remember everything and everyone because the images of Paris would travel with me forever, wherever I went; the rue Mouffetard is carry-on luggage that will be available and on-call wherever I take pen to paper for the rest of my life.

As I write these words on Fripp Island, I realize that I am exactly Hemingway's age when he first began to write *A Moveable Feast* at the Finca Vigia in Cuba in 1957. In his prose, I can feel the tenderness he had begun to feel for the fiery, virile young man he had once been, and the regret for things he had done and said. His love for his first wife, Hadley, infuses the book, as does his pleasure in the company of his firstborn son, John, whom he nicknamed Bumby. It is one of the great books ever written about a writer's life and art. Its ardent sense of place still makes Paris seem like the most glamorous and enchanting place for a writer to be in the world.

I said goodbye to Paris slowly, and it took two weeks to pull it off. Again I went to all the places Hemingway mentions in *A Moveable Feast*. I drank a "black" wine from Cahors because he did, and I had a Rhum St. James at a café near Place St. Michel because Hemingway had done so. I lingered outside the sawmill on the night before I would leave Paris for a car trip to Rome with friends.

Then I walked to the Closerie des Lilas to have a cognac at the restaurant where Hemingway and F. Scott Fitzgerald had dined in Paris. I had stood outside the restaurant many times, committing the menu to memory, but was unable to eat there because it cost a hundred bucks a person at that time, and my budget was too strict to engage in such a guilty pleasure. But I went at dinnertime, in coat and tie, and the maitre d' led me out to a courtyard, where he seated me at a small table beneath an umbrella. I possessed a sense of completion that I have rarely felt before or since in my lifetime. The book I had written I liked very much, and it pleased me very much that the city of Paris had a hand in the writing of it. A waiter appeared and I ordered an Armagnac.

Two men entered the patio with the maitre d', and I thought I recognized one of them. The taller of the two was the familiar one; he nodded to me in passing, and I nodded back. They sat two tables away from me, but I was seated looking straight at them. The shorter one was a reporter, and he began interviewing the taller man. After they had spoken for several moments, I realized that Paris had granted me one last extraordinary gift. As I make my way around this life, I look for signs and baubles and charms and amulets and secret texts that there is a meaning and significance to human life that is under the control of some great moderating force. I like the glimpses of sorcery and fantasy that sometimes enter the human arena at the oddest, most unexpected times. At the table in front of me, I watched and listened as John Hemingway, Bumby, was interviewed by a reporter for the *International Herald Tribune*. I did not go up to introduce myself. I have always regretted that, but I was too struck by the wonder of the moment and the incomparable glory of the great city.

ROASTED WHITE ASPARAGUS WITH PARMIGIANO-REGGIANO

• SERVES 4

1³/4 pounds white asparagus (about 20 stalks)
Olive oil
Shavings of Parmigiano-Reggiano
Coarsely ground black pepper
2 Roasted Lemons (page 51)

1. Preheat the oven to 400°F.

2. Rinse and dry the asparagus. Using a vegetable peeler, peel the bottom half of each stalk.

3. Place the asparagus in a shallow roasting pan, drizzle with olive oil, and place in the oven. Roast until tender, about 20 minutes.

4. Transfer asparagus to serving plates. Top each serving with a couple of shavings of Parmigiano-Reggiano and ground black pepper. Serve a roasted lemon half alongside the asparagus.

Roasted White Asparagus with Shallot Butter While the asparagus is roasting, sauté 2 finely chopped shallots in 4 tablespoons (¹/2 stick) unsalted butter until lightly browned. Transfer the asparagus to serving plates, season with salt and pepper, and top with the shallot butter.

Roasted White Asparagus with Tasso Ham and Pecans While the asparagus is roasting, sauté ¹/4 cup finely chopped pecans in 2 tablespoons unsalted butter until browned. Stir in ¹/4 cup diced Tasso ham and cook until warmed through. Transfer the asparagus to serving plates, season with pepper, and top with pecans and ham.

• • •

SOLE EN PAPILLOTE   I once went on a parchment paper frenzy that lasted about six months. It was the showy moment of presentation when I cut open the packet and the steam rose up in all its perfumed glory that I adored. I have come across no better way to cook seafood. It is also a great way to show off and bring attention to yourself.

• **SERVES 4**

2 leeks (white parts only), cleaned and finely chopped

2 carrots, julienned

4 sole fillets (about 6 ounces each)

Olive oil

Unsalted butter

8 sprigs fresh thyme

Coarse or kosher salt and freshly ground white pepper

1. Preheat the oven to 400° F.

2. Cut four 12 X 12-inch squares of parchment paper.

3. Place an equal amount of leeks and carrots in the center of each parchment square and top with a sole fillet. Drizzle olive oil over each fillet, dot with butter (sparingly), and top with 2 sprigs thyme.

4. Bring the open ends of the parchment together over the center of the fillet and fold the paper over once (along the entire length) to seal it. Gently but firmly continue folding the paper down and crimp the ends into an airtight packet.

5. Transfer the packets to a baking sheet and brush them with olive oil.

6. Bake for 12 to 15 minutes (the paper will begin to brown and the packet will start to puff up), turning the pan once to ensure even cooking.

7. Transfer packets to serving plates, tear (or cut) open the tops and sprinkle with salt and pepper. Serve immediately, while the steam is still rising from the packets.

• • •

ROAST CHICKEN WITH GRAINY MUSTARD SAUCE   When I
lived in Paris while finishing up *The Lords of Discipline,* the nonpareil
food writer Waverley Root wrote an article saying the great French chefs
were ultimately judged by how well they roasted a chicken. The second
great test was how the chef prepared a plate of lamb's kidneys, a subject
I know much less about. In the cooking of meat, there is only one unforgivable crime, which is overcooking until a piece of meat is dry and tasteless and irredeemable. In the world of meat, dryness is taboo unless you
happen to be making beef jerky. The chicken meat here should be tender
and irresistible. The tarragon is *très* French and *très* Julia Child.

• SERVES 4

1/4 cup olive oil

4 tablespoons (1/2 stick) unsalted butter

Two 2 1/2-pound chickens (fryers or broilers)

4 shallots, peeled

4 garlic cloves, smashed

4 sprigs fresh thyme

4 sprigs fresh tarragon

1 teaspoon whole black peppercorns

1 lemon, halved

Grainy Mustard Sauce (see opposite)

1. Preheat the oven to 375°F.

2. Place the olive oil and butter in a small saucepan over moderate heat until the mixture gets foamy, about 3 minutes. Rinse
the chickens (inside and out) under cool running water and pat
dry with paper towels. Fill the cavity of each bird with half the
shallots, garlic cloves, thyme, tarragon, and peppercorns. Rub
each chicken with half a cut lemon and then put it in the cavity,
too.

3. Using a basting brush, coat the birds (on all sides and in crevices) with butter and olive oil mixture. Place in the oven and roast until skin is crisp and meat is thoroughly cooked but still juicy, 55 to 60 minutes. (An instant-read meat thermometer inserted in the thickest part of the thigh should read 165 to 170°F.) About halfway through, rotate the pan so the chickens brown on all sides.

4. Transfer the chickens to a cutting board when done, and let them rest 10 minutes before carving. To carve, use a sharp heavy knife to separate the legs and thighs and the wing portions. Then slide a knife with a thinner blade down each side of the breast bone, scooping out the breast section and leaving the skin intact. Each chicken will serve two people: overlap one leg, thigh, and wing to form a base for one side of breast meat. Top with sauce and serve.

Grainy Mustard Sauce • MAKES 1½ CUPS

> ¹/₂ cup dry Vermouth
> 1 cup Chicken Stock (page 11)
> ³/₄ cup heavy cream
> ¹/₄ cup grainy Dijon mustard
> 1 tablespoon finely chopped fresh tarragon
> 1 tablespoon finely chopped fresh thyme
> Coarse or kosher salt and freshly ground black pepper

Add the vermouth to the chicken stock and, in a large saucepan over moderately high heat, reduce the mixture by half. Place the heavy cream in a small bowl and whisk in about ¹/₄ cup of the hot stock. Slowly whisk the cream mixture back into the hot stock. Whisk in the mustard and reduce the heat, simmering until slightly thickened, 3 to 5 minutes. Add the herbs, season with salt and pepper, and ladle over the chicken.

• • •

BRAISED SHORT RIBS   My wife, Sandra, and I like to cook braised short ribs on those lamentable occasions when we are visited by the loutish and randy sons of her first marriage. I generally tell people that Sandra told me on our first date that she had never married and never had children, but that is a demonstrable lie. What she did do, with extraordinary craft and guile, was to keep her brutish sons out of sight until the marriage vows were spoken, after which the freeloading, broke hucksters made a beeline for my house. They brought the appetites of hippopotamuses with them, along with bags of filthy laundry, tattoos, and holes in every part of their anatomy for the careful placement of earrings, nose pieces, and accessories. They have the IQs of what you might expect of boys raised in Alabama. (That's a joke, Alabama and Doubleday lawyers.)

As a literary aside, I would like to note that my wife wrote her superb novel *The Sunday Wife* about her many years' experience as the wife of a minister. Her main character, the demure and pretty Dean Lynch, seems based with some accuracy on Cassandra's own life, with one glaring exception: Dean Lynch is childless, and after meeting my "sorry" stepsons (my nickname for them), I understand why better than anyone else. The boys are named Jim, Jason, and Jacob, an obvious *J* obsession running through the family. Sandra admitted to me she had already picked out the name of her fourth son if she'd had one—Jesus. Which is exactly what I would cry out when they pulled into the driveway, penniless, unshaven, with their dilapidated automobiles and their wallets full of canceled credit cards. Sandra and I fed them very well, then sent them reeling back to live out their desperate and wild lives with the sad-eyed young women who love them.

Fortunately, the "sorry" stepsons have a terrific sense of humor since they have to put up with this kind of joking on every visit. Jim, Jason, and Jacob are actually marvelous and successful young men: Jim's a doctor and neurobiologist, Jason an artist and a chef, and Jake a therapist, working toward a doctorate.   **• SERVES 4 HEARTY EATERS**

2 bottles dry red wine

2 parsnips, coarsely chopped (about 1 cup)

2 carrots, coarsely chopped (about 1 cup)

1 red onion, coarsely chopped (about 1 cup)

5 pounds beef short ribs, cut flanken or Korean style

Coarse or kosher salt and freshly ground black pepper

1 cup all-purpose flour

3 tablespoons olive oil

2 garlic cloves, finely chopped

1. In a heavy saucepan over medium heat, bring the red wine to a boil. Add the parsnips, carrots, and onion and remove from heat.

2. Place the ribs, flat side down, in a shallow baking pan (large enough to hold the ribs in one layer). When the red wine cools, pour wine and vegetables over ribs. Turn the ribs in wine and cover with aluminum foil. Marinate overnight, turning at least once.

3. To cook the ribs: Remove from the marinade, dry thoroughly with paper towels, and set aside. Strain the vegetables from the marinade, reserving both. In a small heavy saucepan over moderate heat, clarify the marinade by bringing it to a boil and skimming the surface of all impurities. Reserve.

4. Preheat the oven to 350°F. Place rack in middle of oven.

5. Sprinkle the ribs with salt and pepper and dredge in flour. In a large heavy frying pan over moderately high heat, heat 1 tablespoon of olive oil until hot but not smoking. Working in small batches, sear ribs on all sides to form a crust, about 5 minutes total. (This is a messy but necessary step that will greatly add to the flavor of the finished dish.) As the ribs brown, remove them to a large roasting pan. Add more olive oil to the pan and repeat.

6. When all the ribs are browned, add the remaining olive oil, vegetables, and garlic and cook, stirring frequently to loosen any browned bits stuck on the bottom of the pan, 2 to 3 minutes. Stir in the reserved marinade and pour the mixture over the ribs. (If there is not enough wine to come halfway up the sides of the ribs, add warm beef or chicken stock.) Cover tightly with foil. Place in oven until meat is tender and falls away from the bone, about $2^1/_2$ hours. Cool ribs to room temperature before refrigerating overnight.

7. Preheat the oven to 350°F.

8. Remove all congealed fat from surface of the ribs and marinade. Place the ribs in a roasting pan, cover with foil, and place in the oven.

9. In a small saucepan, heat the marinade. Strain and discard solids. Continue to simmer marinade until slightly thickened, 5 to 8 minutes. Keep the sauce warm.

10. When the ribs are heated through, transfer to a serving plate and top with the warm sauce.

• • •

HOT POTATO SALAD WITH VINEGAR   On the market street rue de Seine, near my hotel in Paris, during the winter months a dapper man with a beret made a version of hot potato salad with vinegar dressing. He tried to tell me what Paris was like during the war, and he still did not seem to like Germans very well. He sold cooked artichokes and mushrooms à la grecque and an onion soup that was wonderfully complex. The vinegar he used on the potatoes was homemade, the recipe handed down through generations of his family. I asked for it, but he snorted and refused and said it was a family secret. One unstated theme of this cookbook is that no one ever shares a recipe with me.   • **SERVES 4**

3 thick slices smoky bacon, coarsely chopped

2 shallots, finely chopped

1 $^1/_2$ pounds Red Bliss potatoes (as uniform and as small as possible), scrubbed but not peeled

Olive oil

Best-quality white wine vinegar

Coarse or kosher salt and freshly ground black pepper

2 tablespoons finely chopped fresh flat-leaf parsley

2 tablespoons snipped fresh chives

1. In a small skillet over moderate heat, cook the bacon until it begins to render some of its fat, 2 to 3 minutes. Add the shallots and cook until the bacon is crisp and the shallots are browned. Remove from the heat and set aside.

2. Steam the potatoes in a vegetable steamer until just tender, about 20 minutes. Drain in a colander and cut in half (or into quarters, depending on size). Place the potatoes in a large mixing bowl, drizzle with olive oil, and toss. Repeat with vinegar. The potatoes should be coated but not drenched. (There are no exact proportions of olive oil and vinegar for this salad; it all depends on how absorbent the potatoes are.)

3. Let the potatoes sit for 15 minutes to drink in the dressing. If the potatoes need more vinegar, add it now. (They will probably not need more oil.) Add the bacon and shallot mixture, then salt and pepper to taste.

4. Sprinkle the parsley and chives over the potatoes and toss gently. Serve while still warm.

• • •

CHOCOLATE CRÊPES   When I first got to Atlanta in the early seventies, there existed a trendy little restaurant called the Magic Pan, which specialized in the preparation of crêpe dishes. I even went through my own crêpe period later on in the decade, specializing for a time in a seafood crêpe that contained morsels of crab, shrimp, and scallops. Suzanne makes her crêpes with ease. I have always been one of those cooks who overwatches the batter, then worries it in the pan when it should just be cooking.   **• SERVES ABOUT 8**

3 tablespoons unsalted butter, plus additional

2 large eggs

1 tablespoon granulated sugar

Pinch of salt

1 cup whole milk

$3/4$ cup all-purpose flour

1 tablespoon hazelnut liqueur (optional)

FOR THE FILLING

$9^1/2$ to 10 ounces bittersweet chocolate (such as Scharffen Berger)

Confectioners' sugar for sprinkling

1. To prepare the crepe batter: Melt the butter in a small saucepan over low heat.

2. In a medium bowl, whisk the eggs, sugar, and salt together. Add the milk to the melted butter and pour half the milk and butter into the eggs. Sift in the flour and whisk, then add the remaining milk and butter. Whisk in the hazelnut liqueur, if using. When the mixture is smooth, cover with plastic wrap and refrigerate for 1 hour or overnight to let the gluten expand. Bring to room temperature before using.

3. To make the crêpes: Melt 1 tablespoon butter in a nonstick sauté pan over medium-high heat. Ladle about 2 tablespoons of batter into the hot sauté pan and quickly tilt the pan so the batter spreads evenly. When little bubbles appear on the surface and the edges begin to brown, about 1 minute, lift the edge of the crêpe with a spatula and flip. Cook for another 30 seconds (the second side will not brown as much as the first side).

4. Invert the sauté pan over a plate to remove the crêpe. Continue cooking the crêpes, adding more butter as needed. Stack the crêpes between paper towels or wax paper and keep warm.

5. To make the filling: In a double boiler over hot but not boiling water, melt the chocolate just until soft enough to stir. The consistency of the melted chocolate should be thick, not runny.

6. To assemble: Spread the warm crêpes with a generous tablespoon of warm chocolate. Roll, sprinkle with confectioners' sugar, and serve.

• • •

CRÈME BRÛLÉE   In the first celebrity cook-off I ever took part in, I wowed the audience with my version of the French classic dessert crème brûlée. For the uninitiated, crème brûlée simply tastes better than most other foods, and it can make you fat much faster than other foods. But it is elegant, classy, and silken and should be saved for those occasions that require a touch of grandeur. I finished second among the celebrities that night. My crème brûlée found itself overmatched by a shrimp course entered by a pretty woman named Shirley Franklin. She called her dish Shrimp Niger, and it was wonderful. Today, Shirley Franklin is the mayor of Atlanta.   **• SERVES 4 TO 6**

2^1/$_2$ cups heavy cream
1 vanilla bean
6 egg yolks
^{1}/$_2$ cup granulated sugar
^{1}/$_2$ cup packed light brown sugar

1. Position a rack in the center of the oven and preheat to 325°F.

2. Pour the heavy cream into a large saucepan and set aside. Split the vanilla bean lengthwise and scrape the seeds from inside the pod into the cream. Add the pod.

3. Over moderate heat, bring the cream and vanilla mixture to a low boil. Remove from the heat, cover, and let the mixture steep for 15 minutes. Remove the vanilla pod.

4. In a medium bowl, whisk the egg yolks and granulated sugar until pale yellow. Slowly whisk the egg mixture into the cream.

5. Pour into four to six shallow broiler-proof custard dishes. Set the dishes in a shallow roasting pan and pour boiling water into the pan to come halfway up the sides of the dishes.

6. Bake until the custard is set, about 30 minutes. (The tops will still look jiggly.)

7. Remove the dishes from roasting pan and cool on a rack to room temperature.

8. Preheat the broiler.

9. Press the brown sugar through a fine-mesh strainer onto the custards in an even layer. Wipe excess sugar from rims.

10. Broil about 5 inches from the heat source until the sugar liquefies, then starts to bubble and caramelize. This can take from 1 to 3 minutes. Rotate the pan to ensure even browning and be extremely careful not to burn the tops.

11. Remove the custard dishes and cool on a rack to room temperature. Refrigerate for at least 1 hour before serving.

CHAPTER FOURTEEN

Bridesmaids' Luncheon

When my daughter Megan called from California to let me know that she and her boyfriend were going to get married, I said that I thought it was time that I learned Terry's last name. Megan paused, then I heard her ask her fiancé: "Terry, what's your last name again?" Returning to the phone, Megan said to me, "Giguire. Yeah, that's it. Giguire."

A young woman who was always full of surprises and astonishments, Megan then told me that she wanted a traditional Southern wedding like the ones she had read about in *Southern Living* magazine. I cautioned Megan that there was not a single thing traditional about her madcap and widely traveled life, and that I had never read one article in *Southern Living* that made me conjure up the image of my pretty daughter. But she insisted that it be both Southern and traditional, and that she wanted the ceremony to take place in Beaufort, South Carolina. She had chosen Beaufort because she knew what the town meant to me, and because she had spent every summer on the beaches of Fripp Island. Also, it was her birthplace as well as one of the prettiest towns on the planet to get married in.

"I plan to be a gorgeous bride, Dad," she said. "Just want you to get used to the idea."

"You've been gorgeous since the day you were born, kid," I said.

"Were you there at my birth, Dad?" Megan asked.

"I asked to be. But it was the South. The early seventies. Dr. Keyserling called me a sick sexual pervert and banished me to the waiting room," I told her.

When Megan Elizabeth Conroy was born on November 5, 1970, the moment the masked nurse lifted her up to the window for the first inspection by the proud dad, I was floored by the outpouring of love for the newborn child that both dazzled and overwhelmed me. Love flooded through me like a great, ceaseless river that I could not control. I remember thanking God that Megan was not a boy, for I carried an irrational yet unshakable belief from my childhood that I would treat a son in the same awful way my father had treated me. I also thought, My God, Megan's got my nose. No one on earth will want to marry a girl with my nose. But I pulled myself together and studied her more closely. Megan is beautiful. I amended my thoughts. Even with my nose.

I have never met a soul who did not fall in love with Megan Conroy after being with her for five minutes. There may be such people on earth, but you would not want to know them.

In great joy, Barbara and I brought Megan home to Hancock Street on the Point, where my family and neighbors awaited our return. The dining room table overflowed with food brought by our neighbors. My mother called me aside and said I needed to have a good straight talk with Jessica and Melissa, the two daughters I had adopted after I married Barbara. Their father, West Jones, was a Marine Corps fighter pilot who was killed while giving close air support for the ground troops in Vietnam. When I adopted them, I vowed that they would never feel like second-class citizens in my house. If they did, I would not be worth a nickel as a father or a man.

"Pat, the girls are worried you won't love them as much now that Megan's been born," my mother said. "It's natural. You just need to reassure them."

I found the girls on the couch in the living room. They ran to me, and

I took them up in my arms. Jessica was coming up on five years old, and "the Woo" was two and a half.

"Peg said you two need to talk to me," I said.

The two girls looked at each other, and the Woo nodded for Jessica to speak.

"Do you like Megan more than us?" Jessica asked, up front.

"Nah," I said. "Have you seen her? She cries all the time. Poops in her britches. It's awful. I don't know how we're going to survive this one."

"But she's your real child," Jessica continued. "And me and the Woo aren't."

"No, girls. I got a piece of paper saying that you're my real kids. And I had to pay a lot of money to get those adoption papers."

"You love us that much?" the Woo asked. "More than Megan?"

"More," I said. "I love you a lot more."

"Why?" both girls asked.

"Because I've known both of you a lot longer," I said. "Megan's a pain in the butt. She can't even talk. Can you believe that? And she's so dumb, she doesn't even know I'm her daddy."

"She's just a baby," Jessica said, defending her sister's honor.

"We've got a lot of work to do," I told her. "We've got to make Megan as nice and smart as you two girls."

In truth, as I look back, I had brought Megan home to a house in great and mortal peril. A month before her birth, I had been fired from my teaching job on Daufuskie Island for "gross neglect of duty, conduct unbecoming a professional educator, AWOL, and insubordination." I had found it difficult to gain other teaching jobs with those words glistening on my résumé. In Savannah, Georgia, a deputy superintendent of education was interviewing me for a job when the phone rang. It was the superintendent who fired me getting his two bits in on my qualifications as an educator. The man hung up the phone and said, "Dr. Trammell said you were the worst teacher he's encountered in a thirty-year career in education. You're exactly the kind of teacher we don't want here in Savannah. Our kids deserve better than you."

In the first six months of Megan's life, I would be writing *The Water Is Wide*, shivering with rage at the injustice of my firing. At the time we brought our first child into our home, I had endangered my family, destroyed my reputation, and stumbled awkwardly into my life's work. I began writing sentences that had some weight and gravitas and could stand on their own like beaten egg whites. Something in Megan's birth brought a roundedness and contentment I had never felt. I remember lofting a prayer that she grow into proud womanhood and not inherit a single one of my itchy, disharmonious traits. Naturally, because of the way the world works, Megan grew into the loveliest of women, but she's so much like me that my sarcastic tribe of brothers and sisters have labeled poor Megan "Pat with boobs."

Whenever I pull *The Water Is Wide* from the shelf and read the jumpy sentences of the iridescent, wet-behind-the-ears kid I was back then, to me the book still feels Megan-shaped, even Megan-induced. I was trying to force myself into a career that could support a comely child, her mother, and her frisky sisters. Bearing down, I completed the book in three months, and Megan's infant cries were the background music of that book. I had produced a "Beaufort girl" with my first daughter, the first Conroy ever to be a native of this small town I had thrown my arms around as a fifteen-year-old boy.

Like all children, Megan was a baby, then suddenly I blinked my eyes, and she had transformed herself into a toddler wearing tiger pajamas. While I planted a camellia bush in the side yard, turned around, Megan was walking into first grade. I bought a new fountain pen to write *The Great Santini*, and then watched as Megan blew out ten candles on her birthday cake. Time began to speed up, and I heard something behind me—Megan was walking across the high school stage to receive her diploma from Paul Bianchi. A letter came from Barbra Streisand that she wanted to make a movie of *The Prince of Tides;* a phone rang in the background, and it was Megan telling me she had fallen in love with a boy named Terry Giguire. I spun around in the new terror of aging, wondering who had stolen my life from me and where they had taken it. I looked in the mirror and saw a fifty-four-year-old stranger staring back at me.

In 1995, the year that *Beach Music* came out, I was in a bookstore signing stock with the help of a handsome, cheerful young man who was asking me questions about how I went about turning myself into a writer. I gave him the usual thumbnail sketch about my career, then asked him where he was from.

"Boulder, Colorado," he said.

"No kidding? My daughter went to the University of Colorado," I told him, as he passed me copy after copy of *Beach Music*.

"What was her name? It's a huge place, but maybe I ran into her," he said.

"Her name is Megan Conroy," I said, and the young man gasped aloud as he stepped back from me.

"Hey, pal?" I asked. "Why are you gasping when you hear my daughter's name spoken aloud?"

"Mr. Conroy," he said in total admiration, "your daughter Megan was the biggest party animal in the history of the University of Colorado."

"Thanks, kid. I think," I said, then asked him: "Wasn't the University of Colorado voted the best party school in America by *Playboy* magazine?"

The kid lit up again and said, "Yes, sir. Four years in a row. The same four years that Megan Conroy was there."

That night I called Megan and told her the story.

"Who was that guy, Dad?" she asked. "What was his name?"

"I forget his name, but I'll never forget his story," I said. "What exactly does it mean, Megan?"

"It means, Dad," Megan said without a trace of defensiveness, "that I love to have a good time . . . just like my daddy."

To his everlasting credit, my son-in-law, Terry Giguire, tells my family that he loves that story more than any I tell about my legendary daughter.

The problem with giving Megan an old-fashioned Southern wedding was that Barbara and I did not raise Megan to be an old-fashioned Southern girl. We raised all our girls to be bright, sassy, liberated, and the life of every party they walked into, anywhere in the world. But if my girl wants something, I can do Southern with the best of them. I called my cooking partner, Suzanne Pollak, and told her about Megan's wedding plans. With the extraordinary generosity of spirit that marks her every waking hour, Suzanne offered the use of her house and gardens. She lives in a matchless Southern house with a garden that smells like the inside of a perfume bottle in the spring. My sister Kathy Harvey put in a call to Butch Polk, one of the best football players ever to come out of Beaufort High School, and he promised to put on a Southern barbecue that Terry's California family would talk about the rest of their lives. For the reception, we hired the great Beaufort caterer Steve Brown to fix Southern dishes like crab cakes and shrimp gumbo and dozens of others. Megan bought a wedding dress that had a classic Southern look, and set her father back—let's see—I don't quite remember the price and have been criticized in my life for my powers of exaggeration, so let me be conservative about the actual cost, but it was somewhere near a billion dollars or so. All the engines of small-town Beaufort life were set into motion to give my daughter Megan the traditional Southern wedding she desired.

On the day of her wedding, the bridesmaids and friends arrived in sets. First came Molly Malloy, Bebe Allen, Erin Bradley, and Anna Kramer, all of whom had gone to school with Megan at Paideia School in Atlanta, the last place in America to send a girl to be taught as a traditional Southern girl. The next group was composed of her college friends from Colorado: Julie Lindsay, Katie Gjorolina, Kristin Pierce, Alex DeNeva, and Jenny Hatifield, the radiant young women who had collaborated in Megan's noble quest to be "the biggest party animal in the history of the University of Colorado." Yet another group was made up of family, the sisters of the bride and groom. The prettiest women in the state of South Carolina had gathered under my roof to honor my daughter, and I was moved by the sight of such beauty and freshness and devotion to her. My gift to Megan was that I would prepare the traditional bridesmaids' lunch.

I had selected the menu with the help of both my wife, Sandra, and my cookbook partner, Suzanne. It was tomato season in Beaufort, and there is nothing in the world that tastes as good as a Beaufort tomato picked fresh from Dempsey's Farm on Highway 21. I sliced up a platter full and spread them like a deck of cards, then anointed them with a splash of extra virgin olive oil from Lucca. (Ever tasted Southern olive oil?) Then I threw a handful of basil from our garden over it. I fixed a chilled cucumber soup with fresh dill, then made a squash casserole and a salad with a dressing I had first tasted in a Charleston mansion. The main course was a swordfish salad that I had eaten at Suzanne's house at a dinner party the year before, and I shamelessly stole Suzanne's recipe. The dessert was the part of the meal that meant the most to me. I made Sandra's mother's famous pound cake to honor a woman who had died five years before Sandra and I met. In honor of Pat King, I used her recipe and made a cake that will help her memory live on and that validated her fame as a nonpareil Southern cook. I served the pound cake with fresh peaches and whipped cream, and it was sublime. My daughter rose and toasted me for preparing the finest bridesmaids' lunch any of them had ever tasted. She said it was the only one ever fixed by the father of the bride that they knew of, and I bowed deeply from the kitchen.

The weather turned cool for June, and Megan's wedding was out of a storybook. She and Terry exchanged vows that are ancient and important and moving every time I hear them (or take them). But there is one metaphor of that weekend that I hold dear and priceless. It makes me laugh every time I see it. When the photographs of the traditional Southern wedding came back, I looked at the first photograph and thought, This is what my entire life has been like. This photograph could tell everything about the chaos and dissonance and breakdown of all order and serenity or fealty to custom in my squirrelly life. In the photograph is my handsome son-in-law, Terry, in his tuxedo. His arm is behind Megan, the beautiful bride, looking ravishing in her billion-dollar wedding dress. But what makes this photograph Conroyesque in the extreme is the presence of the sweet-faced Molly Jean Giguire, my one-year-old granddaughter, who is riding on her mother's hip, barefooted and enjoying every single moment of her mother's traditional Southern wedding.

CUCUMBER SOUP   The ripening of the tomato and cucumber fields is one of the clearest augurs of summer's arrival in Beaufort. I like to make cucumber soup with Beaufort cucumbers because it gives me the false sensation of a deep connection with the Low Country. Since most of you will have no access to Beaufort cucumbers, we include the hothouse variety in the recipe. There are many variations of this recipe, most of them delicious.

In Mobile, Alabama, Eugene Walter once fixed me his version, which included fresh-picked strawberries, a combination that sounded revolting to me. But it was cool and refreshing, and even exciting, as he said it would be. I've made this soup with buttermilk, whole milk, skim milk, and heavy cream. The fresh dill is the essential ingredient.

In New York City, I once ordered cucumber soup at the restaurant of the impeccable chef Daniel Boulud. He garnished it with smoked fresh trout, quail eggs (I think), and tomatoes, but he almost ruined it with the subtle addition of cilantro, Satan's own herb. I do not know why I react so strongly to cilantro (which often travels under the equally unsavory alias of coriander), but its addition made it seem as though Monsieur Boulud had thrown a bar of soap into his soup. My aversion to cilantro is so well established that I had a wonderful visit to Bangkok having learned to say only these three words: "No *pai chi.*"

• SERVES 6 AS A FIRST COURSE

3 seedless cucumbers

1 small jalapeño chile, halved, seeded, and chopped

2 shallots, coarsely chopped

1/4 cup plain yogurt (not nonfat)

1/2 teaspoon coarse or kosher salt, or to taste

Finely chopped fresh dill

Sour cream

1. Peel and halve the cucumbers lengthwise. Use the tip of a teaspoon to scoop out the seeds. (This variety typically has very few.)

Cut the cucumbers into small pieces and place in the bowl of a food processor fitted with a metal blade.

2. Add the jalapeño and shallots and process until the mixture is as smooth as possible, about 2 minutes. Pour the mixture into a bowl and stir in the yogurt. Add the salt (you may need more than $^1/_2$ teaspoon).

3. Pour into a storage container and chill in the refrigerator for up to 2 hours. Chill six serving bowls.

4. Ladle the cold soup into chilled bowls and sprinkle with dill. Garnish each serving with a small dollop of sour cream.

• • •

SWORDFISH SALAD   Swordfish salad is an elegant, forgiving recipe that can be made ahead of time. It is easy, and there are only three indispensable rules for success: don't overcook the pasta, don't overcook the swordfish, and don't burn the pine nuts. I chose it for the bridesmaids' lunch because I was frankly overwhelmed by all the details of Megan's wedding.

I hired my old friend Butch Polk to put on an old-fashioned outdoor barbecue the night before the bridesmaids' luncheon. Since the groom, Terry Giguire, and his family came from California, I thought they deserved a taste of the Old South. In the middle of the barbecue, a ten-foot alligator, who lives in the lagoon behind our place, made his evening run past our house. To this day the Californians think I hired that alligator for the pure shock value it gave to my new West Coast relatives.

• SERVES 6

1 pound spaghetti

1 $^1/_2$ pounds swordfish steaks ($^3/_4$ to 1 inch thick)

$^1/_2$ cup fresh lemon juice (about 2 lemons)

$^1/_4$ cup olive oil

1 cup pitted and sliced green olives

$^1/_2$ cup toasted pine nuts

Herb mayonnaise*
Coarse or kosher salt and freshly ground black pepper
Fresh marjoram and tarragon sprigs

To prepare an herb mayonnaise, flavor 1 cup Homemade Mayonnaise (page 57) with 2 tablespoons chopped capers and 1 tablespoon each finely chopped fresh parsley and tarragon. If fresh tarragon is not available, do not substitute dried tarragon. Use whatever fresh herb you can find, such as basil in the summer or thyme in the winter.

1. Preheat the broiler.

2. Cook the pasta according to package directions until al dente. Drain in a colander, but do not rinse.

3. Brush the swordfish steaks lightly with lemon juice (use only half the amount) and broil about 6 inches from heat source until lightly browned, turning once, a total of 6 to 8 minutes. (The second side always takes less time than the first.)

4. Cool the fish to room temperature and cut into bite-size pieces.

5. Transfer the drained spaghetti to a large mixing bowl and toss with the remaining lemon juice (at least $1/4$ cup) and the olive oil. Gently fold in the fish, olives, and pine nuts.

6. Add the mayonnaise sparingly and toss until salad is covered but not drenched with dressing.

7. Refrigerate until the flavors marry, about 2 hours.

8. Season the salad with salt and pepper to taste, transfer to a serving platter, and garnish with herb sprigs.

• • •

SQUASH CASSEROLE I have been looking for an opening to praise fresh mozzarella, as opposed to that tasteless, hardened glop we Americans have used to ruin perfectly good pizzas. With this single squash casserole, which is a breeze to make, I seize my opportunity.

The Ruggieri brothers' shop on the Campo de' Fiori was my favorite place to buy food in Rome. It was the youngest of the brothers who introduced me to mozzarella di bufala, made from the delicious milk of water buffalo that graze the pastures of Campania. The cheese was silken and bone white and freshly made. I had never seen cheese that came packed in water, but this cheese is perishable and needs to be eaten soon after it is made. It is a sweet, delicate cheese with a slight tartness in the aftertaste. I have found it in gourmet cheese shops in New York and California, and American cheesemakers are making gallant attempts to make a fresh mozzarella of their own. If you are ever in Italy, order a Caprese salad: slices of mozzarella di bufala, fresh ruby-red tomatoes, julienned basil leaves—all anointed with extra virgin olive oil. You will not eat a better meal in your life. **• SERVES 6**

1 large red onion, chopped

1 garlic clove, minced

$1/4$ cup diced country ham

$1 1/2$ pounds zucchini

$1/2$ pound fresh mozzarella (or mozzarella di bufala), cubed

$1/2$ teaspoon red pepper flakes

1 to 2 teaspoons chopped fresh rosemary or thyme

$1/2$ cup homemade fresh or dry bread crumbs

1. Preheat the oven to 350°F.

2. In a nonstick medium sauté pan over medium heat, sauté the onion and garlic until wilted and lightly browned. Stir in the ham and cook briefly, about 2 minutes.

3. While onion is sautéing, clean and trim the zucchini and cut into $1/4$-inch pieces. Transfer zucchini to a mixing bowl. Add the mozzarella, red pepper flakes, and rosemary. Stir in the warm onion and ham mixture.

4. Transfer the vegetable mixture to a casserole and sprinkle the bread crumbs on top.

5. Bake until the bread crumbs are browned and the casserole is bubbling slightly around the edges, 45 to 50 minutes. Serve hot.

• • •

SANDRA'S MAMA'S POUND CAKE I have lived a life of many regrets, things I've said that I shouldn't have said, things I have written that caused grief to people I loved, women I should have married, women I shouldn't have married, friends I should have pursued, and friends whose aura was so dangerous I should have sprinted away from them after our first handshake. But I ache when I realize that my current wife's mother, Pat King, died a full five years before I fell in love with her daughter. I hear the stories whenever the rowdy King tribe gathers at the peanut farm in Pinckard, Alabama, where Sandra's father, Elton (Tony), still lives and prospers and fishes every day of his life for bass and catfish.

Pat King was a legendary Southern cook and, to hear her three daughters tell it, a package of kinetic movement who could do everything well except sit still. Her grandsons talk about her Christmas and Easter feasts as if James Beard and Alice Waters had flown into Pinckard to cook them. While at the farm, sadly exiled among Alabama football fanatics, all of whom look and act like extras in the film version of James Dickey's *Deliverance*, I enjoy the endless discussions of Pat King's wizardry in the kitchen. Sandra herself is a marvelous cook, but even she agrees that she could not hold a frying pan to her mother's natural gifts. I've met no one in Alabama who says they ever met a finer cook than the sweet-faced Pat King.

So, in honor of my daughter Megan, and in honor of my beloved wife, I made Pat King's famous pound cake to cap off the bridesmaids' luncheon with a bang. There is one secret that I carry around with me about Pat King: she might have been a superb cook, but she was much better at raising daughters.

3/4 pound (3 sticks) butter, softened
3 cups sugar

8 large eggs, at room temperature

1 teaspoon vanilla extract

3 cups cake flour, sifted twice

Sliced fresh peaches

Whipped cream

1. In preparation, turn a large tube pan upside down; place a piece of wax paper over the bottom and trace the outline. Cut the paper to fit, including a hole for the center tube, then invert the pan and put the wax paper in the bottom. Lightly grease the paper as well as the sides and the center tube of the pan with pure vegetable oil, then dust with flour, shaking out the excess. This method will ensure that the cake can be removed without falling apart. Preheat the oven to 325°F.

2. With an electric mixer on medium speed, beat the butter and sugar until light and fluffy. Add the eggs one at a time, beating well after each, then stir in the vanilla. With a spatula, stir in the flour until thoroughly mixed into the batter, but do not beat, which will cause the cake to be tough. Spoon the batter into the prepared pan, smoothing the top lightly with a spatula so cake will bake evenly.

3. Bake for 1 hour, then check appearance, since ovens vary. Normally it takes $1\frac{1}{4}$ hours. (My mama checked for doneness with one of the clean, slender broom straws she kept for this task; lacking this, a toothpick or bamboo skewer will do.) Let cake rest in the pan on a rack for 10 minutes. To remove the cake from the pan, place a rack over the top, invert, and carefully lift the pan off the cake. Do not shake or force the cake out. If it does not immediately loosen, turn it back over and let it cool for another 5 minutes before trying again. Let cool thoroughly on a rack before slicing, if you can stand to wait. This makes a large and showy, picture-perfect cake.

4. Serve thin slices (it's very rich) with sliced peaches and whipped cream.

CHAPTER FIFTEEN

Why Dying Down South Is More Fun

Southern grief at a funeral of a loved one often gets mollified by the scrumptious feast that follows the ceremony. In the South, you often eat as well after the burial of a family member or friend as you do on Thanksgiving Day or Christmas. It is the custom of the place for friends to bring a dish of delicious food to the home of the deceased—it is one of the binding social covenants that still survive in even the most estranged and disconnected enclaves of the South.

Cooking food for a grieving family and their friends is still one of the classiest ways to send a love note that I can think of. I still get teary-eyed and grateful when I think of the sheer amount and quality of the food that the people of Beaufort and Fripp Island, South Carolina, sent to my house after the deaths of my mother and father. Such generous responses tie you to some places of the earth forever. My family was overwhelmed by the kindness of the neighbors who had loved our parents. They cared for us, fed us wonderfully well, comforted us, and eased the grief of our parents' passing with astonishing grace.

When I lived in Atlanta during the seventies and eighties I developed a signature dish I would deliver to the houses of friends or loved ones on the night before a funeral. I would fix a half-gallon jar of pickled shrimp from a recipe I had brought from the Low Country for special occasions. I missed the Low Country the whole time I lived in Atlanta, and the taste of pickled shrimp was a sure way for me to engage in time travel without leaving the city limits.

When Olive Ann Burns's husband, Andy Sparks, died after a long illness, I brought over the jar full of pickled shrimp, and the author of *Cold Sassy Tree* made me give her the recipe before I left her house that night. I happened to know that Olive Ann had adored her husband and was brokenhearted at his death, but talking about food at a funeral is one of the ways we start to heal ourselves. When the novelist Paul Darcy Boles died a few years earlier, I made the pickled shrimp at the same time I worked on his eulogy. Pickled shrimp is my answer to death in Georgia. In South Carolina, I generally respond with a shy and unexpected gift of Dunbar Macaroni, the only dish in my repertoire whose origins spring from the singular and comely borders of Newberry, South Carolina. I have never tasted or seen a recipe for Dunbar Macaroni outside of Newberry. It is indigenous to the town and part of its history.

In 1962, I was playing the first baseball game of the season with Beaufort High School. The boy who sat next to me in Gene Norris's English class was Randy Randel, the son of the school superintendent. Randy was a superb athlete and a delight in the classroom: mouthy, irreverent, and extroverted.

Mr. Norris would get exasperated with Randy and say, "Sit down in your seat, Randy, you fool. And hush your mouth, boy."

"Norris," Randy would say sadly, "don't forget who my father is, Norris. Your job's hanging by a thread, Gene. One word from me and you're in the unemployment line."

"Don't you dare call me Gene, you little scalawag," Mr. Norris would say. "How dare you threaten me with my job."

"No threat, Gene," Randy would say, grinning at the class. "I'm talking fact here, son."

Randy had asked me to go golfing with him on Easter weekend when his parents were returning to his grandmother's house in Newberry.

Since I was a military brat, I had never gone to anyone's house for a whole weekend in my life. My high school years had been excruciatingly lonely ones. My mother was thrilled that Randy had extended this invitation and gave me permission to go immediately.

Randy was six feet four inches tall and fifteen years old, and he was the best pitcher we had on the team that year. But our coach started Jimmy Melvin, a lanky junior who was hit hard by the visiting Wade Hampton team in the first inning. (Jimmy Melvin's name is now enshrined on the wall of black marble honoring the Vietnam veterans killed in action during that long, dispiriting war.) The coach replaced Jimmy with Bruce Harper, who had a fastball I was afraid of, but Bruce was wild that afternoon. Soon the coach had Randy warming up in what passed for a bullpen at Beaufort High School. (Bruce Harper would walk out of the history of that game and into the history of his time—he would serve with distinction as one of John Ehrlichman's lawyers during the Watergate trials.)

Then it was Randy Randel's time, and he was called on to shut down the Wade Hampton Generals. Already there was talk about Randy pitching in the major leagues one day. He set out to prove that there was substance to this talk. He struck out five of the first seven batters he faced, and the other two batters did not even get the ball out of the infield. Randy Randel had not allowed a hit when he fell to the ground after striking out his fifth batter. When the ambulance finally arrived and a girl named Pat Everette gave Randy mouth-to-mouth resuscitation until Dr. Herbert Keyserling moved her aside and injected a shot of pure adrenaline into his heart, every witness to Randy Randel's fall to the earth had been changed and changed for all time. The doctor said that Randy had been dead when he hit the ground.

In Eugene Norris's English class the next day, Randy's empty seat exuded a devastating sense of displacement and loss. His seat's emptiness filled the room. The whole world seemed misplaced and ill-fitting. My class and I were in a state of shock when Gene Norris walked into the room, cleaning his glasses with his tie.

"I was just thinking about grief and how we express it. Or how we don't. Boys seem to have the toughest time showing how much they hurt, but the boys in here shouldn't. Not in this room. Not among those who loved Randy with you."

The room came apart, and I cracked like an egg. I wept for two days and could do nothing to stop myself. I wrote my first poem about Randy's death and gave it to his mother and father after the funeral. Nor did I have to call off my trip to Newberry because Randy was buried in Newberry with his mother's people in the Rosemont Cemetery. I rode to Newberry with Gene Norris and stayed in his Uncle John and Aunt Elizabeth's house, where I fell in love with Gene's pretty cousin Liz, or "Cuz" as he called her.

I did not know then that love and death could find each other at the same dance. Liz was a fetching and uncommonly lovely freshman at Columbia College, and I was smitten the moment she walked into the room. She walked with a dreamy, sophisticated air that made the high school boys who encountered her unsteady in our loafers.

On the way to Randy's burial service, I asked Mr. Norris, "Does Liz ever date high school boys, Mr. Norris?"

"Of course not," Gene said, dismissing the possibility out of hand. "She wouldn't be caught dead with a high school Harry like you. Liz only dates the cream of the crop of the college boys. From the very best fraternities. Her boyfriend's going to be a doctor. Yes, sir, a doctor."

"If she ever breaks up with her doctor friend, I'd sure be interested, Mr. Norris."

"Of course, you'd be interested, boy," he said. "But she's got big plans with Clemson men and leaders of fraternities. She left you high school Harrys back in the playgrounds a long time ago. Now, quit mooning over my cousin and start thinking about Randy."

When I got to Randy's grandmother's house, I could smell the food all the way up the hill on Main Street where we parked the car. His grandmother, Mrs. Smith, who would soon become Mamaw to me, introduced me to Dunbar Macaroni. She gave me the history, lore, and legend of the dish as she served me a large portion.

"No one knows who Mr. Dunbar was. But we are absolutely sure he was a Newberrian. This dish is native to this town. You'll never find another single soul eating this anywhere. But it's delicious. Though there are two or three versions of the dish, I'm letting you eat mine. I made it the classic way. No frills or fuss."

I knew so little about food and the way it was prepared that all I remember about her Dunbar Macaroni was that she watched me closely as I ate her concoction of cheese and macaroni and onions. It was my first South Carolina funeral, and everything about that day remains bright, vivid, and profoundly sad. Though I had never felt sadder, I had never eaten better in my whole life. There was something scandalous to me about combining mourning Randy with the exquisite pleasures of a Newberry table.

I did not eat Dunbar Macaroni again for thirty years. I was in the middle of finishing the novel *Beach Music* when I got a call from Gene Norris, late at night. He could hardly speak as he told me that his cousin Liz, the one who had infatuated me as a boy, had died in her sleep at the age of forty-nine. Liz had followed her plan with immaculate precision and married that Clemson fraternity man, who then set about to become a doctor. They had lived out their lives as important citizens of Newberry, raised two children, attended the Lutheran church, and had some fine years before it began to go wrong with them. Their divorce was almost final when she was found dead in her bed. Sadness had attached itself to her final years, and Gene would periodically ask me to call Liz to cheer her up when things were really bad. I tried to get Liz to come to a screening of *The Prince of Tides* in New York with Gene, but her lawyer said it could be used against her in court. I sent her a bottle of champagne that Barbra Streisand had sent to my hotel room after that screening. Liz called me to tell me she and several of her girlfriends had made an elaborate ceremony out of drinking that champagne. The note I had written to Liz when I sent her the champagne was hanging by a magnet on her refrigerator door when I gathered with her family after her burial.

I was reading my note to Liz when one of her friends tapped me on the shoulder and said, handing me a plate, "You've got to eat this. It's a Newberry County specialty. We call it Dunbar Macaroni."

I had never seen Liz Norris after that day of Randy's funeral. We would speak on the phone, but our paths never crossed again. As I ate Dunbar Macaroni for the second time in my life, I said a prayer for Liz, and thought how strange it was that her high school Harry had finally caught up with her when it was far too late for either one of us.

PICKLED SHRIMP   When a good friend dies, I take two pounds of shrimp for the mourners. When a great friend dies, I go to five pounds. When I die, I fully expect all the shrimp in Beaufort to be pickled that day.

• SERVES 6 TO 8

1 cup thinly sliced yellow onion

4 bay leaves, crushed

One 2-ounce bottle capers, drained and coarsely chopped

$1/4$ cup fresh lemon juice

1 cup cider vinegar

$1/2$ cup olive oil

1 teaspoon minced fresh garlic

1 teaspoon coarse or kosher salt

1 teaspoon celery seeds

1 teaspoon red pepper flakes

2 pounds large (21–25 count) shrimp, peeled and deveined

1. Mix all the ingredients except the shrimp in a large heatproof glass or ceramic bowl.

2. In a medium stockpot over high heat, bring 4 quarts abundantly salted water to a rolling boil. Add the shrimp and cook until just pink, about 2 minutes. (The shrimp will continue to "cook" in the marinade.) Drain and immediately transfer to the marinade.

3. Bring to room temperature, cover tightly, and marinate overnight in the refrigerator. Transfer shrimp and marinade to a glass serving compote or bowl. Serve chilled.

• • •

CHEDDAR CHEESE COINS   Cheddar cheese coins are the popular old Southern standbys cheese straws, but our recipe majored in economics. They are mouthwateringly good and a welcome addition to any Southern table at any time of the year.   **• MAKES 72**

> 8 ounces extra-sharp orange cheddar cheese, grated (2 cups)
>
> 12 tablespoons (1 $\frac{1}{2}$ sticks) unsalted butter, chilled but not hard
>
> $\frac{1}{2}$ teaspoon cayenne pepper
>
> $\frac{1}{4}$ teaspoon freshly ground black pepper
>
> 2 cups unbleached all-purpose flour

1. Preheat the oven to 375°F.

2. In the bowl of a standing mixer, cream the cheese and butter until well combined. Mix the cayenne and black pepper into the flour. Add the flour mixture slowly to the bowl, stopping to scrape down the sides, until the mixture forms a ball.

3. Lightly flour a dry work surface and roll out the dough until $\frac{1}{4}$ inch thick. Using a 1$\frac{1}{2}$-inch straight-sided biscuit cutter, make the coins and transfer them to ungreased baking sheets. Reroll the scraps as needed.

4. Prick the top of each coin several times with the tines of a fork and bake until golden brown, about 15 minutes. Cool on a rack before serving.

• • •

FRESH HAM   It is worth all the trouble in the world to fix a fresh ham. It is worth all the trouble in the world to fix fresh anything. I cannot think of ham without thinking of Southern funerals, and I do not believe I have ever eaten lunch after a funeral in the South without at least one ham there to feed the multitudes.

• SERVES A CROWD (AT LEAST 12 TO 14) WITH LEFTOVERS

1 large garlic head, cloves separated and finely chopped (about 5 tablespoons)

2 tablespoons dried thyme

2 tablespoons coarse or kosher salt

2 tablespoons freshly ground black pepper

One 16-pound fresh ham, skin on

1. Mix the garlic, thyme, salt, and pepper together in a bowl.

2. Place the ham in a large heavy roasting pan.

3. Cut 2-inch-long slashes in both sides of the ham and poke dozens of holes in it as well. Rub the salt mixture into the holes and over the outside of the ham. Let the ham absorb the seasoning for 1 hour at room temperature.

4. Preheat the oven to 450°F.

5. Roast the ham for 20 minutes at 450°F, then turn the oven down to 325°F. Cook for an additional $3\frac{1}{2}$ hours, until the internal temperature in the thickest part of the ham is 150°F and the skin is a burnished-mahogany color. The skin will crisp to tasty cracklings.

6. Transfer the ham to a large platter, cover with aluminum foil, and let rest for 20 minutes so the juices will redistribute.

7. To carve, remove the skin and cut into strips for cracklings. Carve the ham into thin slices and serve.

• • •

DUNBAR MACARONI Dunbar Macaroni belongs to the town and history of Newberry, South Carolina. This is Julia Randel's own personal recipe that she inherited from her mother, Mrs. Smith. I have seen several recipes that add ground beef or pork, but Julia insists that Dunbar Macaroni was meatless in its original, purest of forms. • **SERVES 8 TO 10**

1 1/2 cups elbow macaroni

4 onions, chopped

Two 16-ounce cans whole tomatoes, preferably San Marzano,
    mashed, without their juice

3/4 pound sharp cheddar cheese, grated

4 tablespoons (1/2 stick) butter

Salt and freshly ground black pepper

1. Preheat the oven to 350°F.

2. Cook the macaroni. Drain and set aside.

3. Cook the onions in 3 cups boiling water for 5 minutes. Drain. Add the tomatoes and cook over low heat for 10 minutes, until liquid has evaporated. Add the cooked macaroni, cheese, butter, salt and pepper. Mix together and pour into a large greased casserole dish.

4. Bake for 30 minutes, or until lightly browned. Serve hot.

• • •

COUNTRY HAM WITH BOURBON GLAZE

Now that I am older, I have eaten far too many slices of good country ham on biscuits in my lifetime at funerals too numerous to count. But this is the best recipe I know for anyone nervous around hams. Down here, when Southerners die, the pigs grow nervous.

• SERVES A CROWD (AT LEAST 12 TO 14) WITH LEFTOVERS

One 12- to 14-pound bone-in cured ham

1/2 cup apple juice

1 teaspoon ground cloves

FOR THE GLAZE

1/2 cup best-quality maple syrup

1/4 cup bourbon

1/2 cup plus 1/4 cup apple juice

1. Unwrap the ham and let it come to room temperature, at least 2 hours. This helps the ham absorb the liquid used in cooking, making the meat more flavorful.

2. Preheat the oven to 325°F.

3. Pull away most of the rind (in many cases, this has already been done) of the ham and trim the excess fat to an even $\frac{1}{4}$ or $\frac{1}{2}$ inch. Using a sharp knife, score the fat lightly in diagonal lines to create a diamond pattern. Put the prepared ham, fat side up, in a sturdy, shallow baking pan and place in the oven. Mix the apple juice and ground cloves with 1 cup water and pour into the pan. Bake for $1\frac{1}{2}$ hours.

4. To make the glaze: In a medium bowl, combine the maple syrup, bourbon, and $\frac{1}{4}$ cup apple juice.

5. Without removing the pan from the oven (just pull out the rack, provided it is sturdy enough), pour the glaze over the top of the ham. Add the remaining $\frac{1}{2}$ cup apple juice to the pan and continue cooking for another 45 minutes, basting frequently. (You are looking for about 140°F on an instant-read meat thermometer.) Remove the pan from the oven and allow the ham to cool on a rack before carving and serving.

• • •

BISCUITS

• MAKES 12

2 cups self-rising flour (preferably White Lily)

$\frac{1}{2}$ teaspoon salt

3 teaspoons baking powder

$\frac{1}{2}$ teaspoon baking soda

5 tablespoons cold unsalted butter, cut into 5 pieces

1 scant cup buttermilk

1. Preheat the oven to 450° F. Place rack in middle of oven.

2. In a large bowl, sift together the flour, salt, baking powder, and baking soda. Add the cold butter pieces to the flour and cut in with two knives (or rub butter into flour with your fingers). When the mixture resembles coarse crumbs the size of peas, pour almost all of the buttermilk in and stir with a wooden spoon just until dough forms one piece. If the dough doesn't come together, add the remaining buttermilk.

3. Turn the dough out onto a dry, lightly floured work surface. Using a wooden rolling pin, roll into a rectangle about $^1/_2$ inch thick. Use a biscuit cutter or the open end of a glass to cut rounds of dough.

4. Place the biscuits on an ungreased cookie sheet. The scraps of dough can be gathered and rolled again one more time. If not baking the biscuits immediately, cover them with plastic wrap and refrigerate for 2 to 3 hours.

5. Bake for 12 to 14 minutes or until lightly browned on top. Serve hot.

• • •

GRITS CASSEROLE   This is the best grits casserole I have ever eaten. Grits provide an empty canvas for all kinds of experimentation. I have cooked the casserole using different kinds of cheese, thrown in a nugget of garlic or a ragout of wild mushrooms. Grits is a food that forgives almost any kind of messing around or tomfoolery by a cook. The best grits I have ever tasted come from Anson Mills out of Columbia, South Carolina. Of course, they are stone-ground.   **• SERVES 6**

> $^1/_2$ teaspoon coarse or kosher salt
> 1 cup slow-cooking stone-ground grits
> $^1/_2$ pound andouille sausage, chopped
> $2^1/_2$ cups grated sharp cheddar cheese
> 3 large eggs, beaten

¼ cup heavy cream

Tabasco sauce

Coarse or kosher salt and freshly ground black pepper

1. In a large saucepan over high heat, bring 4 cups water to a boil. Add the salt and slowly pour in the grits. Reduce the heat and cook, stirring occasionally, until grits are done, about 40 minutes.

2. Preheat the oven to 350°F.

3. In a small saucepan, sauté the sausage until it is slightly crispy, 8 to 10 minutes. Set aside.

4. Remove grits from the stove and add the cheese, stirring until smooth. Beat in the eggs and cream. Add the sausage and season to taste with Tabasco and salt and pepper.

5. Pour the grits into a 2-quart soufflé dish and bake until they are set and lightly browned on top, about 40 minutes. Serve hot.

• • •

CURRIED POACHED FRUIT

• SERVES 8 TO 12

1 lemon

One 2-inch piece ginger, peeled and sliced

½ cup granulated sugar

4 pears, peeled, cored, and thickly sliced

4 peaches or apples (depending on the season)*

1 cup pineapple, cut into ½-inch pieces

1 cup cherries, pitted, or ½ cup dried cherries

4 apricots, pitted and quartered, or ½ cup dried apricots

1 cup seedless green grapes

6 tablespoons unsalted butter

½ cup dark brown sugar

1 tablespoon curry powder

Dried fruit also can be substituted for fresh. If using fresh peaches, blanch the peaches in boiling water for 15 seconds. Peel and halve the peaches, remove the pits, and thickly slice. If using fresh apples, peel, core, and thickly slice.

1. Using a vegetable peeler, cut strips of zest from the lemon (not including the white pith). Squeeze juice for the poaching liquid.

2. Make the poaching liquid by combining the lemon peel and juice, ginger, 4 cups water, and the sugar in a large saucepan. Bring to a boil, then reduce the heat and simmer, covered, for 15 minutes.

3. Place the fruit in poaching liquid. If the liquid does not cover the fruit, gently push the fruit down to submerge it. Return the mixture to a boil, reduce heat, and simmer until the tip of a sharp knife can easily pierce the fruit, 5 to 10 minutes. (Since cooking time varies with the ripeness of the fruit, test frequently.)

4. Drain the fruit in a colander. Discard poaching liquid.

5. Preheat the oven to 300°F.

6. In a large skillet, melt the butter. Stir in the brown sugar and curry powder. Carefully fold in the fruit (so as not to mash it) with a plastic spatula. Transfer to a glass baking dish and bake for 30 minutes. Serve hot.

• • •

GEORGE WASHINGTON'S PUNCH   This recipe came to us from the Reverend William Ralston. It was actually the Mount Vernon Christmas punch he got from Martha Washington Jackson, which she had from her aunt, Mrs. George A. Washington (Quennie Woods, who lived at Sewanee). They were both part of the collateral Washington family.

Father Ralston told us that he feels that the special thing about this punch is the way all those alcohols mix and blend. "It is as smooth as velvet," he said. "It also does not leave you feeling 'punchy' the next day, although you certainly can drink too much of it. It also makes the base for the world's best old-fashioned—add soda water and an orange slice. Divine!"

• **SERVES A CROWD**

1 quart strong brewed English Breakfast tea, sweetened
1 gallon good-quality bourbon
1 gallon sherry
1 quart sweet vermouth
1 pint best-quality Jamaican rum
1 pint yellow or green Chartreuse (I prefer green)
4 bottles champagne, or more to taste
12 lemons, each cut into 4 wedges
1 quart maraschino cherries, without stems but with their juice

Combine the first six ingredients. When it is time to serve the punch, add champagne—as much as you wish. Add lemon wedges and cherries to the punch and serve. (The punch is much improved if allowed to stand for at least 1 week before serving.)

An ice ring (made in a Bundt pan filled halfway with water and the cherries) looks good and helps keep the punch cold when serving.

CHAPTER SIXTEEN

Oyster Roasts

W hen I first arrived in Beaufort, South Carolina, in 1961, I had never eaten an oyster, nor entertained any plans to do so in the future. Though I grew up surrounded by salt marshes and rivers, my mother had a landlubber's disdain for all varieties of seafood, but held a special contempt for the lowly and despised oyster. I remember her wrinkling her nose as she held a pint of oysters aloft, saying, "I wouldn't eat one of these balls of mucus in a famine."

But we had come to the land of the great winter oyster roasts, where friends and neighbors gathered on weekends armed with blunt-nosed knives, dining on oysters that grown men had harvested from their beds at dead low tide that same day. At an oyster roast on Daufuskie Island thirty years ago, Jake Washington came up to me as I was devouring, with great pleasure, oysters he had gathered from the Chechessee River earlier that day. The afternoon was cold and clear, and I washed the oysters down with a beer so icy that my hand ached even though I was wearing shucker's gloves. Among Daufuskie Islanders and folks from Bluffton and Hilton Head, there is a running argument about which river produces the most delicious and flavorful oysters: the Chechessee or the May River. I have partaken of both, and the sheer ecstasy of trying to make the subtle distinctions that make arguments like this arise makes me shiver with pleasure.

"You like those oysters, teacher?" Jake asked me. "They taste good?"

"Heaven. It's like tasting heaven, Jake," I answered.

"You know what you're tasting, teacher?" Jake said. "You're tasting last night's high tide. Them oysters always keep some of the tide with them. It sweetens them up."

Once when my boat broke down on the May River while going to Daufuskie, I drifted into an oyster bank and spent the hours awaiting rescue by opening up dozens of oysters with a pocketknife. Of all the oyster bars I have frequented in my life, none came close to the sheer deliciousness of those tide-swollen oysters I consumed that long-ago morning, which tasted of seawater with a slight cucumber aftertaste. The oyster is a child of tides and it tasted that cold morning like the best thing that the moon and the May River could conjure up to crown the shoulders of its inlets and estuaries. A raw oyster might be the food that my palate longs for most during the long summer season in Beaufort when we give our oysters their vacation time and they grow milky from their own roe. But then I remember my first roasted oyster, dipped in hot butter and placed on my tongue. As I bit into it, its succulence seemed outrageous, but it made my mouth the happiest place on my body. That first roasted oyster ranks high on my list of spectacular moments I have experienced while meandering through the markets and restaurants of the world—my first taste of lobster, truffle, beluga caviar, escargot, and South Carolina's mustard-based barbecue.

An oyster roast must take place on a cold day for it to work its proper magic. You should invite only those friends who have never heard of Proust's *Remembrance of Things Past.* It is not a milieu that induces euphoria among highbrows and intellectuals. You'll seldom hear talk about quantum physics or quadratic equations as newspapers are spread out over picnic tables. There will be a lot more pickup trucks than Lexuses in the parking lot, and the dress code is decidedly casual. The expectant hum of the crowd is what hunger sounds like. Great sacks of oysters are cut open with knives, and several men, who know exactly what they are doing, tend to an oak fire with a piece of tin laid over it on cinder blocks. It does not have to be tin, but it has to be a metal that will not melt into the fire. When the tin is iridescent and glowing from the fire, several men shovel bushels of oysters, many in clusters, onto the slab of tin and cover the oysters with wet burlap sacks.

The crowd cheers when the first oysters are shoveled on because we know the process is quick. Another cheer arises when the heat forces the first batch of oysters to pop open, the juices of the oysters hissing against the tin and causing a redolent, noisy steam to rise in the air like a secret fog. The men with the shovels then distribute the roasted oysters to the restless waiting crowds, who grab them up, hot as bricks in a kiln, warming their gloved left hands as they pry the shells apart with their right hands. There is no labor at an oyster roast. The fiery heat has done all the work for you. Your one job is to eat as many oysters as you can while they are still steaming off the fire. A lukewarm oyster is beside the point and always a disappointment to the spirit.

I love to dip my oysters in a bath of hot butter, but other Low Country people swear by the catsup and horseradish, or cocktail sauce, route. Yet I have known people who carry whole lemons and who would not even consider adding another condiment to such a distinct and natural taste. Others believe that any addition at all is a form of heresy, and they eat their oysters as God made them, savoring that giddy, briny essence of the Low Country as it comes from its shell.

Always, in the Low Country, you eat more than you should at an oyster roast. I never have left an oyster roast without thinking that I should not have eaten the last seven oysters I forced down. But how do you turn your back on something so enchanting and delicious? For the half-shell people, an oyster roast always sounds like an abomination unto the Lord, but the tradition dates back to the Yemassees, Kiawahs, and other tribes that once roamed these forests. Is a roasted oyster ever as good as a chilled oyster on the half shell? Perhaps a Chilmark, a Sailor Girl, a Point Reyes Pacifica, a Cotuit, or that Rolex of oysters, the snooty Belon— No, it's not, not to me, but it is still terrific all the same. The camaraderie and the gossip and the sheer goodwill of the crowd set the oyster roast apart for me as something particularly Southern and indigenous, a rite that poor people have access to because our rivers are open to everyone and our oyster banks are fecund and public and healthy.

My favorite oyster roast was not planned. When *The Lords of Discipline* came out, I was spending the night with my friends Dana and Sallie Sinkler at their house on Wadmalaw Island. Before dinner, Dana and I rode out in his boat to an oyster bank across the river, where we gathered the evening meal with tongs. With a boatful of oysters, we recrossed the river at sunset, the water turning gold around us, and the wake of our boat kicking up a more startled form of gold behind us.

Before we left, Dana had started his own oak fire in his hearth and had laid a piece of tin across it. We roasted the freshly harvested oysters in Dana and Sallie's living room. Sallie brought bread and bacon-laced coleslaw out of her kitchen. There was beer and wine and grand talk as we sat in front of the fire, and I could feel our friendship deepening while we opened the oysters and told each other the stories of our lives.

Last year, I bought two bushels of oysters from an oysterman on St. Helena Island for a roast of my own. The Low Country is always capable of astonishing me anew.

"Sir, are these oysters local?" I asked after paying him.

"No, sir. Gotta be honest. I harvested these oysters over three miles from here."

OYSTER ROAST

$1/2$ pound fresh bratwurst sausages

$1/2$ pound smoked bratwurst sausages

$3/4$ pound Mexican chorizo sausages

12 dozen oysters, well scrubbed

4 dozen littleneck clams, well scrubbed

One 12-ounce bottle beer (not dark)

ACCOMPANIMENTS

Low Country Aioli (see below)

Cocktail sauce

Lemon wedges

Melted butter

You'll need about 2 yards burlap for the grill method or heavy-duty aluminum foil, as well as 12 oyster knives and 12 oven mitts or thick kitchen towels.

CHARCOAL GRILL METHOD FOR SAUSAGES AND OYSTERS

1. Prepare the grill for cooking with about 7 pounds of briquets. (You'll need about 15 pounds of briquets total.) Or use a gas grill.

2. Prick the sausages in several places with a fork, then grill, covered, turning occasionally, until browned and cooked through, about 10 minutes. Transfer to serving platters.

3. Scatter about 12 additional briquets over the glowing coals and replace the rack. Fold the burlap into a triple layer slightly smaller than the grill surface and soak it completely with water. Put 3 to 4 dozen oysters directly on the grill rack, cover with wet burlap, and roast, with grill cover up, until the shells just begin to open (about $1/16$ inch) or give slightly when squeezed with tongs, about 10 minutes. (If necessary, sprinkle more water over the burlap to keep it moist.)

4. Serve the oysters, with accompaniments, as they open, removing them with tongs, and roast any unopened oysters a few minutes longer, replacing burlap. Roast the remaining oysters in two or three batches in the same manner, adding about 12 more briquets between batches to keep the fire hot and resoaking burlap thoroughly.

5. In a 6- to 8-quart pot, steam the clams in beer over medium-high heat, covered, until clams open, about 10 minutes (discard any unopened clams after 15 minutes). Transfer the clams as they open to a platter. Carefully pour the clam broth into cups, leaving any sediment in the pot, for dunking in case the clams are sandy.

STOVETOP-OVEN METHOD FOR SAUSAGES AND OYSTERS

1. Preheat the oven to 500°F.

2. On the stovetop, heat two heavy, ridged grill pans or skillets over moderately high heat until hot but not smoking, then cook the sausages, turning occasionally, until browned and cooked through, 15 to 20 minutes.

3. Heat a large, deep roasting pan on the bottom rack of the oven until very hot. Remove from the oven and quickly fill with 3 to 4 dozen oysters and 1 cup water, then cover the pan tightly with heavy-duty foil. Roast the oysters until the shells just begin to open (about $1/16$ inch) or give slightly when squeezed with tongs, and roast any unopened oysters a few minutes longer, covered with foil. Roast the remaining oysters in two or three batches in the same manner.

4. Steam the clams as described in step 5 above.

Low Country Aioli • **MAKES ABOUT 3$1/2$ CUPS**

$1/2$ sweet onion, quartered

$1/2$ pound tomatoes, halved crosswise

1 large green bell pepper, halved lengthwise, cored, and seeded

1 fresh habanero or jalapenño chile, halved

1 tablespoon olive oil

1 $^1/_2$ tablespoons finely chopped garlic

$^1/_2$ teaspoon coarse or kosher salt

2 cups Homemade Mayonnaise (page 57)

$^1/_2$ teaspoon freshly ground black pepper

1 to 3 teaspoons white wine vinegar

1. Preheat the oven to 450°F and set rack in upper third of oven.

2. Toss the onion, tomatoes, bell pepper, and chile with the oil in a shallow baking pan and arrange, cut sides down, in one layer. Roast, turning onion once or twice, until vegetables are charred and tender, 15 to 20 minutes.

3. Discard skins from tomatoes and bell pepper. Chop the tomatoes and drain in a sieve, discarding juices. Finely chop the onion and bell pepper. Mince the chile.

4. Mash the garlic and salt into a paste. Blend together mayonnaise, garlic paste, and black pepper in a food processor. Add the chile, about one-quarter at a time, tasting for desired heat.

5. Transfer to a bowl and stir in the tomatoes, bell pepper, onion, and vinegar.

The aioli can be made 1 day ahead and chilled, covered.

• • •

CORN BREAD   • MAKES TWO 10-INCH LOAVES

3 cups white cornmeal

1 cup all-purpose flour

1 teaspoon baking powder

1 teaspoon baking soda

2 teaspoons salt

2 large eggs, lightly beaten

3 cups well-shaken buttermilk

12 tablespoons (1 $^1/_2$ sticks) unsalted butter, melted

1. Heat two well-seasoned 10-inch cast-iron skillets in the upper and lower thirds of the oven while preheating it to 450° F.

2. Whisk together the cornmeal, flour, baking powder, baking soda, and salt. Add the eggs, buttermilk, and 1 cup melted butter, then quickly stir together.

3. Remove the hot skillets from the oven. Divide the remaining $^1/_2$ cup melted butter between them, then divide the batter between pans. Bake in the upper and lower thirds of oven, switching positions of pans halfway through, until golden and a cake tester inserted in the center comes out clean, 15 to 20 minutes total.

• • •

SPICY SLAW

• SERVES 12

1 $^1/_2$ cups Homemade Mayonnaise (page 57)

$^1/_2$ cup cider vinegar

$^1/_2$ cup sugar

1 tablespoon Tabasco sauce

2 teaspoons coarse or kosher salt

$^1/_2$ teaspoon freshly ground black pepper

4 pounds mixed cabbages, such as green, red, and savoy, thinly
   sliced

3 cups halved cherry tomatoes

1 large sweet onion, thinly sliced

3 cucumbers, peeled, seeded, and diced

1 small red bell pepper, cored, seeded, and cut into thin strips

1 small yellow bell pepper, cored, seeded, and cut into thin strips

Whisk together the mayonnaise, vinegar, sugar, Tabasco, salt, and pepper until the sugar is dissolved, then toss with the vegetables.

The slaw may be made 1 day ahead and chilled, covered.

• • •

APPLE COBBLER
• SERVES 12

FOR THE APPLE FILLING

8 tablespoons (1 stick) unsalted butter, cut into pieces

8 pounds Granny Smith apples, peeled, cored, and each cut into 8 wedges

1 $^1\!/_2$ cups sugar

2 teaspoons finely grated orange zest

$^1\!/_2$ cup apricot preserves

$^1\!/_3$ cup brandy

FOR THE BISCUIT TOPPING

3 $^3\!/_4$ cups self-rising flour (preferably White Lily)

6 tablespoons plus $^1\!/_4$ cup sugar

$^1\!/_4$ teaspoon salt

$^1\!/_2$ pound (2 sticks) cold unsalted butter, cut into bits

1 $^3\!/_4$ cups plus 2 tablespoons chilled heavy cream

1 large egg yolk

2 tablespoons heavy cream (not chilled)

1. To make the filling: Divide the butter between two wide, heavy 5- to 6-quart pots. Heat over moderately high heat until foam subsides, then sauté the apples with the sugar and zest, dividing them evenly between the pots and stirring, until apples are slightly softened, about 5 minutes.

2. Transfer the apples with a slotted spoon to two $2^1\!/_2$- to 3-quart buttered shallow baking dishes.

3. Transfer all apple juices to one pot. Stir in the preserves and brandy and bring to a boil, stirring occasionally. Divide the mixture and pour it over the apples. (This may be made to this point 1 day ahead and chilled, covered. Bring the apple filling to room temperature before proceeding.)

4. To make the biscuit topping: Preheat the oven to 375°F. Place rack in middle of oven.

5. Pulse the flour, 6 tablespoons sugar, and salt in a food processor just until blended. Add the butter and pulse just until the mixture resembles coarse meal. Transfer to a large bowl and add the chilled cream, stirring gently with a rubber spatula to form a dough. (The dough will be sticky at first, but it will stiffen slightly as the flour absorbs the cream.)

6. Knead the dough on a lightly floured surface four to six times with floured hands (do not overwork dough, or biscuits will be tough). Roll out the dough $^3/_4$ inch thick, flouring the surface as needed, and cut out 12 to 14 rounds with a cookie cutter, rerolling scraps as necessary. Arrange the rounds on top of the apples, about $^1/_2$ inch apart.

7. Stir together the yolk and unchilled cream and brush on the biscuits. Sprinkle the $^1/_4$ cup sugar generously over the biscuits.

8. Bake until biscuits are golden and cooked through (lift one to check if the underside is cooked), 35 to 45 minutes. Serve warm.

The cobbler can be baked 1 day ahead and chilled, covered. To reheat, put the chilled cobbler, uncovered, in a cold oven, then bake at 375°F until the apples are bubbling, 25 to 30 minutes.

CHAPTER SEVENTEEN

Men Grilling

It was William B. "King Tut" Harper who not only sold me my first car but also taught me the joys of grilling steaks on a well-laid fire. In everything he did, King Tut was a craftsman who sneered at imprecision, indecisiveness, or anything he considered second-rate. "If you're going to do something, boy, learn to do it right. If not, let someone else do it."

Each Sunday afternoon at six, he rose from his recliner, walked out to his back porch overlooking Factory Creek in Beaufort, South Carolina, and lifted up a large bag of charcoal. With great care, he distributed the coals evenly in the pan of his grill. With a master's touch, he arranged the charcoal in a cone-shaped mound, then drenched each briquet with just the right amount of lighter fluid, that amount being a secret to all but him. For five minutes, the charcoal marinated as King Tut looked out toward the setting sun, which had begun to ignite the creek with soft gold.

"Got to give the lighter fluid time to soak the charcoal, boy," King Tut said to me.

Taking a blue box of kitchen matches, he lit a single match, held it straight up for a moment, and then tossed it with a priestlike flick of his hand toward the charcoal, which ignited in a satisfying but muffled explosion. "We'll give it a spell. Then we'll check to see if the fire's right."

"How will we know it's right?" I asked.

"Because we're men," King Tut said, scoffing. "Men just know these kinds of things. It'll look right. That's how we'll know."

When the flames died down and the coals were molten and the same color as the sun-fired creek, King Tut placed three large T-bone steaks on the grill with the deftness of a card dealer. He was the first cook I had ever known who held religious beliefs against cooking beef until it was well done.

"I'd rather feed it to my beagle," he said. "You don't overcook a good steak. That's a sacrilege."

"Who taught you how to cook, King Tut?" I asked.

"Hush, boy. I'm grilling," he said, his voice carrying both softness and scorn. "Grilling's serious business. Go in and tell Maw I'll be bringing the steaks in sixteen minutes. Git, now!"

The air was filling up with smoke, and the smell of beef hitting the fire brought the beagle out of the doghouse and teased the palates of fishermen returning to the boat landing a mile down the creek. King Tut turned the meat once and once only, and the steaks were uniformly striped by the lines of the grill. Those Sunday night steak dinners at the Harper house remain some of the finest and most hospitable meals I have enjoyed on the planet. The thought of those beautiful cuts of meat laid over a fire with such ritual and devotion are among the most mouthwatering memories of my boyhood.

Later King Tut taught me to wrap Vidalia onions and Idaho potatoes in foil and cook them in the glowing coals before putting on the steaks. He introduced me to the glories of garlic salt, Worcestershire sauce, red wine vinegar, sour cream, and a dozen other condiments. Cutting through blackened foil and catching that first aromatic explosion of steam from the grilled onions was the first experience I had of the pure sensuousness of cooking. Watching King Tut eat what he had cooked was one of the great pleasures of dining at his table. He ate with utter concentration, savoring every bite of his perfectly seasoned meal. On Sunday nights during my high school and college years, I hated not being at the Harper house. Because my own father could not boil an egg, I had never seen a man cook anything until I came to King Tut's grill and learned of the rapture of the lucky men who step outside to light the fires that feed their families the best meals of their lives. Whenever I recall King Tut hunched over his grill, I think of fire and meat and small talk and getting things right and the coming of nightfall and the smell of the inrunning tide. What King Tut was passing on to me was ancient, and he let me love him freely because he knew the responsibilities of being a father. Without knowing it, he prepared me for a lifetime of cooking for family.

When I was moving my family from Atlanta to Rome in 1981, a group of men I had cooked dinner for once a month planned a party in honor of my imminent departure. The novelist Terry Kay came up with the idea of barbecuing an entire pig in the woodsy backyard of Cliff Graubart, who lived on three acres of land a couple of miles from Grant Park. Terry Kay, the author of *To Dance with the White Dog*, loves playing "redneck" more than any white Southerner I have ever been around, and he can talk for longer than anyone has any reason to listen on such arcane topics as the proper way to plow a cotton furrow or the burial of a good mule. I find such conversation tedious in the extreme, and I do all I can to keep Terry's mind from drifting back to those far-off days of his childhood when he and twelve siblings grew poorer and poorer with each passing year. It's my belief that by the time I reach the age of seventy, Terry Kay will not even have managed to survive his hookworm-ridden childhood. In spite of all that, we let him cook the pig.

Terry dug the pit in Cliff's backyard and stacked up concrete blocks three feet high. He then fashioned a makeshift grill using strong hay wire and rebar, weaving the wire through the rebar, so it did not collapse under the weight of the pig. When I arrived late Friday afternoon, Terry had already started a fire in the fire barrel using several cords of dried hickory, whose smell can induce Proust-like reveries in Southerners everywhere. Terry stacked wood on a grate in the fire barrel, and once the fire was raging, he shoveled out the red-hot ashes that dropped to the bottom of the barrel. Those burning coals, spread evenly about the pit, would cook the pig. It was a continuous process that would go on all through the night.

"Where's the pig?" I asked as I walked up to the fire.

"It's in Cliff's bathtub," Terry replied.

"Cliff's Jewish," I said.

"So?"

"It is my experience that Jews and Muslims are funny about finding pork in their bathtub," I said.

"It wouldn't fit in the refrigerator," Terry explained.

We watched as Cliff drove up with Bernie Schein and Frank Smith, and they walked into Cliff's house carrying wine and groceries. A moment later, we heard a scream that was both primal and terrified.

"Cliff found the pig," Terry said.

"Hey, Kay!" Cliff shouted from the back porch. "There's a pig in my bathroom."

"I know, Graubart," Terry said.

"Did you see the one in your bed?" I asked.

"Do you know that I shower in this tub, Kay?" Cliff said. "Tell me the truth. In that hokey, poverty-stricken, chicken-growing, cotton-picking, country-song-singing, grits-eating childhood of yours, did you ever put a pig in your parents' bathtub? Or were you too poor to have a bathtub in North Georgia?"

"We had the creek," Terry said, winking at me. Then we heard wild, hyenalike laughter coming from the house.

"Bernie found the pig," I said.

We learned all the secrets of barbecuing a pig that night from Terry Kay. After the pig had cooked for three hours, he began to sop the slow-browning meat with a mixture of water, apple cider vinegar, and salt. With his country-boy knowledge, Terry had made a sop mop by tearing up an old T-shirt and tying the strips around a broomstick. Terry proved to be a vigorous and relentless sopper.

"You've got to keep the meat moist, boys," he said to us. "The rest of the night is going to be dip and sop, dip and sop."

"This is the most boring thing I've ever done," Bernie said.

"I think this might have been the worst idea any of us ever had," Frank said. "I vote that we throw Kay out of the group. All in favor?"

All four of us raised our hands in favor while Terry dipped and sopped to his heart's content. We raised our glasses of red wine and toasted each other and made promises that the group would gather in Italy for a reunion. For an hour, we talked about what our group had meant to us, and the pleasure we took in one another's company and conversation and the respite it gave us from families and jobs and the great pressures of modern life.

"It hasn't been all roses," Bernie said. "This group has had its share of rough times."

"Name them," Cliff said.

"There was that time you found a pig in your bathtub," Bernie said.

"Yeah, and it's been agony listening about Terry's deprived childhood," I said.

"The pain of it," Bernie said. "I don't know how any of those poor Kay kids survived."

"They got by like they always did—dipping and sopping. Just dipping and sopping," Frank said.

"I get weepy when I think of Terry and his poor family," I said.

"It's enough to break a man's heart," Bernie added.

Terry roared at us in his gruff, theater-trained voice: "You boys leave my family be."

"They were godlike people. Godlike Southerners," Cliff said.

At midnight, I stood up and announced, "Boys, this has been a pleasure, and I have enjoyed every moment of it. But I went to college so I didn't have to stay up all night barbecuing a hog. If you need me, you can find me in Cliff's guest bedroom."

"Why am I sitting against a tree when I could be sitting in a nice armchair in Cliff's house?" Bernie asked, rising to join me.

"I'm Jewish," Cliff said. "I'm outraged to find a Methodist cooking treyf in my backyard."

"In solidarity with Cliff, I'm going to the house, too," Frank said.

Terry Kay spent the night cussing and turning the pig all by himself. When the hundred guests gathered the next evening, we fed them the best barbecue I have ever eaten. I have never been praised with as much promiscuous gusto as I was for that moist, vinegar-anointed meat from that barbecue in Atlanta over twenty years ago. I found friends moaning over their paper plates, and people returning for seconds and thirds. A sensitive man, Terry Kay, who was not talking to any of us because of his justifiable anger at our defection, left the party early. I heard a woman ask Bernie who cooked the pig, and was not surprised when he answered, "I did. Pat and Frank and Cliff helped."

Cliff caught the spirit quickly, and said, "I'm exhausted. We were up all night."

"None of us have slept for twenty-four hours," Frank added.

"Terry Kay told me that he cooked the pig," the woman said.

The four of us laughed and shook our heads. Then I said, "Give Terry credit, boys. It was his idea, but we stayed up to cook the pig. Terry Kay went to bed."

PORK—PIECE BY PIECE

There are five major sections of a pig:

- Leg, where the fresh ham (page 197) comes from
- Loin, where almost everything else meaty and tender comes from, roasts and chops and tenderloin strip
- Side, source of bacon and spareribs
- Shoulder/butt, provides shoulder roast (sandwich meat) and smoked butt
- Picnic shoulder, the smoked picnic roast and smoked hocks

STUFFED PORK CHOPS I was not a great and fervent fan of pork chops until I used this recipe. I discovered I loved these pork chops when I gussied them up and sent them to finishing school.

> Four 1 1/2-inch-thick rib pork chops (about 1 pound each)
> Stuffing (see below)
> 1 tablespoon unsalted butter
> 1 tablespoon olive oil
> 1 cup white wine or chicken stock
> 1/4 cup tangy grainy mustard
> 1/2 cup heavy cream

1. With a small sharp knife, make a horizontal pocket in the meat side of each chop, deep enough to hold the stuffing without puncturing the top or bottom of the chop. (The pocket should be almost to the bone.) Fill with just enough stuffing to keep the pocket slightly open (1/4 to 1/3 cup per chop; the stuffing should be compressed so that it sticks together).

2. In a large skillet with a tight-fitting lid over medium-high heat, melt butter and oil until foamy. Brown the chops, turning only once, for about 3 minutes on each side.

3. Reduce the heat to low, cover the skillet, and cook the chops until medium well done, about 8 minutes per side. (Or brown the chops on top of the stove and finish the cooking in a preheated 350°F oven for 15 to 18 minutes.) To check for doneness, make a small slit near the bone with the tip of a paring knife and peek inside, or check with an instant-read meat thermometer inserted near the bone; it should read 115°F.

4. Transfer the pork chops to serving plates, letting them rest for about 5 minutes to let the natural juices redistribute. While chops are resting, deglaze the pan with the wine, stirring well to scrape up any browned bits. Bring to a low boil and reduce by half. Stir in the mustard and slowly whisk in the heavy cream until well incorporated and sauce is thick enough to coat the back of a wooden spoon.

5. Spoon the sauce over the chops and serve, passing extra sauce on the side.

Stuffing

• **Makes about 2 cups**

    4 thick slices smoky bacon, coarsely chopped
    2 shallots, finely chopped
    2 tablespoons olive oil (optional)
    2 cups cleaned greens, such as mustard greens, kale, or collard
        greens, cut into long, thin strips
    1/2 cup Pepperidge Farm Corn Bread stuffing

1. Warm a heavy skillet over moderate heat. Add the chopped bacon and cook until fat is rendered and bacon is almost crisp, about 10 minutes. Remove and reserve bacon (leaving behind as much bacon fat in the pan as possible).

2. Sauté the shallots in the bacon fat (if there is not enough, add olive oil). When the shallots are soft but not yet browned, about 2 minutes, add the greens. Cook over medium-high heat until greens are wilted, 3 to 5 minutes for collard or mustard greens, up to 10 minutes for kale.

3. Remove from the heat and add the reserved bacon and the stuffing. Stir to combine.

• • •

CANDIED BACON   One cannot make bacon in a way that I could not like it. This recipe brings elegance and sweetness to an already fabulous product. The recipe approaches decadence, like putting perfume on a pig.   • SERVES 2

> 6 thick slices bacon
>
> 1 tablespoon light brown sugar
>
> 1 teaspoon Dijon mustard

1. Preheat the oven to 375°F.

2. Arrange the bacon on a sturdy baking sheet. Place a smaller baking sheet on top of the bacon: the weight of the top pan will keep the strips flat while they cook.

3. Bake until almost crisp, about 20 minutes.

4. In a small bowl, mix the sugar and mustard together into a lumpy paste.

5. Remove the bacon from the oven and transfer (draining the grease) to a clean baking sheet. Using the back of a spoon, coat the top of each bacon strip with the mustard mixture. Return to the oven for 5 more minutes. Remove the bacon, turn the slices over, and repeat. Bake until the bacon looks brown and lacquered, about another 5 minutes.

6. Using tongs, remove the bacon and set on a rack over paper towels to drain. Serve warm.

• • •

COLLARD GREENS   Collard greens are soul food pure and simple. In 1971, while living near San Francisco, I had a car cut me off and wave me down while I was driving through the Presidio. A huge black man got out of his car and approached my own. Oh, oh, I thought, he saw my South Carolina license plate and has decided to kill me because of the crimes my people committed against his people. But he surprised me with his large magnetic smile. I got out of the car and we shook hands.

"Where you from in South Carolina, man?" he said.

"Beaufort," I answered.

"Man, I'm from Charleston. Don't you miss the Low Country?"

"More than I can tell you."

"I saw your license plate and I just had to talk to someone from home."

We talked for fifteen minutes and he told me the names of three soul food restaurants that served good collard greens, fried chicken, and pot likker— two in Oakland and one in San Francisco. He told me he prayed every day for a good-paying job to open up in Charleston and that he was worried about raising his children among the "hippies and wackos." He missed fishing for bream in the Edisto River and going after blue crabs with string and a chicken neck. Everything I loved about the South was contained in this ebullient homesick man. He told me the name of two Baptist churches in San Francisco. "The old-time religion. Man, these people believe some weird shit out here." He embraced me when we said goodbye, and as he drove off I regretted not getting his name and address. I would have liked to have been his friend for the rest of my life. This recipe is dedicated to him. • **SERVES 4**

> 4 ounces salt pork, diced
>
> 1 tablespoon olive oil
>
> 1 medium onion, coarsely chopped (about $3/4$ cup)
>
> One 1-pound smoked ham hock or country ham bone
>
> 4 pounds collard greens, picked over and cleaned, with stems
>   removed and leaves cut into 1-inch strips

One 35-ounce can whole tomatoes, preferably San Marzano, broken
up into small pieces and drained

1. To make the pork stock: In a medium, at least 8-quart stockpot over moderate heat, sauté the salt pork in the oil until lightly browned, 6 to 8 minutes. Add the onion and cook until the salt pork is crisp and the onion is well colored, 8 to 10 minutes. Add 3 quarts water and the ham hock. Bring to a boil, turn down the heat, and simmer slowly (so the surface of the liquid has some movement) until the water is infused with flavor, at least 1 hour or up to 2. Remove ham hock, cool, and strip the meat from the bone (reserve the meat for Pot Likker Soup, page 226). (The pork stock can be cooled to room temperature, transferred to a storage container, and refrigerated overnight.)

2. Add the collards and tomatoes to the pork stock and cook on medium heat until the greens are wilted, 30 to 40 minutes. Serve hot.

• • •

SOUTHERN RATATOUILLE WITH BACON This is called Southern ratatouille because it contains bacon. Southerners cannot seem to cook anything without flavoring it with some part of a pig. I still cannot spell or pronounce ratatouille, even with the bacon in it.

• SERVES 1 AS A MAIN COURSE OR 2 AS A SIDE DISH

2 thick slices bacon, coarsely chopped

1 large red onion, finely chopped (about 1 cup)

2 garlic cloves, finely chopped

2 small zucchini, peeled and diced into $1/4$- to $1/2$-inch cubes (about
$1^1/2$ cups)

2 small yellow squash, diced into $1/4$- to $1/2$-inch cubes (about $1^1/2$
cups)

1 large ripe tomato, coarsely chopped (about $1^1/2$ cups)

1 cup fresh corn kernels (about 2 ears)

Chopped fresh chives, thyme, basil, or mint

1. Warm a large heavy skillet over moderate heat. Add the bacon and cook until fat is rendered and bacon is just crisp, about 5 minutes. Add the onion and garlic and continue cooking over medium heat until the onion is softened and begins to brown.

2. Raise the heat to moderately high and add the zucchini and squash. Cook, stirring occasionally without turning, until lightly browned but still crisp-tender, 5 to 8 minutes. Stir in the tomato and cook until softened, translucent, and beginning to break apart, about 5 minutes. Add the corn and cook, stirring frequently, for another 2 minutes. Add the herbs and mix gently. Serve at once.

• • •

POT LIKKER SOUP

I used to order pot likker every time I went to eat at Mary Mac's in Atlanta, a sacred institution of Southern cuisine on Ponce de Leon Avenue near Peachtree. The simplest version of pot likker is this: cook a bunch of greens with a goodly portion of fatback, pour the liquid into a bowl, and serve it. A shake of pepper vinegar livens it up. It calms a Southerner's nerves and brings a sense of order back to the world.

This is a simple, rough country soup; don't even try to fancy it up. Remove the fat from surface of refrigerated pork stock (page 225). For each serving, bring 1 cup pork stock to a low boil. Add 2 canned tomatoes (break up the tomatoes with your fingers), some cooked collard greens, and a sprinkling of salt pork. Simmer the soup for a few minutes, then sprinkle with shreds of meat from the ham hock and serve with corn bread on the side.

PORK BUNS

3 cups unbleached all-purpose flour

2 teaspoons baking powder

1 teaspoon salt

$^1/_2$ cup boiling water

Olive oil

Pork Filling (see below)

1 cup crumbled blue cheese

Chutney

1. Place the flour, baking powder, and salt in the bowl of a food processor and pulse to combine. With the motor running, add the boiling water and then add $^1/_2$ cup plus 2 tablespoons cold water in a thin stream until the mixture forms a ball. Process for 1 minute longer and turn the dough out onto a floured surface. Knead briefly, cover with plastic, and let sit for 15 minutes.

2. Divide the dough into 8 equal pieces. Working with one at a time (leaving others covered), roll the dough into an 8-inch circle and brush with a little olive oil.

3. Spread one-eighth of the pork filling and one-eighth of the crumbled cheese evenly on the dough, leaving about a $^1/_2$-inch border around the edge. Roll the dough up like a jelly roll, as tightly as possible. Holding one end of the resulting tube on your work surface, pull the other end around as tightly as possible and pinch the two ends together, making a smooth round. Repeat with the remaining dough. As you fill each bun, place it on a baking sheet and cover with plastic wrap. (The filled buns can be cooked immediately or covered with plastic wrap and refrigerated for up to 2 hours. Bring to room temperature before cooking.)

4. Preheat oven to lowest setting.

5. Using the palm of your hand, slightly flatten each bun. On a lightly floured work surface, use a rolling pin to roll each bun out into circle about 6 inches in diameter.

6. Heat two large sauté pans over medium heat. When the pans are hot, coat lightly with olive oil (swirling it around for even distribution). Place 2 dough rounds in each pan and cook until the surface of the buns is flecked with light brown spots, 3 to 5 minutes per side. Remove the buns from the pans and keep them warm in a low oven while cooking the remaining buns. Serve hot, passing chutney on the side.

Pork Filling   • MAKES ABOUT 2 CUPS

> 3 tablespoons olive oil
> 2 red onions, thinly sliced (about 2 cups)
> 1 pound ground pork shoulder
> $3/4$ teaspoon coarse or kosher salt
> $3/4$ teaspoon freshly ground black pepper

1. In a large skillet over medium-high heat, heat the olive oil until hot but not smoking. Add the onions and cook without turning until they begin to brown, 5 to 8 minutes. Using a spatula, flip the onions over to brown on the other side, 3 to 5 minutes. The onions should be well colored but not burned.

2. Add the pork and cook, stirring occasionally, until the meat loses its color, 3 to 5 minutes. Add the salt and pepper and let cool. (The filling can be refrigerated for up to 1 day before making the buns.)

• • •

ROAST SUCKLING PIG   There is no reason for anyone to figure out how to roast a pig on their own when so many people do it so well and are happy to tell you how. This recipe, from Betty Fortson, chef at Bolan Hall Plantation in Beaufort, South Carolina, makes an all-day job seem doable.

• **SERVES 10 TO 14**

1. First, you need a good butcher. To feed 10 to 14 people, a real suckling pig won't have enough meat (it might serve 3 or 4). Ask for a baby pig around 30 to 35 pounds. If the pig is too large for the oven, have the butcher cut it in half and either bake the halves in two ovens or bake them one after another if you have only one oven. The butcher must also remove the eyes and break the jaw.

2. Preheat oven to 350° F. Place rack in middle of oven.

3. Once your pig is home, scrub it well inside and out with warm water. Dry, then rub it outside and inside with canola oil. Salt and pepper liberally (inside and out) and add a dash of Accent.

4. Crumple aluminum foil to the size of a small apple and insert in the jaw. Bake for 3 to 4 hours. Test during last hour with a sharp knife. The skin should be crackling crisp. If meat begins to fall apart, stop cooking. Obviously, as pork, the pig must be well done.

5. Insert a small lady apple in the pig's mouth. Use green grapes for eyes. If the pig is cut in half, place the halves together on a large, parsley-surrounded platter. Cover the cut with large bunches of green grapes. The result should be spectacular.

CHAPTER EIGHTEEN

Vidalia Onions

W hen I lived in Atlanta during the seventies and eighties, a fetishistic whoop of pleasure would go up along the aisles of the Piggly Wiggly or Kroger or Bi-Lo by wild-eyed aficionados who would let the uninitiated into the secret that the Vidalia onions had arrived in the produce department. I witnessed a pretty Atlanta Junior Leaguer eating a Vidalia onion like an apple as she completed her shopping. A friend of mine would buy a dozen bags of Vidalias on the first day they were available and concoct strange methods to preserve the sweet onions far into the winter months. Once he allowed me access to his cellar and I pulled back at the sight of grotesque, truncated women, until he explained that he used his wife's ruined panty hose, filled them with the precious Vidalias, and then hung them from the ceiling. "There's not one onion that is touching another onion. Too much spoilage that way."

"You like onions a lot more than I do," I said.

"I like Vidalia onions more than anyone on earth," he said, his onions hiding but safe in a place where a woman's legs used to go.

Since those early days in Atlanta, I have become a dedicated advocate of the Vidalia onion. First, let me teach you how to pronounce it because

I have seen the word mangled by some of the most famous cooks on earth. It is *vie-dale-ya*. It is an onion so sweet that you think the fields around Vidalia, Georgia, must be sugary or connected to hives of underground bees. Indeed, they are delicate and subtle and they do not overpower salads or sandwiches. I like to peel them, put them in aluminum foil, hit them with a splash of sesame oil and soy sauce, and grill them over an open fire or throw them in the oven for an hour. They take to my Pickled Shrimp (page 196) with gladness.

The only anti–Vidalia onion fanatic I have ever encountered is my former high school English teacher, Gene Norris. Gene opines (and no one else in the history of the South can make an art form out of opining) this way: "When I want an onion, I want something with kick in it, something that will bite me back, something with some substance to it. I don't want no sweet onion that's trying to be more like a potato than a good old onion from my mama's garden. I want an onion that's got some sass and backbone to it. Why celebrate an onion that prides itself on not tasting like an onion? Makes no damn sense to me."

What little opposition the Vidalia onion has received in its triumphant march across the country has come from the unreconstructible Gene Norris. I bought a bag of them in a grocery store in Blue Hill, Maine, this past summer, and I was always pleased when they arrived on California Street when I lived in San Francisco. But what I love most about the Vidalia onion is that it led me straight into the path of the greatest Southern story I have ever heard. I call it the perfect Southern story because all the participants are Southern, because it involves peculiarity, madness, liquor, good high humor, football, snappy dialogue, and more liquor.

My next-door neighbor in Ansley Park was the most fanatical Tennessee football fan I have ever met. When I first moved into the house on Peachtree Circle, I walked out to my office in the back and passed Knox Dobbins washing his car in the driveway we shared. His face was awash with grief, and he leaned against the hood of his car as though he were about to vomit or split open with abdominal pain.

"Are you all right, Knox?" I asked.

"It's okay. I'll be fine," he whispered. "The Volunteers are losing by two touchdowns."

I nodded in silence and walked up the steps to my office. When I came down an hour later, Knox was on his back in the driveway doing the "dying cockroach" with the spray from the hose hurtling straight up into the air and falling back on him.

"The Vols won it by a field goal," he shouted.

Later that season, Knox invited me to a football game when Tennessee was playing Georgia in Athens. The only caveat he gave was that we would be forced to sit on the Georgia side because the tickets came from a banker who graduated from the University of Georgia. Knox was worried that he could not sit on his hands for an entire game without rooting for his beloved Vols. That did not turn out to be the major problem of the game.

When I took my seat near the fifty-yard line on the Georgia Bulldog side, a diminutive but formidable lady in her late seventies sat to my immediate left, and she drank from a silver cup filled with ice. She was drinking freely of a brown liquid known as Wild Turkey. She introduced herself and said she'd never seen me, and where was the son of a bitch who usually occupied that seat? I assumed she meant the banker who provided the tickets, but did not know for sure, so I turned and studied the Tennessee lineup with Knox, who had compendious insider knowledge of the entire Volunteer team.

When we rose for the kickoff, I experienced a moment of sheer anxiety when the birdlike woman to my left began to bark like a Georgia bulldog. "Arf, arf, arf, arf, arf, arf, arf!" You get the picture, but it did not let up, so after five minutes I was nearing hysteria as the woman's barking increased in intensity and volume. She would quit barking only for the several delicious moments when she took a fast swill from her drink and shouted into the sunshine-sweetened air: "Let the big dog drink!"

The barking continued unabated as I became claustrophobic, which began to make breathing difficult. Finally, in desperation, I said, "Madam, do you plan to bark like a bulldog for the entire game?"

She stopped, flashed her ferocious eyes at me, and said, "You're just like that son of a bitch who usually sits here."

"Yeah, I can see why it must be a pleasure to surrender those tickets to a stranger."

"I'll bet you're for the goddamn Tennessee Volunteers."

"I wasn't when this game began, but I sure am thinking hard about it now," I said.

She answered me by barking, "Arf, arf, arf, arf, arf," until halftime, when she mercifully stopped, took a last swallow, and screamed at me, "Let the big dog eat."

The silence seemed funereal when the woman stopped barking. Then she surprised me by turning friendly. "Hello. Now, son, I've got to rest my vocal chords for the second half. So tell me all about yourself. Where you from, honey?"

"Madam, I'm from Beaufort, South Carolina," I said.

"Beaufort, South Carolina!" she screamed. "I love everything about Beaufort, South Carolina, everything about that pretty little river town. But do you know what I love most about Beaufort?"

"No, ma'am, I don't."

"I love to get drunk in Beaufort, South Carolina." Then she turned to Knox Dobbins and said, "Sweetie pie, where you from, sugar?"

Knox answered, "I'm from Knoxville, Tennessee."

Again she screamed. "Knoxville, Tennessee? I know everything there is to know about Knoxville, Tennessee. Everything, honey. You know what I love most about Knoxville, Tennessee, the really great thing?"

"No, ma'am, I can't imagine," said Knox.

"I love to get drunk in Knoxville, Tennessee."

There was a pretty young woman sitting next to Knox whom neither of us knew, but who had been dragged into the dance of the bulldog-woman by mere happenstance and the laws of nearness.

"Hey, sweetheart, you look down here, darling. Where are you from, girl?"

"My hometown is Valdosta, Georgia," the young woman replied.

"Valdosta, Georgia? Now there's a place to remember. There's a town you can love. Do you know what I love most about Valdosta, Georgia? The very best thing you can say about Valdosta?"

"No, ma'am, I don't."

The older woman paused, took another drink of bourbon, and said, "I love your goddamn onions."

I told that story once in South Dakota and once in New Hampshire. The audience waited for me to complete the story or get to the point. That's why I know it is the perfect Southern story—it doesn't travel well.

FRIED RINGS

Line a baking sheet with brown paper bags and set aside. Thinly slice 2 Vidalia onions crosswise, about $\frac{1}{8}$ inch thick. In a large frying pan over medium heat, heat 2 cups peanut oil (or enough oil to come 3 inches up the side of the pan). While the oil is heating, mix 1 cup all-purpose flour with 1 teaspoon sea salt and 1 teaspoon freshly ground black pepper on a plate. Dredge the onion slices in the flour mixture and coat well. Fry the onions in batches (as many as will comfortably fit in pan) until golden brown, about 2 minutes. Using a slotted spoon or tongs, transfer the onion slices to the paper bags to drain. Sprinkle lightly with salt and serve piping hot.

• • •

SALAD RINGS

Slice a Vidalia onion and separate into rings. Place in a large bowl and cover with cold water (including a few ice cubes) and 1 tablespoon white wine vinegar. Refrigerate for a couple of hours. Drain the onions, toss with a dressing made from 4 parts olive oil and 1 part white wine vinegar, and season with sea salt and freshly ground black pepper. Serve the salad ice-cold.

• • •

RING SANDWICHES

Cut homemade-style country bread into thin slices and spread unsalted butter on one side of each slice. Lay half the bread out, buttered side up, and arrange razor-thin slices of Vidalia onion over the surface. Sprinkle with sea salt and top with another slice of bread, buttered side down. Cut in half and serve.

CHAPTER NINETEEN

The Greatest of All South Carolinians

t the moment I first met Alex Sanders, the mythical and larger-than-life former president of the College of Charleston, it was on a hillside in North Georgia, where he stood holding a brace of live Maine lobsters in a doughnut box while he taught a group of children a magic trick. We were the guests of two ebullient Georgians, Joe and Emily Cummings, on the first of twenty-five annual weekends when a specially selected group of friends would gather for sparkling conversation and superb food. I had always thought I had a good personality until I met Alex Sanders, and I found myself gripped by a kind of autism during that memorable encounter, when Alex dazzled the entire entourage with stories about the South that seemed epic in scope and definitive in nature. That evening, we met at sunset, with the long shadows moving across the hills and the last light sliding across the mountain lake like icing slow to cool.

Emily Cummings, our hostess, pointed toward the disappearing sun and shouted to her musical and talented family, "Oh, look. The sunset. The sheer beauty of the world."

Her husband, Joe, a wordsmith of great note, added, "By God, this light is a changeling, even a barbaric thing. Thus, this noble orb, engorged with mercury and gold, vanishes even as we speak the name of harsh, demonic night . . ."

I was new to all this and found it interesting, indeed. Long prepared for these sudden paganlike moments of ecstasy, the four Cummings children, aged eight to eighteen, rushed to their parents' side and all six of them began humming, tuning, and harmonizing their voices, sounding much like musical instruments warming up in an orchestra pit.

Alex Sanders and his wife, Zoe, watched my reaction to all this with great bemusement. I saw Alex smile as my face turned to pure astonishment when the Cummings family bade farewell to the fast-disappearing sun by bursting into song:

"Day is done, yes, the day is done.
 Day is done
 Yes, oh Lord, day is done."

I am not speaking here of a shy, Trappist-like praise of the spilling of time as in Lauds or Matins. It looked like the finale of *Show Boat* or *West Side Story*, with everyone singing at the top of their voices, their arms extended, Joe down on one knee, and Emily thrusting an umbrella out toward the mountains and beyond.

Alex Sanders noticed my puzzlement and utter surprise at the suddenness and spontaneity of the scene as the valley rang with the echoes of the hymn.

Then Alex spoke: "Ah! I could not help but notice—this is your first time with the Family von Trapp."

I fell in love with Alex Sanders that weekend, simply one of the many over the years who have been overwhelmed and ambushed in the field by the sheer immensity of his charm. By a roaring fire on the second day, Alex told some of the greatest stories I had ever heard, and I had to fight the urge to retreat to my room to record them in my journal while their fresh, persimmon-like details still burned along the taste buds of memory. In firelight, Alex had the head of a Javanese tiger and a serenity that enabled him to hold court without resorting to coarseness or testosterone.

He waited his turn, then used a matador's skill in controlling the pace of his narrative, and by changing the rhythm of his great accented voice, he could move us the way the matador could change the direction of a bull's charge by the flick of the wrist and the false billow created in that acreage of red cape. His phrasing was eloquent, colloquial, his pitch perfect. Wonderful writers surrounded him, and all of them found themselves bested and awed.

I will always remember Alex sitting in his flannel shirt with the smell of burning wood around us as the fires of autumn lit up the ridge of Tate Mountain with the surprising beauty that withering grants to its high forests. Alex's stories matched the uncommon colors of fall, where the trees flared up in all the vividness of wild roses gone to seed, the wings of hairstreaks and hummingbirds and all the last rainbows of the dying year. Rarely had I encountered stories so original, so strong with delightful detail, so perfect. Like wood smoke, his stories were born of fire, then carried away through air.

Whenever I have been in the presence of Zoe and Alex Sanders, the food has always been fabulous, the company unparalleled, the drink free-flowing and plentiful, and the conversation thrilling, heady, life-changing. As a couple, they have turned the dailiness of life into an art form and invited anyone who crosses their path to learn all its steps and secrets. As the College of Charleston knows, the now-retired President and Mrs. Sanders live out their lives at full speed, incapable of holding anything back. Both are fine cooks, and I have eaten like a deposed Italian king when I've found myself a lucky guest in their house. Zoe has as inimitable a reputation and mystique as a hostess as her husband does as an orator or storyteller or judge or educator. She is pretty, fiercely competent, fiery in her beliefs, and tenacious in her loves and enthusiasms.

Once, I sat with friends as Alex and Zoe fixed a fish stew that I remember being as good as any bouillabaisse that I ordered in the back-streets of Marseilles. The rouille they composed to top that soup in cloud-like dollops was a lovesong to garlic. I can summon up visions of past meals that have included ice chests loaded down with shrimp that had been swimming offshore that morning; oysters gathered during the last low tide; salads glistening with olive oil and darkened with raindrops of balsamic vinegar; fennel and red peppers blistered on the same grills where marinated flank steaks will follow; quail and wild rice swimming in gravy; sirloin steaks as large as my head hanging off serving platters; grouper and salmon and mahimahi coming off their bones in nuggets of white flesh that tastes like seaborne butter to the palate.

Both Alex Sanders and I have been accused of being prone to grotesque exaggeration in our careers, and there is great merit when that accusation is directed at Alex. But in my own defense, I can never convince people outside the South that I know someone as pointlessly colorful, outrageous, and bone-jarringly amusing as Alex Sanders himself. Alex helped me understand that the South I grew up in is so over-the-top and overbaked that I see myself as a shy minimalist trying to ink black-and-white woodcuts of my native land. Southerners all know that the South is too bizarre and out of control for its own good. I always find myself having to surrender some of the juice, hold back on the cayenne and Tabasco, for the sake of credibility itself.

When *The Prince of Tides* came out in 1986, I sat in the Four Seasons Restaurant in New York answering questions from a hostile reporter. As I dined on sweetbreads poached in white wine, I never thought I would be conducting much of the interview about Alex Sanders while a journalist skewered my brightest work.

"I found the white porpoise scene in your novel a little much," she said, toying with her salad. Critics are mostly bulimic, rail-thin—no great appetites there. "Homage to Herman Melville. Right?"

"Wrong," I said. "Alex Sanders told me the story."

"Who is Alex Sanders?"

"The greatest of all South Carolinians," I answered. "I thanked him in the acknowledgments."

"You thanked everyone in the acknowledgments," she said. "But there's no white porpoise, right?"

"Wrong. I saw the white porpoise swimming in Harbor River when I was at Beaufort High School."

I could tell she did not believe me, but she went on with the next question. "In your book you have a Bengal tiger at a gas station. How ridiculous."

"I'm sorry," I say, eating happily. "Another story from Alex Sanders. That was Happy the Tiger at an Esso gas station on Gervais Street in Columbia. I once fed Happy a chicken neck after I got my car washed."

"Let's go on," she said, her voice skeptical. "The moving of the town? To make way for a plutonium plant?"

"Want to go to the town?" I asked. "It's called New Ellenton."

"You claim it's true."

"I could get you a radiation burn at the plant, if you're so inclined."

She looked over her notes, then said, "And you're going to tell me Alex Sanders told you this story."

"It's one of his best," I said.

"Do you pay Alex Sanders royalties?"

"If I were a good and decent man, I certainly would. But I prefer to simply rob him of all his material and take full credit for it. He does the same to me."

"Do you ever have any ideas of your own?" she asked scornfully.

"Every once in a while I borrow from my meager pantry of ideas. But not often."

"What does this Alex Sanders do? Is he employed?"

"He's the chief justice of South Carolina's Court of Appeals, and he teaches at Harvard Law School."

She studied me for a moment, then said, "You're exaggerating again."

"Hotshot reporter like yourself could find out in a jif," I said, my voice revealing my irritation.

"You sound hostile."

"You find me dishonest."

"I'm skeptical," she said.

"That makes me hostile."

"Does the great Alex Sanders find you hostile?"

"He finds me perfectly delightful in every possible way," I said.

"Why?" she asked.

"Because I feel the same way about him. I'd rather spend an evening with Alex Sanders than anyone I've ever met. You'd feel the same way if you knew Alex. Everyone does."

Again, her eyes went to her notes, and her hostility was like a condiment to the meal. She said, "Let's go to the old chestnut. If you could invite any three people in history to a dinner party, who would they be?"

"Alex Sanders. Alex Sanders. Then Alex Sanders again."

"You're making fun of the question," she said.

"I certainly am. You want me to answer Jesus of Nazareth, Genghis Khan, and Eva Braun. Something like that."

"Something like that," she said, then she looked around at the décor of the unsurpassable Four Seasons. "Why did you want to eat in a place like this? I find it pretentious."

"It was recommended to me by Alex Sanders and his lovely wife, Zoe."

The reporter rose up to shake my hand and said, in parting, "I haven't believed a word you've said."

I found this strange encounter in one of my journals and wanted to include it in this book because Zoe and Alex are unlike any two people I have ever met. They entered my life like two sharply tanged sorbets, coming in the middle of the meal to cleanse the palate and ready you for the feast that is on its way from the kitchen. Always, they have surprised me with their uncanny and inexhaustible generosity.

When I last saw Alex, he told me about selling a litter of Boykin spaniels from the back of a pickup truck to a group of rich Yankees at William Buckley's house in Camden, South Carolina. Then he launched into one of the greatest love stories I've ever heard, about a shepherd in France who falls in love with a beautiful French reporter. The reporter climbs for six hours to reach the upper pastures where the shepherd tends his flocks in plain sight of the Alps. But I only hint at these stories with the hope that I live long enough to include them in future novels I have stolen from the brimming imagination of the greatest of all South Carolinians, Alex Sanders.

SOUPE DE POISSON   Near the docks of Marseilles, in a restaurant that looked more dangerous than enchanting, I followed the maitre d' to a small table with a starched, no-nonsense tablecloth; a glacial waiter moved toward my table. My guidebook said the restaurant served one of the best bouillabaisses in Marseilles, where the dish marked its provenance. I had eaten Zoe and Alex Sanders's fish soup on two occasions— once in the mountains of Georgia at Joe and Emily Cummings's house, and once in their own house in Columbia. I noted that these were two of the finest home-cooked meals I had ever eaten. This soup is celebratory and generous of spirit, and you fall in love with the friends who take the time to make it for you. It is a soup of great simplicity, yet the taste resonates along the palate.

I thought I was going to catch grief from the waiter for dining alone because Julia Child had forewarned in her book *Mastering the Art of French Cooking* that bouillabaisse was best made for a table of six. The French waiter asked me if it was my first time eating bouillabaisse in Marseilles, and I said in pidgin French that it was. "The bouillabaisse of Paris is not bouillabaisse," he said in one of the only French sentences I've ever understood.

When he emerged later from the kitchen, I could smell the meal racing ahead of him in the air. He set it in front of me and told me to inhale the steam rising from the broth. The smell was clean and deep, as though I were living inside an aquarium. I took a spoon and made sure I shaved off the southern portion of the rouille, a piece of sole, the scented broth, and a piece of the toasted French bread at the bottom. It was good beyond my powers to dream.

France, ladies and gentlemen. France.

• SERVES 6 AS A FIRST COURSE

4 cups Fish Stock (page 12)
2 tomatoes, coarsely chopped

Pinch of saffron threads

3 pounds any combination of fresh fish, cleaned, skinned, and cut
   into large dice*

12 slices baguette, lightly toasted

Rouille (see below)

Using at least four or five types of fish makes the soup more interesting: cod, mahimahi, tilapia, sea bass, grouper, halibut, snapper, trout, monkfish, catfish, or swordfish. Avoid strong-flavored fish like bluefish or mackerel.

1. In a medium stockpot, bring the fish stock to a simmer. Stir in the tomatoes and saffron and continue to simmer until the flavors marry, 8 to 10 minutes.

2. Gently place the pieces of fish in the simmering stock and continue simmering until the fish is cooked through but still slightly translucent in the center, about 5 minutes.

3. Put 2 slices of toast in each wide, shallow soup bowl. Ladle the soup into the bowls. Place a spoonful of rouille in the middle of the soup and serve. Pass the remaining rouille at the table.

Rouille

Use Homemade Mayonnaise (page 57) for the framework. Add 5 finely minced garlic cloves to the whisked egg yolks and a crushed small dried red chile when the mixture is transferred to the food processor.

• • •

GRILLED FENNEL AND PEPPER SALAD · SERVES 6 TO 8

4 fennel bulbs, cleaned, trimmed, and quartered
4 large red bell peppers, cored, seeded, and quartered
Olive oil
Coarse or kosher salt and coarsely ground black pepper
Fresh mint leaves
Balsamic vinegar

1. Toss the vegetables in olive oil, add salt and pepper to taste, and marinate for at least 45 minutes.

2. Light a medium-hot fire. Grill the fennel, cut side up, for 3 minutes. Turn and grill for another 3 minutes, or until lightly charred. Grill the peppers for 2 minutes a side until lightly charred.

3. Arrange the fennel and peppers on a serving platter. Sprinkle with fresh mint. Pass balsamic vinegar on the side.

CHAPTER TWENTY

Frank Stitt

There are austere rules in the writing of novels that vex the young writer every bit as much as the rules of finesse and discipline and cuisine vex a headstrong apprentice. Young masochists are drawn toward melodrama and coincidence; thus young writers and young cooks have much in common. As do older writers and master chefs.

I speak now of coincidence and the detached collisions of fate. In the early eighties, I spent an extraordinary week in New York City, where I attended plays and thrilled to an opera with my agent, Julian Bach, having dinner at the Four Seasons afterward. Like a bird-watcher, I keep a list of great restaurants that I would like to eat my way through during my passage on this earth. I crossed off Lutèce and La Côte Basque on this journey, during which I presented the full outline of *The Prince of Tides* to my lovely editor, Nan Talese. But Julian Bach and Nan Talese were not coincidences, rather part of the natural architecture of my life.

On the Delta flight back home to Atlanta, fate cleared its throat as I heard a handsome young man in the aisle seat across from me whistling softly. I am not the kind of man who starts up conversations with strangers on airplanes and who then pulls out pictures of his children to show to any passenger within earshot. When I travel, I prize my anonymity and solitude and have no desire to be seated next to a compulsive chatterbox. The whistling from the right drew my attention, but it was the stack of cookbooks that riveted me. In a neatly stacked pile, the young man was looking up recipes from the very best cookbooks published in that year. These were on the cutting edge and the outer rim— it was long before the dawning of the era of the celebrity chefs and the Food Network, but that revolution was in the air. Already, extra virgin olive oil had started to appear in Southern supermarkets, bringing sex, at last, to Southern kitchens. Arugula, watercress, and daikon radishes were making shy appearances in produce departments in my part of the world, and Paul Prudhomme had already made his mark in New Orleans, initiating the era when you could not meet a redfish that someone had not blackened. In my hometown of Atlanta, the glittering era of Pano & Paul's had begun, Buckhead began to strut with restaurants bucking for four stars, and I heard a Frenchman say you could get a better Russian meal at Nicolai's Roof's downtown location than you could in Moscow. Cuisine was breaking out all over the South, as luxuriant and uncontrollable as kudzu. The man across the aisle from me was about to change the history of his home state of Alabama forever.

"Sir," I said, watching him scribble in his notebook, "those cookbooks you're reading, they're wonderful."

"I think I just spent the best week of my life working in the kitchens of these four chefs," he said. "It's amazing what you can learn in just a week. My name is Frank Stitt, sir."

"Mine is Pat Conroy," I said. "Are you a chef?"

"Yes, I am, though I've never run my own place," Frank said. "I'm about to open a restaurant."

"Can I ask where?"

"Birmingham, Alabama," he said.

"It's a wasteland for good food," I said. "I was there a month ago."

"It won't be a wasteland anymore," Frank replied with a confidence that both surprised and delighted me.

"If you're any good at all," I remember saying, "you're going to be a very rich man."

Frank appraised me with care and then said, "I'm good. I'm very good."

He said it with a measure of conviction and authority that carried much weight with me. Frank declared it like a man with keenly earned self-knowledge, an awesome respect for the art of cooking, and a firm knowledge of the great gift he was about to bestow on his home state. He spoke with enthusiasm about the chefs who trained him in France, and he was already comfortable speaking in the vocabulary and techniques of Escoffier, Joel Robuchon, and Alain Ducasse. I could not mention a restaurant that he did not have knowledge of. His long apprenticeship was now over and Frank Stitt was coming home to deliver the goods to Alabama.

The Highlands Bar & Grill changed the way the people of Alabama thought about food. It was a revolution in the center of a neighborhood that was going slightly to seed but was about to start its renaissance. The quality of its restaurants is an important gauge for a city to measure its call to greatness. Frank Stitt put Birmingham on the culinary map the day he opened his restaurant. Later I heard from a white-shoe lawyer in one of those Atlanta law firms with enough WASP names to start a hive that the Highlands Bar was better than any restaurant in Atlanta. That's long before the kinks were worked out and long before Frank hit his amazing stride. I made it to the restaurant in the first six months of its existence and discovered that Frank Stitt was a far, far better chef than anyone who had ever crossed the Chattahoochee River from Georgia or entered the Birmingham city limits under the cover of darkness after a lost weekend in New Orleans.

Here is what you get in a Frank Stitt meal and what you get with every recipe in his magnificent cookbook, *Frank Stitt's Southern Table:* the full measure and passion of a man on fire with devotion to his chosen work. He gives you all the artistry at his command every time you sit down for a meal, and he does not tolerate lapses in the kitchen or produce that is not the freshest available. I have eaten at the Highlands Bar & Grill over twenty times and have never eaten a single meal that was not superb—the restaurant remains the best reason to move to Birmingham that I can think of. I would call Frank Stitt the best chef in America, but that would cause undue jealousy in the ranks of other chefs whose powers of cruelty are exceeded only by genocidal despots and serial killers with bad tattoos. So let me simply state that I think that Frank Stitt is *one of* the best chefs in America, and America is starting to come around to my position.

I have watched with interest the growing reputation of Frank and his restaurant on the national scene. Whenever I go to Birmingham, I return to the Highlands or its sister restaurant, Bottega, where I look forward to the changes and improvements in the menu. Frank works miracles with pork, as I discovered when I ordered a tenderloin with a bourbon and molasses glaze that I thought was the best thing I ever put in my mouth. But I had said the same thing about the soft-shell crab with brown butter and bacon vinaigrette and, on the same night, the basmati rice salad with chilled crabmeat, crescents of avocado, roasted peppers, and slivers of olives and mushrooms folded into a lemon mayonnaise that was both delicate and fragrant. I could write poems about the seared duck breast and his Louisiana rabbit simmered in red wine. Even the lowly Southern dish of grits Frank uses as a palette that he fills with slices of country ham and tosses with wild mushrooms, with a dusting of Parmesan cheese, grated fine.

At the Highlands Bar & Grill, there is a sensibility at work in the smallest of details. When Frank offered me a watermelon margarita, I could think of no more nauseating a combination of tastes than a sweet fruit and tequila. Naturally, I was wrong and watermelon has seemed a noble fruit, as kingly as pineapple, since that encounter. Frank's bar makes a better gin martini than New York's Plaza Hotel, and his Chilton County Bellini is far superior to the one served at Harry's Bar in Venice, where it was invented. You can enjoy those drinks at the best raw oyster bar outside New Orleans, where the Apalachicola oysters have been harvested from the Gulf of Mexico on the day you consume them. They are cold and salty and Gulf-born. Just when you think that an oyster on the half shell is the most perfect food on earth, Frank will present you with baked oysters with watercress and a bread crumb crust, or his oyster pan roast with crawfish and buttery croutons, or spicy baked oysters with caramelized onions, pan juices, and chiles.

But then there are the lamb shanks with favas and the cobia with beet relish and how can I leave out the Gulf triggerfish or the magic he works with South Carolina quail or his ravioli with sweet potatoes, mustard greens, and country ham? I cannot do justice to Frank if I fail to praise his foie gras with corn bread or his roast leg of lamb with spring vegetable ragout, or the wine list that grows and mellows and deepens in complexity with each passing year. I have even failed to mention the desserts, which are often the weak spot of restaurants with the raw ambition displayed by the Highlands Bar & Grill. But Frank's desserts are the stuff of both dreams and paradise, and I have heard men say aloud in front of their wives that they would marry the pastry chef as they scooped up clouds of the cinnamon crème anglaise or moaned over the crème brûlée. The waiters are classy and well trained. Frank's beautiful wife, Pardis, runs the front with elegance and panache. His chef de cuisine is masterful and the cooks know what they are doing. The knife work is deft and Zen-like, and every night the men and women of Frank Stitt's Highlands Bar & Grill know that they are in the process of making both history and art.

The food world is coming around to my opinion formed so many years ago. Recently, I was in another airplane to Atlanta when I read that *Gourmet* magazine had named the Highlands Bar & Grill the fifth-best restaurant in the nation. In the same year, Frank won a James Beard award for being the best chef of the Southeast. The inimitable R. W. "Johnny" Apple of the *New York Times* made one of his baptismal visits to the restaurant and left shouting kudos and benedictions like all the rest of us.

Over a year ago, my wife and I joined Frank and Pardis for a spectacular meal at Alain Ducasse's restaurant in New York. It was a meal for the ages, and a great joy to watch Frank smell each dish as it arrived steaming from the kitchen, his eyes lighting up with lapidary pleasure as each dish arrived on our table. The restaurant is as formal and plush and forbidding as the Highlands Bar & Grill is welcoming and all-inclusive. The meal was Proustian and fabulous and indescribable, as all the great meals are.

When Sandra and I said farewell to Frank and Pardis Stitt that night and walked toward our hotel with all the clamor and splendor and mystery of the great city swarming about us, we both agreed that Alain Ducasse is a splendid chef, but we also both agreed that he is no Frank Stitt.

The following three recipes came to me directly from Chef Frank Stitt of Birmingham, Alabama.

GRILLED FIGS WITH PROSCIUTTO, WALNUTS, AND
LEMON-MINT CREAM This is one of my favorite summer hors d'oeuvres—perfect for passing around at a party still sizzling from the grill. Make this only with absolutely fresh ingredients: perfectly ripe figs, the finest prosciutto, and the freshest walnuts. Richard Olney was the inspiration for this dish. He loved figs more than almost any other fruit and was especially fond of their affinity for cured ham. We first passed this now-late-summer menu standard at an event in the gardens of the Joseph Phelps winery. The salty ham and the just-beginning-to-warm plump fig is one of the sexiest bites ever.   • SERVES 4

1 handful fresh spearmint, plus sprigs for garnish

Juice of 1 $^1/_2$ lemons

$^1/_2$ cup heavy cream

Coarse or kosher salt and freshly ground black pepper

8 ripe Black Mission figs

16 walnut halves

16 very thin slices prosciutto di Parma

4 fig leaves

1. Prepare a hot grill.

2. Finely chop the mint and place in a mortar with the lemon juice. Pound with the pestle and strain into a medium mixing bowl. Add the cream. Season with salt and pepper and stir to incorporate. The acidity of the lemon juice will thicken the cream.

3. Halve the figs and place a walnut half on the cut side of each. Wrap a slice of prosciutto around the fig, only slightly overlapping where the prosciutto ends meet. (The perfect slice of prosciutto has an outer edge with some of the snow-white fat included.)

4. Char the figs on the hot grill for 30 to 45 seconds per side. The figs should just be warmed through and the prosciutto crisp in parts. These contrasting textures make this a wonderful dish. Place 4 figs

on each fig leaf and serve with the bowl of mint cream on the side, garnished with mint sprigs.

• • •

RED SNAPPER WITH CRAWFISH MEUNIÈRE   Red snapper has been the reigning queen of Gulf Coast seafood for over seventy-five years and with good reason—the delicate, white, flaky, moist flesh fits almost everyone's idea of what fish should be. Sautéed red snapper is a wonderful thing unto itself. When you mix plump little buttery crawfish tails with lots of lemon and fresh mint, you've created a plate of springtime goodness. Don't hesitate to substitute crabmeat for the crawfish, if you wish. This recipe calls for a quick sauté of the fish. Then the same pan is used to create the ultimate fish sauce—a meunière. Its origin, the story goes, began with the miller's wife who would use some of the mill's flour to dust the fish before cooking. She would then add a bit of shallot and white wine to make a sauce, finishing it by whisking in a little butter, lemon juice, and fresh mint at the last second. The only way we improve upon this age-old formula is to enliven the dish with a little crawfish or crabmeat. One of my favorite restaurant experiences is digging into the speckled trout with crabmeat meunière at Galatoire's in New Orleans (and at Highlands Bar & Grill). Such meals are some of life's great moments. If you can't get your hands on impeccably fresh red snapper, opt for wild striped bass, speckled trout, flounder, or pompano. **• SERVES 4**

> Four 6- to 8-ounce red snapper fillets (or other fresh white fish; see headnote)
> Coarse or kosher salt and freshly ground white pepper
> $^{1}/_{2}$ cup all-purpose flour
> 2 tablespoons clarified butter
> 4 tablespoons ($^{1}/_{2}$ stick) plus 1 $^{1}/_{2}$ teaspoons unsalted butter
> 2 shallots, finely minced

$^3/_4$ cup white wine

$^1/_2$ pound crawfish tail meat or jumbo lump crabmeat

Juice of 1 large lemon

1 small bunch fresh mint leaves, chopped at the last moment (to
    yield 2 tablespoons)

Hot pepper sauce, such as Tabasco or Cholula

1. Check to be sure that all of the bones have been removed from the fish and any little scrappy ends are trimmed so that the fillets are uniform and will cook evenly. Season the fish with salt and pepper on both sides. Dust the fish with the flour and shake off any excess.

2. Heat a large heavy sauté pan over high heat. Add the clarified butter and heat until almost smoking. Place the fillets in the pan, skin side up. Lower the heat to medium and cook until light golden brown and the outer edges begin to turn opaque, about 3 minutes. Turn the fillets and cook until just done, about 3 minutes more, depending on thickness. Remove the fillets to a rack.

3. Pour out any clarified butter remaining in the pan and add the $1^1/_2$ teaspoons butter along with the shallots. Cook over medium-low heat until the shallots soften, about 1 minute. Add the white wine and crawfish tails and raise the heat to high to reduce the liquid by more than half.

4. When the wine has reduced, begin to whisk in the 4 tablespoons butter quickly, bit by bit, shaking the pan while whisking. Once the butter is incorporated, lower the heat so that the sauce does not boil, or it will separate. Quickly add the lemon juice along with the freshly chopped mint. Season to taste with salt, white pepper, and a dash of hot pepper sauce. Taste and adjust seasonings, then pour the sauce over the snapper and serve immediately on hot plates.

• • •

CURED PORK CROSTINI WITH SWEET POTATO BRANDADE

A traditional *brandade* is made of salt cod, potatoes, and garlic bound with olive oil. In the south of France, brandade is often used as a spread on crostini. Here we're having a little improvisational fun. Instead of cured fish, we use cured pork, and instead of the typical potato, we use local sweet potatoes. You can substitute roasted or grilled pork tenderloin and still have delicious results, but if you have the time, try this cure. **• SERVES 8 AS AN APPETIZER**

1/2 cup sugar

1/2 cup coarse or kosher salt

4 garlic cloves, crushed, plus 1/2 garlic head

8 whole black peppercorns, crushed

4 whole allspice berries, crushed

1 whole star anise, crushed

1 dried hot chile

1 pound pork tenderloin, trimmed, and silver skin removed

2 large sweet potatoes, peeled and quartered

1/4 cup slab bacon cut into 1/2-inch cubes

1 teaspoon extra virgin olive oil

Freshly ground black pepper

2 tablespoons olive oil

8 slices baguette, about 1/4-inch thick

Fresh cilantro sprigs

1. In a medium saucepan, combine the sugar, salt, crushed garlic, peppercorns, allspice, star anise, chile, and 4 cups water and bring to a boil. Simmer for 15 minutes and then pour the contents into a nonreactive container that is narrow and deep enough to keep the pork tenderloin submerged. Let the brine cool completely in the refrigerator. Once cool, add the pork and let cure overnight or for up to 2 days in the refrigerator.

2. Place the sweet potatoes and garlic head in a medium saucepan and cover with water by 2 inches. Add a good pinch of salt and bring to a simmer. Cook until very tender, about 30 minutes.

3. While the sweet potatoes are cooking, place the bacon in a sauté pan and cook until crisp, about 8 minutes. Set aside. Drain the sweet potatoes, then purée them through a food mill or ricer. Return the purée to the pan and add the bacon and its rendered fat along with the extra virgin olive oil and salt and pepper to taste. Stir vigorously to combine. Keep the potatoes warm.

4. Preheat the oven to 425° F.

5. Remove the pork from the brine and pat dry. In a heavy, ovenproof sauté pan, heat 1 tablespoon olive oil over high heat and sear the pork on all sides. Place the pan in the preheated oven and cook until medium (internal temperature of 145° F), 10 to 15 minutes. Transfer to a rack to rest.

6. Brush the baguette slices with the remaining 1 tablespoon olive oil, sprinkle with salt and pepper, and toast in the oven for 5 minutes.

7. Spoon a little sweet potato brandade on top of each crostini, spreading it evenly. Slice the pork thinly and arrange a few slices on top of each crostini. Allow the colorful brandade to show along the edges by folding the pork slices for an attractive presentation. Garnish each crostini with a few sprigs of cilantro and a grind or two of black pepper and serve.

CHAPTER TWENTY-ONE

Eating in New Orleans

In the lucky life I have had as a writer of books, I will never duplicate the astonishment and surprise I felt when Houghton Mifflin
introduced the world to *The Prince of Tides* at the American
Booksellers Association in New Orleans. I had been content with my
career, which was modest but successful; that I could be publishing books
in this country, with a background like mine, seemed further proof of the
deepest American ideal. I had been caught off guard by the explosive
reception to the new novel by the booksellers and the gushing, wide-eyed
enthusiasm of my publishing company. Several of my friends had read
the book and had delivered lukewarm responses. The novelist Michael
Mewshaw read it in Rome and suggested I cut it into twelve novels. Nan
Talese told me she liked it a lot, but I thought she spoke from her good
breeding and editorial politesse. One friend said I was an anti-Semite and
another said I hated the South.

It was only when the best reader of my life, Bernie Schein, checked in
that I started thinking that I had hit on something big in this novel.
"Goddamn," Bernie said when I answered the phone.

"You like it, Bernie?" I said. "Tell me the truth."

"Goddamn. Goddamn. Goddamn. Goddamn."

"You really like it, Bernie?"

"Goddamn, son. If this ain't a son of a bitch, I'll kiss your ass on the pitcher's mound during this year's All-Star Game."

All writers need friends like Bernie Schein and neighbors like the lawyers Knox and Carolyn Dobbins. Since we shared a driveway, we became inseparable friends. They would often stop me as I came out of the office I had over the garage.

"Finished yet?" Knox would ask me every time. For years I shook my head no.

Then in 1985, Carolyn asked me, "Finished yet, Pat?"

And I said, "I just wrote the last sentence."

Carolyn squealed, then ran toward me, and I danced her around the yard. When they finished reading the book, they invited me over to the house for a celebratory drink. They toasted me and predicted great success for the book.

"We both think it's going to be the main selection of the Book of the Month Club," Carolyn said.

"No, it'll never get that. I'll be lucky to be an alternate," I said.

Knox said, "You don't know what you're talking about. You're not a member of the Book of the Month Club and we are. It's going to be a main selection. It's a lock."

"Why do you think so?" I asked.

"Because it's about everything in the world," Carolyn said. When *The Prince of Tides* was named the main selection of the Book of the Month Club, I invited Knox and Carolyn to be my special guests at the luncheon the Book of the Month Club had in my honor. I wanted to thank them for their generosity, their openness, and their amazing powers to see into a future that I didn't see.

But it was the city of New Orleans where I felt the chambers of my fate click into high gear. Everything about that weekend in the spring of 1986 seemed magnetized, lustrous, and fine. In *The Prince of Tides* I had let my passionate love of story loose from the cage after a long imprisonment; it became possible after I read Gabriel García Márquez's *One Hundred Years of Solitude* and John Irving's *The World According to*

Garp. Those two marvelous books freed something inside me and made me take note of my own work and realize I was holding back and keeping a tight rein on my imagination because of cowardice and a deep fear of the judgment of critics and other writers. The first sentence of *One Hundred Years of Solitude* dazzled me, and I said out loud to myself, "I don't know how to write. I couldn't write a sentence this complex if I had to." So I pressed myself to get better by growing bolder and more ambitious. I had tired of life among the parakeets, and I was eager to test the hot thermal currents from which the great condors with their immense wingspans surveyed their vast domains. But with all this bold talk and inflated thinking, I was not sure the world was ready for a book that contained the capture of an albino porpoise, a giant rapist who would be killed by a Bengal tiger, and the moving of an entire town to make way for a nuclear power plant. In Atlanta, at a party in Ansley Park before I left for New Orleans, a friend of mine who had read the book yelled at me from across the room, "Hey, Conroy! Who else writes about the birth of a child, only it's not just a child—it's twins? And it's during a hurricane and the river is flooding and the father has just been shot down in Germany and is going to be saved by a German Catholic priest? Have you ever thought about just writing a normal novel?"

No, come to think of it, I never had, but my friend's send-up of *The Prince of Tides* still strikes me as accurate and hilarious. I was nervous about going to New Orleans and witnessing the novel's reception among the booksellers of America. But here is what is never disappointing in New Orleans: the wonderful food cooked by some of the most imaginative chefs in the world.

On Friday night, my elegant editor, Nan Talese, picked up my wife and me in a limousine to take us to dinner at a new hot restaurant in the New Orleans suburbs. Writers of the world, it is a good sign when your editor arrives in a limo to take you anywhere. It is a telling sign when she starts booking you into rooms with minibars. By the time we reached the restaurant, I was disoriented and had no idea about where in Louisiana I was. But the restaurant had smells coming out of the kitchen that were heavenly, so it boded well for the evening.

We were seated at a table beautifully set with bone-white china, good cutlery, and a tablecloth you could have performed inpatient surgery on. There were candelabras and chandeliers, and the waiters were well-groomed and well-schooled. The women at the table—I have never seen this done in another restaurant—were provided with small, raised, and inlaid pillows on which to rest their pretty but weary feet. I heard a feminist writer at another table say, "What the hell is this bullshit?"

My two British publishers were already at the table, Mark Barty King, who is known in publishing circles as the handsomest man in the world, and Paul Sherer, the head of the London division of Doubleday. Royce Bemis, the Houghton Mifflin rep from Atlanta and my good friend, had brought one of his booksellers from Emory University, a pretty woman named Cassie Fahey. All of us studied the menu with sublime happiness as people at tables nearby raved about the quality of the food. When the appetizers arrived, they were hot to the touch and ambrosia to the taste buds. We began sharing one another's appetizers, plates moving across the table with crab in puff pastry that tasted as though blue crabs had actually been born in the pastry, never needing the armor of their cartilage. There were mussels in a cream and wine sauce that were the best I had ever eaten, as well as an artichoke heart wrapped in aspic.

When the main course arrived, I tasted quail roasted with pancetta and fried oysters nestling in a bed of hollandaise, and a lamb shank that seemed to have been braised in red wine, but there were hints of garlic and peppers and even, I thought, a touch of rich coffee to top off the bouquet. I lingered over my grouper, which for me has always been the tastiest fish that the Atlantic Ocean seems capable of producing. The chef had steamed the grouper in paper, flavoring it with olive oil, garlic, ginger, and wine, and once again, I think, I tasted the pungent salty afterbite of soy sauce. The table toasted the success of *The Prince of Tides,* and I toasted right back and felt like a million bucks as the waiter began to bring out desserts. The crème brûlée and cheesecakes and sorbets, the decadent cakes and sinful pies I tasted that night as the sharing of plates continued were magnificent. I think it would have ranked as a perfect meal, except for its unfortunate finale.

My editor is as proud a woman as I have ever been around, and I grew up in the South. Her grooming is perfect and one could purchase a small used car for the cost of one of her suits. I was sitting beside Nan when she whispered an urgent message in my ear: "This restaurant doesn't take credit cards! Did you bring any money, Pat?"

"Not a penny, Nan," I said.

"We need to talk to the headwaiter. Would you come with me? I've never been so embarrassed," she said.

The headwaiter repeated the restaurant policy of no credit cards and no checks and sent us into the kitchen to plead with the chef, who was also the owner. Nan and I entered the hectic atmosphere of a kitchen in full throttle, and a dark flame of a man moved out to meet us.

Nan said, "I'm a New York publisher in town for the ABA, and I'm told you don't take credit cards. I've never heard of a restaurant that doesn't accept credit cards."

"Welcome to my establishment, madam," the chef said. He did impervious as well as any man I have ever seen. This guy carried himself with the sangfroid of Auguste Escoffier and displayed the presence of a field commander in the Marine Corps. "We do not accept credit cards, but my staff and I do wish to be paid for our labors. I hope the meal was adequate."

"The best I have ever eaten, my friend," I said.

The chef nodded and said again, "My staff and I simply wish to be paid for our services."

"This is such a dreadful rule," Nan said, but she had met her match. Then she began removing her many gold bracelets, soon holding a king's ransom out to the stern-jawed chef.

"I shall leave my bracelets with you while I go back to the hotel, get the money, and come right back here," Nan said with some desperation in her voice.

The chef shook his head no and said again, "We wish to be paid for our labors. Nothing less, nothing more."

"Hey, pal," I said, "I don't know you, but I'd take that jewelry and pray this woman never comes back to this restaurant."

"My staff and I work hard. We deserve compensation for our labors. I suggest you return to your table and tell the others of your dilemma. Someone at the table has the money, I assure you."

So poor Nan returned to the table, told of her utter humiliation by a priggish, dreadful man in the kitchen, and asked to borrow the money to pay for the meal. One of the English editors pulled out a bright wad of traveler's checks from Barclays and paid the bill in full. I suggested right then that Nan get the chef to write a cookbook and publish it before he got famous, but Nan was miffed and declared she would not publish a word written by that man.

The weekend in New Orleans was triumphant and unrepeatable. It will never happen to me again, but then it never happens once to most people. I am deeply appreciative. I got to hear one of my literary heroes, Walker Percy, deliver a speech, then Houghton Mifflin threw me a party at the house where Frances Parkinson Keyes (one of my mother's favorite writers) lived and worked. The great Walter Cronkite introduced me to the booksellers, and I spoke to them before the comedian Carol Burnett followed with her speech.

I spoke to the booksellers about my mother's dream of my becoming a "Southern" writer. I told of my growing up in the household of a fighter pilot and the forces that shaped me as a boy. Then I told them about the publication of my first book, *The Boo*, which I published myself out of ignorance and provinciality. I silenced the laughter when I told them about the death of the mother who had raised me to be a writer. When I sat down, my life had changed forever. There was a huge line when I got to the Houghton Mifflin booth. It was against the rules for a line to form on the convention floor, but the chief of sales, Steve Lewers, said he didn't give a damn, paid a hefty fine, and let the booksellers line up by the hundreds. The first person in that line was Walter Cronkite, and I have never forgotten that graceful gesture.

If I could choose background music for that time in New Orleans, I would choose the "Triumphal March" from *Aida* without a moment's hesitation.

But here is the memory I carry most strongly from that storied weekend. Fifteen years later, I was walking through the den where my wife, Cassandra, was watching a show on the Food Network. A dark-haired chef, a dark flame of a man, was filleting a grouper with great expertise. I stared at the man and said to Sandra, "I know that guy."

"How do you know him?" my wife asked. She and I were still new to each other, and new to an addiction to the Food Network, so she didn't know the chef's name either.

Slowly, it returned: the image of Nan Talese removing the bracelets from her arm in the kitchen of a world-class restaurant. I put it all together and realized that Nan and I had met Emeril Lagasse in the earliest stages of his career. I adore his show and think he's sexy as hell. I love it when he shouts out, "Bam! Let's bring it up a notch or two." I roar my approval along with the bedazzled audience.

When I mentioned to Nan that I had identified the chef of that restaurant in New Orleans as Emeril Lagasse, I could not help but taunt her. "You never listen to my advice. You should have published Emeril's first cookbook."

"He was a perfectly dreadful man," Nan said.

"No, he and his staff simply wanted to be paid for their labor," I said, laughing on the phone.

EMERIL'S BARBECUED SHRIMP WITH ROSEMARY BISCUITS

"These shrimp aren't really barbecued. Instead, this is my take on a classic New Orleans dish where whole shrimp are baked with butter, olive oil, and spices. When Emeril's opened, we took the dish up another notch and created this amazingly rich sauce for sautéed shrimp. The barbecue base will keep for a month, tightly covered in the refrigerator. Try the same sauce with oysters, adding the oysters to the sauce after it has reduced enough to coat the back of a spoon." —Emeril Lagasse

• SERVES 4 TO 6

FOR THE BARBECUED SHRIMP

2 pounds medium shrimp in their shells

1 tablespoon Emeril's Original Essence or your favorite Creole seasoning

$1/2$ teaspoon freshly ground black pepper

1 tablespoon vegetable oil

1 cup heavy cream

2 tablespoons unsalted butter, cut into pieces

FOR THE BARBECUE SAUCE BASE

1 tablespoon olive oil

$1/2$ cup finely chopped yellow onion

1 teaspoon salt

1 teaspoon coarsely ground black pepper

3 bay leaves

1 tablespoon minced garlic

3 lemons, peeled, white pith removed, and quartered

$1/2$ cup dry white wine

2 cups shrimp stock

1 cup Worcestershire sauce

FOR THE ROSEMARY BISCUITS

1 cup unbleached all-purpose flour

1 teaspoon baking powder

$^1/_2$ teaspoon coarse or kosher salt

$^1/_4$ teaspoon baking soda

3 tablespoons cold unsalted butter, cut into small pieces

1 tablespoon minced fresh rosemary

$^1/_2$ to $^3/_4$ cup buttermilk

1. To prepare the shrimp: Peel and devein the shrimp, leaving their tails attached. (Reserve the shells, if desired, to make the shrimp stock.) Season the shrimp with Emeril's Original Essence and black pepper, tossing to coat evenly. Cover and refrigerate while you make the sauce base and biscuits.

2. To make the barbecue sauce base: Heat the olive oil in a medium, heavy saucepan over medium-high heat. Add the onion, salt, pepper, and bay leaves and cook, stirring, until the onion is soft, about 2 minutes. Add the garlic, lemons, and white wine and cook for 2 minutes.

3. Add the shrimp stock and Worcestershire sauce and bring to a boil over high heat.

4. Reduce the heat to medium-low and simmer until the sauce is reduced to $^1/_2$ cup, about $1^1/_4$ hours.

5. Strain the sauce through a fine-mesh strainer into a clean container, pressing on the solids with the back of a spoon. Set aside until needed. (The sauce base can be refrigerated in an airtight container for up to 3 days or frozen for up to 2 months.)

6. To make the rosemary biscuits: Preheat the oven to 400°F.

7. Sift the dry ingredients into a large bowl. Work the butter into the flour mixture with your fingertips or a fork until the mixture resembles coarse crumbs. Stir in the rosemary. Add $^1/_2$ cup buttermilk a little at a time, using your hands to work it in just until incorporated and a smooth ball of dough forms. Add up to an additional $^1/_4$ cup buttermilk if necessary, being very careful not to overwork the dough, or the biscuits will be tough.

8. On a lightly floured surface, pat the dough into a circle about 7 inches in diameter and $^1/_2$ inch thick. Using a 1-inch round cookie cutter, cut out 12 biscuits.

9. Place the biscuits on an ungreased baking sheet. Bake until golden on top and lightly browned on the bottom, 10 to 12 minutes. Keep warm.

10. To finish the shrimp: Heat the oil in a large skillet over high heat. Add the seasoned shrimp and cook, stirring, until they begin to turn pink, about 2 minutes. Add the cream and $^1/_4$ cup barbecue sauce base, reduce the heat to medium-high, and simmer, stirring, until reduced by half, about 3 minutes.

11. Remove the shrimp from the pan with tongs and transfer to a platter. Over medium-low heat, gradually whisk the butter into the sauce. Remove from the heat.

12. Place 2 or 3 biscuits on each plate. Divide the shrimp among the biscuits and top each serving with the sauce. Serve immediately.

CHAPTER TWENTY-TWO

Julian Bach

My longtime literary agent Julian Bach and I moved in different circles, and I consider it a small miracle that he entered my life at the precise time I needed him most. The superintendent had fired me from teaching the children of Daufuskie Island, and I was in the fierce process of handwriting the book that became *The Water Is Wide*. My firing had attracted some national attention. Betsy Fancher had written a brilliant article in *South Today* that was carried on the wires to California. Joe Cummings came down from *Newsweek* and my name attracted the adjective "controversial" for the first but not the last time in my life. I had completed two hundred pages on yellow legal pads when a journalist named Richard Bruner came to my door to change the direction of my life. He took down the details of my story with the efficiency and craft I had come to admire in print journalists. After he completed the interview, I showed Richard Bruner my writing room, which was covered with the manuscript pages and a copy of my first, self-published book, *The Boo*.

"You need an agent for this new book, pal," he said. "How did you pay for the printing of *The Boo*?"

"I told Willie Scheper at the bank that I had written a book about The

Citadel and he offered to write me a check for three thousand dollars on the spot."

"Did you sell any?" he asked.

"Sold them all," I said. "Our first printing was for fifteen hundred copies and we just went back to press."

"You really need an agent, son." Richard Bruner wrote Julian Bach's name, phone number, and address on a sheet of paper. "Julian's good. I'd say he's the best."

In three tight paragraphs I wrote down every word I would say to Julian Bach if I could get him to come to the phone. I practiced in front of a mirror, hoping I sounded sincere but not maudlin, resolute but not desperate. For one hour I sat by the phone summoning the courage to place the call. Even I understood that an encounter with Julian Bach could play a huge role in whatever career as a writer I might have. I dialed his number in New York and tried to sound professional and dignified when his receptionist, Diane Cusumano, answered the phone. For some reason I thought Diane would put up more of a fight to keep an amateur out of her boss's life, but Diane was accommodating and sweet and before I was ready for my grand entrance onto the stage of Julian Bach, a most impatient, authoritative male voice was on the line.

"Yes, yes, what is it? Who are you and why are you calling me?"

"Mr. Bach," I read, shaken, "I have written a book about a year I spent teaching on a Carolina sea island."

"Who are you? What's your name? How did you get to this office?"

I had not written that information down. "I taught eighteen black children for a year before I was fired."

"Do you have a name, young man? Where are you calling from?"

"My name is Pat Conroy, and I live in Beaufort, South Carolina."

"Get to the point. Who sent you to me?"

"A man named Richard Bruner."

"Oh, Dick, of course," Julian said. "Look, I get lots of calls from kids who want to write; most of them turn out to be losers. Get me a freshly typed manuscript by Friday and I will put it with my weekend reading. I make no promises." He slammed the phone down without saying good-bye, hurting my Southern-boy feelings.

I walked downstairs and joined my wife, Barbara, and my mother in the kitchen.

"Did you call Mr. Bach?" Barbara asked.

"I think he said I've got a New York agent," I said, as the two women in my life screamed out of relief and pressure.

"I have to get him a freshly typed manuscript by Friday," I said.

"Does he know you don't know how to type?"

"No, I was ashamed to tell him."

"Don't worry," Barbara said, rushing to the phone. "I'm calling every-one we know in Beaufort who types. We'll give them each one chapter and tell them to get it back to us tomorrow."

My wife and mother marshaled a small battalion of friends in the town of Beaufort who drove or ran to our house as soon as they were called to action. Ting Colquhoun and Betty Sams hurried over from their nearby houses. My English teacher Millen Ellis arrived as Harriet Keyserling was coming through the back door. All night, those friends came crossing through the front door to receive a chapter of my hand-written manuscript.

"We need it back tomorrow morning," my mother would shout. Barbara would say, "Pat's got himself a New York agent."

All returned the next morning with their chapters completed. Barbara began putting the manuscript together, but we instantly stumbled on one problem, which we had not anticipated. Some of those glorious typists who banged out pages for Julian Bach had used onionskin paper, others long yellow sheets, and still others short blue sheets. Since I didn't type, I didn't know about the existence of pica or elite or that kind of typescript that looks like handwriting. Harriet Keyserling had typed her chapter on her personal stationery. The first chapter's pages were numbered one to twenty, the second chapter's one to seventeen, the third chapter's one to twenty-five, and so on.

But Julian Bach wanted to have it for his weekend and, by God, he would get it for his weekend read. Jack Colquhoun was waiting for me at the post office when I arrived at closing time. He boxed the manuscript and shipped it special delivery to Julian Bach Jr. Literary Agency, 3 East 48th Street, New York, NY 10017. His phone number was Plaza 3–4331. Cable address: Turtle News, New York. Jack mailed it off as we embraced in the mailroom.

Friday I received a phone call from Julian Bach telling me that the manuscript had arrived. Then he said, "Pat, I have to tell you, I haven't read a single word of it, but it's the cutest thing I've ever seen. It's being passed around to everyone in the office. It's making quite a hit."

I hung up the phone, mortified. A sense of shame washed over me that I could not shake or control. What I had wanted most of all was to attract the admiration of a New York agent, not his laughter and certainly not his scorn. Since I had not held a job in six months, my mother and wife had leapt through a window of opportunity opened by the unforeseeable arrival of Julian Bach in my life. But it was I who should have acted in a professional manner; it was my name on the manuscript and my name on the return address. I thought I had lost my greatest chance to discover if I was a real writer or not. I was bereft and told no one about my conversation with Julian Bach. Later that week I drove to a chicken farm outside Allendale to apply for a job. The farmer asked me if I was that teacher who'd been fired down in Beaufort County, and when I answered in the affirmative he tore up my application and said he needed someone he could trust with his chickens. In a season chock-full of low points, that was as bad as it got.

Three weeks later the letter arrived from the Julian Bach agency and the shock of seeing that address from the fabled city of New York nearly brought me to my knees. I felt astonishment, despair, and then hopelessness. If this man turned my book down, I had no idea what would happen to me and my family. So much was riding on this single letter that I did not rip it open at once. Instead I went to the back door, got into my 1969 yellow Volkswagen convertible, and drove across the bridge and out toward the beach. I took the left at the dirt road that led to Dataw Island, a magnificent hunting preserve owned by my good friend the historian Larry Rowland. One of the many ways Larry was a good friend was his presentation of a key to the gate of Dataw. I had free access not only to the island but to the graceful, music box–like house that his father had built with his own hands.

Parking the car by the house, I took the letter to the end of the dock and sat there staring at it. For fifteen minutes I studied the name of the Julian Bach agency, but I was paralyzed by fear of what it might say. Looking at the river, then back at the small white house where I would one day house the Wingo family in *The Prince of Tides,* I opened the letter and began reading it. Today, that letter hangs on my den wall in Fripp Island. Here is what it says:

> *Dear Conroy-Conrack, warmly. I have read all the material you sent and so has Wendy Weil, my associate—and we find it exceptionally exciting. More than you may yet realize, you were born lucky. You are a natural writer. Few people are. This is what we are about to do* [here is where I began to fall in love with Julian Bach]*:*
>
> *Pencil in numbers on all your pages and hereby Conroy-Conrack, you must pledge that you will never again submit a manuscript to anyone without numbering the pages so that your agent or editors can refer to page 79 or 179.*

I skittered around the floating dock like a water bug and I warwhooped and screamed out my divine relief and rush of pleasure at the moment a New York agent told me I was a natural writer. I yelled, I screamed, I danced from one end of the dock to the other, and then topped off my performance by falling on my back, pumping my arms and legs toward the sunlight, doing the "dying cockroach," which I could do with blithe expertise after days as a Citadel cadet. I swore to the river and to the sun and to the God who made me that I would be a client of Julian Bach's for the rest of my life, no matter what happened.

The rest of the letter was strategic and businesslike until Julian got to the very last paragraph, where he expressed his belief that this was the first of many books I would write, both fiction and nonfiction, adding that he thought there would be movie deals, magazine assignments, and anything else I might want to do. He welcomed me to his agency and said he would be proud to serve as my agent. There was a party at the Conroy house that night and everyone came, with my heroic typists as the guests of honor.

Two months later Julian Bach called me from New York. "Pat, are you sitting down? I have some great news for you."

"What is it?"

"Houghton Mifflin—the publisher of Thoreau, Emerson, Henry James, and Emily Dickinson—wants very much to publish *The Water Is Wide*. But here is the really great news, Pat," he said, enjoying a long silence. "Seventy-five hundred dollars."

I frowned, shook my head, and then said a line Julian Bach has never let me forget: "But, Julian, I can get it done a lot cheaper down here."

There was what I can only call a stunned silence when I heard Julian clear his throat to say, "Pat, you do realize that it is *they* who pay *you* to publish and not the other way around? My God, people must be naïve in Beaufort, South Carolina."

So my life began with Julian Bach as my literary agent, and he became my portal to and illuminator of the great city of New York. He loved all facets of New York life and introduced me to grand opera, to theater, and to all the great restaurants of Midtown, where Julian was most comfortable. On my first trip to Manhattan he took me to his favorite, L'Argenteuil, an exquisite French restaurant. Although I'd never had asparagus before, L'Argenteuil was where I first tasted the white asparagus for which the restaurant was named. Julian threw the first New York literary party for me and Barbara, held in the garden of his Turtle Bay home. When Julian pointed out his neighbor, Katharine Hepburn, coming down the back steps, I felt like a figure in an F. Scott Fitzgerald novel, and the feeling has never quite left me. My pledge to stay forever with Julian Bach held true. We were together almost thirty years, never having had a single argument or raising our voices to each other. When I think of the word "gentleman," a word of great sanctity to me, I think of Julian Bach. He is elegant, mannerly, and precise. I can think of only one flaw that has caused me any irritation in the long years we've been together. Julian has a strange habit of never saying goodbye on the telephone. One minute you are talking to Julian and the next minute you are not. At first it was maddening, but then endearing when I found out he treated every other human being the same way.

When Julian retired in 1999 I gave the keynote address and tried to make it a good one. The night was an emotional one for both of us as I traced our careers together from a dock in Beaufort to a writing career in New York publishing, through publication parties and movie openings and long celebratory meals at the Four Seasons. What a grand time we had, and I wouldn't change a single thing about it.

As we walked out of the IMG building on Seventy-first Street, Julian and I walked behind our pretty wives, Hope and Sandra. Then Julian told me of a provision in his will where, upon his death, I was to be flown first-class to New York City, put up in the finest hotel, and fed at the finest restaurants if I would do him the honor of delivering his eulogy. "It would be the highest honor," I told Julian Bach. I squeezed his arm before he entered his car, and I said, "Thanks so much for taking that phone call thirty years ago."

"Don't think about it, old boy," Julian said. "Thanks for making it."

I will try to deliver a wonderful and joyous eulogy to Julian Bach one day. But I will promise everyone who ever knew him—I will never, never tell him goodbye.

Fried Vidalia onion rings, 235

Fruit. *See also specific fruits*

   curried poached fruit,
      202–3

   iced fruit tea, 93

G

Garlic

   Low Country aioli, 210–11

   roasted, on pizza bianca,
      125–26

   rouille, 243

Gelatin

   melon ring with mint and honey-
      lime dressing, 21–22

George Washington's punch,
   203–4

Gooseberry pie, 39–41

Grapes, in curried poached fruit,
   202–3

Green peppercorn butter, 161

Greens

   collard greens, 224–25

   pot likker soup, 226

   in stuffing for pork chops,
      222–23

   wilted broccoli rabe, Italian
      sausage with crispy sweet
      potatoes and, 136–37

Grits

   breakfast shrimp and grits,
      87–90

grits casserole, 201–2

Gumbo, 90–92

H

Ham. *See also* Prosciutto

   country ham with bourbon glaze,
      199–200

   fresh, 197–98

   grilled figs with country ham, walnuts,
      and lemon-mint cream, 251–52

   pot likker soup, 226

   Smithfield ham spread, 30

   squash blossoms stuffed with
      cheese and, 140–41

   squash casserole, 186–88

   Tasso, roasted white asparagus
      with pecans and, 166

Herbs. *See also specific herbs*

   herb mayonnaise, 186

   omelet fine herbs, 69–70

Honey-lime dressing, melon ring
   with mint and, 21–22

I

Iced fruit tea, 93

Insalata mista (mixed lettuces and
   greens), 148

Italian sausage with crispy sweet
   potatoes and wilted broccoli rabe,
   136–37

Vegetables. *See also* Salad(s); *specific vegetables*
ratatouille, 72–73
ribollita, 123–24
Vidalia onions
dip, 32
fried rings, 235
ring sandwiches, 235
salad rings, 235
Vinaigrette, sherry, roasted beets with blue cheese and, 68–69
Vinegar, hot potato salad with, 172–73

W

Walnuts
grilled figs with country ham, walnuts, and lemon-mint cream, 251–52

in roasted beets with blue cheese and sherry vinaigrette, 68–69
White chocolate-pistachio cookies, 23
Wild mushroom sauce, 114–16

Z

Zabaglione, Frascati, roasted figs with, 137–39
Zucchini
blossoms, fried or stuffed, 140–42
ratatouille, 72–73
Southern ratatouille with bacon, 225–26
squash casserole, 186–88

PAT CONROY is the author of *The Boo, The Water Is Wide, The Great Santini, The Lords of Discipline, The Prince of Tides, Beach Music,* and *My Losing Season.* Mr. Conroy won the James Beard Award for food writing in 2002.

SUZANNE WILIAMSON POLLAK, the author of *Entertaining for Dummies,* was the spokesperson for Federated Department Stores on the subject of cooking and home entertaining.

A NOTE ABOUT THE TYPE

This book was set in a digital version of Monotype Walbaum. The original typeface was created by Justus Erich Walbaum (1768–1839) in 1810. Before becoming a punch cutter with his own type foundries in Goslar and Weimar, he was apprenticed to a confectioner, where he is said to have taught himself engraving, making his own cookie molds using tools made from sword blades. The letterforms were modeled on the "modern" cuts being made at the time by Giambattista Bodoni and the Didot family.